Life Histories of the Dobe !Kung

ORIGINS OF HUMAN BEHAVIOR AND CULTURE

Edited by Monique Borgerhoff Mulder and Joe Henrich

Life Histories
of the Dobe !Kung

Food, Fatness, and Well-being
Over the Life Span

Nancy Howell

UNIVERSITY OF CALIFORNIA PRESS
Berkeley · Los Angeles · London

University of California Press, one of the most distinguished university presses in the United States, enriches lives around the world by advancing scholarship in the humanities, social sciences, and natural sciences. Its activities are supported by the UC Press Foundation and by philanthropic contributions from individuals and institutions. For more information, visit www.ucpress.edu.

Origins of Human Behavior and Culture, Vol. 4

University of California Press
Berkeley and Los Angeles, California

University of California Press, Ltd.
London, England

Library of Congress Cataloging-in-Publication Data
Howell, Nancy.
   Life histories of the Dobe !Kung : food, fatness, and well-being over the life-span / Nancy Howell.
      p. cm.—(Origins of human behavior and culture, vol. 4)
      Includes bibliographical references and index.
      ISBN 978-0-520-26233-1 (cloth : alk. paper)—
   ISBN 978-0-520-26234-8 (pbk. : alk. paper)
      1. !Kung (African people)—Food.   2. !Kung (African people)—Nutrition.   3. !Kung (African people)—Health and hygiene.   4. Food habits—Kalahari Desert.   5. Food—Caloric content—Kalahari Desert.   I. Title.
   DT1058.K86H7 2010
   613.2089'961—dc22

2009041299

Manufactured in the United States of America
19 18 17 16 15 14 13 12 11 10
10 9 8 7 6 5 4 3 2 1

The paper used in this publication meets the minimum requirements of ANSI/NISO Z39.48-1992 (R 1997) (*Permanence of Paper*).

Cover image: Elderly !Kung man embracing a child. Photo by Richard Lee.

The publisher gratefully acknowledges the generous support of the General Endowment Fund of the University of California Press Foundation.

Contents

Acknowledgments

This book consists of the application of new questions to old data, and so the acknowledgments in my earlier book, *Demography of the Dobe !Kung* (Howell, 2000), apply to this one too, especially thanking the !Kung San people who made the fieldwork such a pleasure, and my colleagues from the Harvard Kalahari expedition of 1967–1969: Richard Lee, Irven and Nancy DeVore, Patricia Draper, Mel Konner, Marjorie Shostak, Henry Harpending, and John Yellen, who taught me much in the field and more from their publications. Some of these have done fieldwork since 1969 and I have incorporated some of what they have brought back into my understanding of the !Kung. Other colleagues who have studied the !Kung and taught me something of what they learned include Ed Wilmsen, Polly Wiessner, Matthias Gunther, Trevor Jenkins, John Hansen, Stewart Truswell, Elizabeth Cashdan, Jackie Soloway, Lorna Marshall, John Marshall, Elizabeth Marshall Thomas, Nick Blurton Jones, and Kristen Hawkes. I apologize for not referencing all the examples and insights I have derived from my colleagues, but if I removed all the derivative ideas from this account, there would be little left, and if I summarized them all, the book would be excessively long and unfocused.

I appreciate too those who took my earlier book seriously and applied some of its methods to their studies or took questions far beyond what I had understood, especially Nicholas Blurton Jones, in his studies of the Hadza, and Kim Hill and Magdelena Hurtado, in their studies of the Ache.

These studies stimulated me to make a proposal in 1995 to the Center for Advanced Study in the Behavioral Sciences for a "special project" on hunter-gatherers, which provided stimulation for this work. Most of the work of this study was carried out while I was a Fellow at the Center for Advanced Study in the Behavioral Sciences, Stanford, California in 2002–2003. I am grateful for the financial support provided by sabbatical leave from the University of Toronto and by the John D. and Catherine T. MacArthur Foundation, Grant #32005-0 to the Center for Advanced Study. I appreciate the help and stimulation of Fellows at the Center in 2002–2003, especially Kristen Hawkes, and also contributions to this work from Lynn Gale, the statistical consultant; Jenny Hayes, the computer advisor; editorial consultant Kathleen Much; and all of the very helpful staff.

In the event, the "special project" on hunter-gatherers at the CASBS took so long to organize that by the time the project was scheduled, most of the people included in the original proposal had moved on to other topics or preferred to go to the field rather than spend a year collaborating in the pleasant surroundings of Stanford. Kristen Hawkes and I worked in parallel at the Center during the 2002–2003 academic year on projects designed to advance understanding of human adaptation by hunting and gathering, and I appreciate her input to my thinking on many levels. Others who were consulted and who provided stimulation and special insight during that year include Ron Lee of the Department of Demography at University of California, Berkeley, and Monique Borgerhoff Mulder and Sarah Hrdy and their colleagues at the University of California, Davis.

During 2002 and later in Florida, Pat Draper came to visit, and we worked intensively for a few weeks on an integration of our databases and wrote two coauthored papers on longevity and on effects of kinship relations on children's growth (Draper and Howell, 2002; Draper and Howell, 2006). I appreciate the encouragement and stimulation that Pat Draper has provided to keep me working on this project, and her generosity in sharing data.

My long-ago ex-students, Eric Roth and Moyra Brackley, at the University of Victoria, British Columbia, provided support and stimulation during a visit to the University of Victoria campus in December 2007, where the manuscript was completed. I appreciate their encouragement and practical help. Maureen Morin of the University of Toronto organized and polished the figures and tables. Rea DeVakos and the staff of the t-space data archive at the University of Toronto have been and continue to be supportive of my wish to make the original data available widely. My colleagues in the Department of Sociology at the University of Toronto have been helpful and interested in this research. And my family, especially my sister, Sue Sobeck, and my son, David Lee, provided welcome encouragement and understanding.

Fort Myers, Florida

CHAPTER 1

Another Look at the !Kung

A Life History Approach

In 1967 I was privileged to go to southern Africa to live with the !Kung Bushmen in the Kalahari desert. I was in the final stages of my Ph.D. in sociology at Harvard, and recently married to Richard Lee, who had already spent a year and a half living with the !Kung San people and learning their language. Richard was a lecturer at Harvard at that time, and he applied to the U.S. National Institute of Mental Health with his longtime collaborator Irven DeVore (a new professor at Harvard then) for funding to support a substantial study of the !Kung, involving fourteen scholars, including me. When they were awarded the grant in 1966, I hurried to finish my dissertation before the !Kung project started.

RESEARCH WITH THE DOBE !KUNG

Richard and I flew to Johannesburg, consulted with colleagues, bought a truck, and loaded it up, adding supplies at each stage of the journey. We drove first to Gaborone, the new capital of Botswana, to get final research permissions; then to Francistown, where we left the paved road parallel to the only railroad line in the country to drive west and north to Maun, on the Okavango delta. We rented a mailbox at the post office in Maun, and bought our last-minute supplies from their few general stores and a garage, and finally drove in our new truck to Nokaneng, a small town on the edge of the Kalahari. There we offloaded all but one of the drums of petrol we had brought from Maun, to create a storage system that would allow us to move safely between Maun and the isolated Dobe area on the Namibian border, where we were headed. From Nokaneng, in July 1967, we drove the last eight-hour stretch across the waterless 100 km or so that we called "the Middle Passage," to the string of ten waterholes on the Botswana-Namibia border that maps call the Xangwa (or Gwanwa) area, but which we always called the Dobe area. The name Dobe, easy to spell and pronounce (doe-bee), refers to one of the smallest waterholes there, where Richard had been welcomed into the !Kung kinship system in 1964 during his earlier visit.

That was a long time ago. The results of the research we did over the next two years have been described in detail in a book of preliminary research reports (Lee and DeVore, 1976) and in research monographs (Howell, 1979; see also Lee 1979) and the dozens of articles and books cited there and published since that time. The research that the fourteen of us as a research group carried out from 1967 to 1969 included studies of the biology, culture, social structure, economics, and psychology of the !Kung (or the *ju /'hoansi*, as they call themselves and are increasingly often called by scholars).[1]

My own research focused on the demography. After learning the language well enough to make my questions understood, and after pre-testing the format with Richard Lee's help, I started a data collection of reproductive histories of the 165 ever-married women in the Dobe area alive in 1967 to 1969. Eventually I got them all, plus another twenty-five reproductive histories from adult women who visited the Dobe area but who did not usually live there, which I ended up not using. This data collection included all of the marriages and marriage terminations, pregnancies and pregnancy terminations, and a history of survival of each of the husbands and children mentioned by the 165 adult women.

This work was interspersed with occasional "campaigns" of data collection with Richard Lee. We took the truck to each of the ten water-holes in turn to visit each of the thirty-five or so villages, usually staying at each waterhole for a few days to make sure we had covered all the residents there. Richard and I conducted censuses in October 1967, November 1968, and April 1969, and in addition we collected measures of height, weight, and skin-fold thickness in August 1968, October 1968, January 1969, and April 1969. We measured weights, especially

1. I continue to refer to the !Kung to avoid confusion between my earlier work and this book. They are the same people as the *ju /'hoansi* and they never called themselves the !Kung.

of children, continuously, wherever we had people and the scale in the same place, but the "campaigns" were especially organized to include all of the members of the population, to look for seasonal changes in weight and height. These sweeps through the population also provided occasions for successive stages of my estimations of the ages of individuals, which consisted of rank ordering the people in local areas by age, and then merging those local age-ranks into a single rank order, later fitting a curve from stable-population theory to the rank order to estimate individual ages, and then checking the plausibility of the resulting estimates.[2]

These data collections were designed to be holistic inventories of the contemporary Dobe !Kung people, including everything that was possible to observe about an ongoing population of people that would allow us to describe in detail how their society operated. Howell (2000) details the data collection and analysis of the fieldwork from 1967 to 1969.

RESEARCH RESULTS: *DEMOGRAPHY OF THE DOBE !KUNG*

Briefly, the book *Demography of the Dobe !Kung* shows one way to construct a demographic description of a small population in which there are no historical records and people don't know their own ages. After sorting out the interrelated issues of the age estimates and the population age structure, I presented a chapter on causes of death during recent decades, and then the life tables, for the two sexes, and for different periods of time. The study revealed that mortality was high overall (an approximate Expectation of Life at Birth of thirty years and an Infant Mortality Rate of 200 deaths in the first year per 1,000 births) but that most !Kung appeared to be remarkably healthy (strong, energetic, cheerful) most of the time. Next, in that book, the fertility history of the women was laid out, first for the older post-reproductive women; and then for the younger women who were still building their families, showing that the fertility is remarkably low for a population that marries young and doesn't use any methods of contraception. The !Kung were found to have a Total Fertility Rate of about 4.6 children born to women who survive to the end of the childbearing period, which is a remarkably low level of natural fertility.

2. Howell 1979 is the original *Demography of the Dobe !Kung* (Academic Press, New York), and Howell 2000 is a second edition of that book (Aldine de Gruyter, New York), with a new preface, a new final chapter, and an enriched bibliography. As only the 2000 version is in print at this time, I will cite it in this document, but readers who find only the 1979 version in their local library should know that pages 1–359 are identical. Methods of age estimation are described in detail in Chapter 2 of that book.

To examine the interactions of fertility and mortality, a computer micro-simulation program called AMBUSH was invented and used (Howell and Lehotay, 1978; Howell, 2000). The program is a stochastic model that shows what happens when you start with a population identical to the !Kung as we observed them in 1968 and simulate a future based on the observed probabilities of birth and death for varying periods of time in the future. The simulations can be thought of as an answer to the question: If there were a continent with 100 (or any number) of independent populations with the probabilities of survival and reproduction that the !Kung have, what range of variation would we expect to see in their functioning? The simulations are not entirely realistic (some of the complexities of life are not included in the models) but they are helpful for confirming the plausibility of the estimates of the real population and for stimulating thinking about the fluctuations that one would expect in such populations, without any complex causal processes. The simulations are best thought of as a variety of the null hypothesis, valuable in a world in which hunting and gathering societies are few and far between. Unfortunately, the AMBUSH program is no longer available for use as it was written in a machine language, IBM Assembler, which is no longer usable, but alternative simulation programs are readily available now.

The original work went on to look at detailed aspects of the population in some detail, to describe marriage, divorce, widowhood, and remarriage, and to explore the networks of kinship ties of consanguinity (birth) and affinity (marriage) generated by the demography. The analysis based on the women's fertility and mortality is repeated for the men, in condensed form. The population was found to be essentially stationary (not growing) as a result of the balance of their moderate fertility and mortality. The people are shown to be small in size, short and thin, and we considered the possible importance of thinness in keeping fertility low, as proposed by the Frisch hypothesis (Frisch, Revelle, et al., 1971). Computer simulations were used to spell out implications of the population parameters over long periods of time, specifically the degree of inequality in reproductive success to be expected in successive generations, and the numbers of living kin to be expected by people of varying ages and sex.

The first edition (Howell, 1979) ended with some predictions about the future to the year 2000; the second edition (Howell, 2000) evaluates those predictions (they were pretty accurate) and discusses the ways that population has changed from the late 1960s to the year 2000, and the probable trends in future decades. *Demography of the Dobe !Kung* included pretty much everything I knew about the !Kung at that time and could infer from the models that I developed. When data archives became available at the University of Toronto Data Library in the 1990s, the raw data from these studies were entered to be made available to any interested researchers who cared to access it. My impression is that few researchers have used the raw data, but many researchers have used the published versions of detailed empirical descriptions of the !Kung (Howell, 2000) in their studies, for comparative or exemplary purposes. Later in this chapter, we will consider a new generation of data archives.

RECONSIDERING THE !KUNG

Why, then, one might ask, is there any need for another book on the same people, based on the same data? Some scholars have complained that the Dobe !Kung case has already been vastly overused in archaeological and ethnographic modeling: Isaac (1990) refers to a "Sanitation phenomenon" in understanding early human societies, and suggests that the field should give the !Kung a rest. There is no new data in this book (although some of the old data are described in more detail than has been done before). The !Kung way of life has changed so much since the 1960s that any new data collected now would be interesting but it would not illuminate the hunting and gathering way of life. In any case, I have not done any fieldwork since 1969, although I was pleased to have the chance to go back to Dobe with Pat Draper for a short visit in 1991–1992 (Howell, 2000). Others in the research group (Richard Lee, Patricia Draper, Henry Harpending, Megan Biesele, and Polly Wiessner) have continued to do fieldwork when they get the chance, but this book is not based on their new data.

What I have is the old data set, some new but mostly old ethnographic background to that data, and the conviction that there is still much to be learned from it. The niche for another book on the !Kung arises from new questions that have been raised, and new models that have been proposed, from the great advances made by the many multidisciplinary colleagues who have contributed to what Roth (2004) has called "anthropological demography" and "human behavioral ecology" or evolutionary biology since the original analysis was completed in 1978. In the course of using the old data to try to answer these new questions, I am trying to make the data more accessible to other scholars, in the hope that it can be used by others to explore the current set of questions and perhaps also others that haven't been thought of yet.

My first book on the !Kung came out of the field of demography (the study of population), with some influence from social-cultural anthropology and sociology. Demography and anthropology seemed quite distant disciplines in those days, but since that time some demographers (Watkins, 1995) have enthusiastically embraced data collection methods and insights from anthropology into demography to enrich the sometimes thin descriptive understanding of populations that are studied by demographers from census and vital statistics registration records. Some circles in anthropology have welcomed the more rigorous models and more systematic data collection methods from demography into their field, in their publications, and in training offered to young anthropologists in graduate programs. By now (2010) most graduate programs in anthropology seem to have some expertise in demography, and some have a great deal.

Roth (2004) argued in a recent book that there are two distinct streams of interest in demographic studies in anthropology, "anthropological demography" consisting of social-cultural anthropologists (and some demographers) who are largely interested in understanding the contributions that demography can make to understanding social structure in the populations that anthropologists study. The other, "behavioral ecology," is primarily made up of biological or physical anthropologists looking for insight into human evolution. Both streams are interesting: it is odd that they tend to ignore each other. Perhaps this is because they draw upon different disciplines for their expertise, and there are only a few scholars like Roth who have mastered both streams of research and methods.

Theoretical and empirical studies of other hunting and gathering peoples (and some horticulturalists and pastoralists) since 1979 have also posed new questions and have suggested new techniques of analysis. There are now detailed accounts of the Ache of Paraguay (Hill and Hurtado, 1996), the Hadza of Tanzania (Woodburn, 1968; Dyson, 1977; Hawkes, O'Connell, et al., 1991; Blurton Jones, Smith, et al., 1992), the Agta of the Philippines (Early and Headland, 1998), the Ganj of New Guinea (Wood, 1980), the Aka (Hewlett, 1988), and Efe Pygmies (Bailey and Peacock, 1988) of West Africa, and the Yanamamo of the Amazon basin (Divale and Harris, 1976; Chagnon and Irons, 1979; Early and Peters, 1990; Early and Peters, 2000), and many more. When research methods and theoretical models that were developed in those studies are applied to the !Kung, as I do in the following pages,

I am impressed by how much we gain in explanatory power. But let me warn the reader that I do not attempt here to review these findings in any systematic way, or make systematic comparisons between these populations and the Dobe !Kung. That would be a good thing to do, but I am not the person to do it. My ambition is smaller: I use the stimulating work of colleagues on other small-scale populations to help me understand the only case study that I have any confidence that I can understand, that of the Dobe !Kung. My goal is to better understand the !Kung, and to leave it to others to generalize about hunters and gatherers or small-scale societies.

The Life History Model

Life history theory is another holistic attempt to integrate a wide range of observations of life in human societies (Alexander, 1987). To paraphrase Roth (2004), all life history theory rests on the principle of allocation, which states that energy used for one purpose cannot be used for another. Energy allocations between the essential life processes of (1) maintenance, (2) growth, and (3) reproduction are viewed as a series of trade-offs made over an individual's life course. Individuals are distinguished by stages of life that correspond to these energy allocations, and these stages are related to the age and sex categories that we have used before. We consider the ways that evolution has worked upon these life stages to produce the adaptations of the hunting-gathering way of life, both those features that are true of all hunter-gatherer groups and those that are peculiar to the !Kung. The task of the present work is to specify the questions that arise from life history theory, consider the ethnographic knowledge that may pertain to the answers to these questions, and then to operationalize the numerical data available to produce the best approximation of an empirical answer to the question posed that I can manage. Readers will note that I rarely present any statistical tests on the answers to the questions in the chapters that follow. And there are many more figures than tables that show the numerical data. I like to look at the patterns of data more than focus on the "bottom line." The process is more exploratory than confirmatory, more suggestive than definitive.

Incorporating the studies of mortality and fertility established in the earlier work, I focus in this study on the food calories that people produce and consume, and that they use to fuel the activities of their daily life that determine their life stages. Note that I account for the same

daily calories of the population in three ways: (1) how the calories are
acquired from the environment, (2) how they are distributed and redistributed by individuals within the population, and (3) the amounts in
which they are consumed by various individuals.

Production of calories was a major focus of others in the "Harvard
Kalahari expedition" during the 1967–1969 studies, especially Lee (1979)
but also Konner and Worthman (1980), Draper (1975), and Wilmsen
(1982). The means of production consisted of hunting and gathering, but
also lactation, and some wage work and agricultural work that is outside
of the traditional way of life of the !Kung (which we acknowledge as a
complication, although it isn't our primary interest here).

Consumption of calories has not been so well studied directly for the
!Kung: We have information on gains and losses in weight over time that
reflects consumption, but we didn't directly measure consumption of
food. The utilization of calories includes growth, maintenance of body
size and condition (basal metabolism), the physical activity of work and
other activities, and reproduction. All of these together account for the
calories required by the population.

Further, we will look at these flows of calories from the environment
through the producers to the whole population in the social forms the
people use to organize the production, consumption, and use of calories:
Individuals differ, especially by their stage of life, in their ability to par-
ticipate in these flows of calories, and individuals are gathered into
households, the primary consumption unit; households are gathered
into living groups (also called camps or villages), which are the primary
production unit; and villages are spread through the environment to
maximize access to natural resources, gathered around named waterholes. In this book, we will come to understand these social structural
units as determinants of how food is produced, distributed, and used by
individuals, and also as products of these processes, resulting from the
interactions of individuals at different stages of the life history process
to channel the flows of calories.

The redistribution of calories from producers to consumers is not an
automatic process: The concept of "sharing" poses as many problems
as it solves. But kinship is the primary form of social structure of the
!Kung, the redistribution of the calorie resources is critical to the population, and after we look first at the residential units in which people live
and share resources, we will turn our attention to the effects of consanguine and affinal kinship on energy allocation processes. We account for
as much variance as we can by focusing on the units of residential and

kinship association, but it is clear that we can only account for a certain low proportion of the allocation process. The rest must be a product of variables not included in our kinship model, including sharing outside of kinship channels. The motives, methods, and means for that sharing will be discussed in the final chapter.

The model being constructed here is original in details but not in overall design. Richard Lee's classic study (1979) and an earlier paper (1969) weave together most of the same variables used here and come to similar conclusions: Mine is an independent approach that both builds on and confirms most aspects of Lee's analysis, and examines some questions that arise from it.

In summary, let us be clear about the goals of this book, particularly those it does not aspire to reach. First, it is not a systematic comparison of the !Kung to the very fine work that has been done in recent decades on comparable populations of hunters and gatherers, such as the Ache and the Hadza, and simple horticultural societies.

Second, this book is not a review of the very interesting literature that has developed on behavioral ecology over the past twenty-five years, and makes no claim to completeness of references to or discussion of this literature. I mention literature only where it is useful in pursuing the goals of this project, and I apologize in advance to authors of much very valuable literature for not mentioning their work, even if I found it extremely interesting.

Finally, it is not a test of any part of the theoretical framework of life history analysis that has been developed, but merely an empirical application of some concepts and some questions that arise from that theoretical body to a database that I created for other purposes.

Richerson and Boyd (2004) offer a thoughtful warning to people like me who want to focus entirely on a single data set:

> A good set of data . . . is a beautiful thing to behold. Foolish, of course, is the empiricist who thinks that even the most beautiful set of data captures any complex phenomenon completely, especially one who thinks that the data from his own case applies without exception to a diverse system such as human culture. However, data are the ultimate arbiter. More than just testing hypotheses, data often start us thinking in the first place.
>
> (Richerson and Boyd, 2004)

The data will be central to this book, with the hope that it starts us thinking about some additional aspects of the puzzles of the !Kung adaptation, and provides the ultimate arbitration between competing models.

It is amusing to note that Henry Harpending and Pat Draper, in their "comments" in the Current Anthropology debate on the "revisionist issue" (Harpending and Draper, 1990), said in passing ". . . Like the devil with a bible, anyone is free to take the data and generate whatever image is desired."

Archiving and Replicating This Research

I use this body of !Kung data collected in 1967–1969 to address some questions in life history analysis in this book, but I disclaim any aspiration to have the last word on the subject of how life history theory applies to the !Kung. On the contrary, I invite the reader to join the process of applying these questions to the !Kung data, by downloading all or some of the data to the reader's computer for manipulation. These data are now in the public arena, and no permissions are required to use them for any purpose. I think the downloading process and analysis will go easily once it is underway, but following along the process used in this work may make it easier for students and professionals alike to understand the data.

The methods of data collection used to create the database used here will not be explained in detail in this book, as the interested reader can go to the earlier work for a full account of the collection and analysis of the raw data (Lee and DeVore, 1976; Lee 1979; Howell, 2000) and can go to the t-space archives (http://tspace.library.utoronto.ca) for access to the many files that result from using the data in this work. A goal of this work is that it is laid out so that any motivated reader can replicate everything I have done here, and contrast the results I produce with any alternative formulations that the reader may think of. Variables can be added, subtracted, recoded, or redefined to apply to any of the theoretical questions defined below, and statistical techniques can be applied to take the analysis beyond the point where I leave it.

The t-space data archive contains the whole set of raw data, and the many subfiles that were created to analyze the variables considered in this book. Some of the subfiles are limited to certain age groups or genders; others concentrate on certain variables. Figures and tables in this book are labeled with the unique web address of the data file that produced it,[3]

---

3. There are many data files in the archive because it is most convenient to create a file containing only the variables to be immediately explored on the individuals who can contribute to that particular analysis. Readers can create their own specialized data files if they wish, building on the ones used here, which will be stored on their own computer until or unless they choose to archive them.

so that the reader can use either the SPSS data analysis package (available by license at most universities, and also for sale from the software company that created it) or MS Excel to re-create what I have done here, before modifying the analysis in any way that seems useful.[4]

The unit of analysis of most of this book is that of the individual !Kung person in the 1968 population. Individuals have identification numbers as well as names, date of birth, and other identifying characteristics.[5] Most of the characteristics studied (the variables) are simple and straightforward observations of the individual at that time. It seems to me valuable to preserve the simplicity and comprehensibility of the original data collection to the greatest extent possible.[6] Most of the data presentations in this book will be exploratory, as befits the small and unique population that is being described. Statistical analysis is kept to a minimum because it is implicitly based on the assumption that the data used are drawn as a random sample from a large universe, to which one wants to generalize. In this work, however, the Dobe !Kung cannot be said to represent a sample of all hunter-gatherer populations, all African hunters, or even all San people. My focus is relating the variables explored here—body size, food production and consumption, and sharing and redistribution—to all that we know about the population of the !Kung San of the Dobe area as we observed them in the 1967–1969 period. Statistical analysis is valuable to help recognize and test patterns in the raw data. But the raw data itself is even more valuable, and skipping over the raw data to go directly to statistical analysis of hypotheses generated seems a great waste and even disrespectful to the !Kung, who co-operated so willingly in the data collection. In this book we will stay close to the raw data, using descriptive techniques like scattergrams and cross-tabulations, moving the richness of direct observation of the !Kung only

4. To access the data, go to http://tspace.library.utoronto.ca, and click on "Communities and Collections," and then on "Dobe !Kung." Note that each file has an identifier or URI, the "handle" of the file. Most files come in two versions: the SPSS version (filename.sav) and an alternative MS Excel version (filename.cvs). This research used the SPSS version, so generally the documentation is more complete in that format, and the tables and figures will look somewhat different if created in Excel.

5. Issues of the privacy rights of identifiable individuals are reduced by the forty-five years that have passed since these data were collected. Almost all of the individuals identifiable from the archived research results are now deceased, and privacy was not a concern of the !Kung in the 1960s. The value of the data would be greatly reduced if we removed identifying information, as the links between individuals known to exist at that time could not be maintained.

6. Only a few variables considered here (the Body Mass Index Differences of Chapter 3, and the Caloric Balance measure of Chapters 5–7) are complex, computed variables that are not immediately understandable.

a step of abstraction away from the reality of their lives. More complex statistical procedures, like multi-variate analysis, will only be used at a few points where it seemed important to check a hypothesis that is not obvious to the naked eye.

I like to think of the archived data as a way to preserve the concrete results of the hard work that I and the other anthropologists in residence at Dobe in 1967–69 carried out, for the benefit of students, teachers, and researchers who were not there at the time but who may be able to make continued good use of our efforts. The analysis in this book illustrates one way that the old data can be reorganized to address a new set of research questions. And of course the life history analysis considered here is not the only possible use for the old data set. Readers may consider what other models of small-scale societies may be illuminated by this data, and may return to this data set in future years or decades, when new models that have not been proposed yet make their appearance.

POVERTY AND SOCIAL CHANGE IN THE DOBE AREA

Before we begin the reconsideration of the Dobe !Kung in the 1967–1969 period, there are two additional issues that I want to address directly in response to questions from students and colleagues. The first is the question of poverty and malnutrition of the !Kung; and the second is the question of how much social change has already occurred during the twentieth century, and the extent to which the !Kung are really hunters and gatherers in a world dominated by agricultural, urban development and technology. Readers may be interested in considering these questions before turning to the details of the model under construction, or you may turn to the next chapter to begin the study report.

Poverty of the !Kung

The !Kung represent a dilemma for modern observers, who are simultaneously charmed by the beauty of the !Kung adaptation to living simply in a wild environment, and are appalled by the extreme poverty of their lives, without property, without education, with minimal governmental assistance, without any means of security provided by the outside world. With their small bodies and their constant concern with the management of scarcity, !Kung San people are as poor as people can be and continue to reproduce their social group reliably. The so-called revisionist scholars (Wilmsen, 1989; Wilmsen and Denbow, 1990) insist that it is untrue and irresponsible to describe the Dobe !Kung adaptation as "original affluence" or anything like it.

If poverty is defined as inequality, however, the !Kung are not poor. Within their society, everyone has more or less the same level of ownership and access to resources. And if poverty is defined as lacking control over one's own activities, the !Kung are rich, as each person, or at least each competent adult, can decide for himself or herself where to live, who to marry or divorce, what people to live with, and what work to do, within the guidance of their cultural norms. Their society is not based on money or property, but on harvesting food and the other necessities of life directly from the natural world. In the 1960s, people owned nothing more than their clothing, perhaps a blanket, a pot, and a few dishes and tools that they carried from place to place as they moved their villages frequently around the territory circling their waterhole. Their only wealth was human capital, consisting of health, vitality, and knowledge of how to live in the Kalahari, plus their network of kinship ties to others.

It is possible to be well nourished and at the same time very thin, but that is surely more dangerous than it would be to be well nourished and also a bit more plump. In the world as a whole we see a strong correlation between being very thin and being positively poorly nourished, but that is not as true of the !Kung San as it would be of people whose diet primarily consists of a starch with a little meat and vegetable material. The thin !Kung we saw at Dobe in the 1960s typically ate quantities of meat, nuts, roots, fruits, and vegetables. They have many sources of protein, vitamins, and minerals. They are short on fats and calories and positively deficient on processed starches and sugars by world standards. We need to think explicitly about the nature of malnutrition and poverty in their society and in ours, so that our preconceptions about poverty don't blind us to the realities of their life.

The !Kung adaptation consists of applying their own energy and work to the natural products of the environment—plants and animals—to obtain all the things that the people need to live, such as food, shelter, tools, medicine, and decoration. The !Kung ask for supernatural help in solving their problems, but in their traditional way of life neither ask for nor receive any supplements to their own energy to solve their problems, with two exceptions. The first is their only domesticated animal in the traditional hunting and gathering way of life, the dog. Dogs are included in village life, although they are rarely deliberately fed by humans, usually getting their own food and indeed providing food for humans by their help with hunting. Dogs were domesticated very early in human prehistory (Cartmill, 1993): Indeed, some experts believe that it is more accurate to describe dogs as having domesticated themselves by hanging around human settlements and making themselves useful as guards against animal intruders into the village, and as "cleaners" who keep the village free of decaying organic materials by eating spilled food and human feces. !Kung dogs are only semidomesticated, in that their owners do not systematically control the reproduction of the dogs, do not feed them consistently, and do not eat them.

The second exception to the generalization that the !Kung have no supplementary sources of energy is that they help each other. The !Kung do a lot of what Richard Lee calls "sharing" and later we will see that sharing is precisely the key to understanding how they can live in the sparse Kalahari environment with some security even if not with surpluses or with ease. Their tendency to help one another with food, with work, and with caring of various kinds will be a major focus of this reconsideration of the !Kung data collected in 1967–1969. A shortfall of the necessities of life is not a fatal problem if others fill the gap, whether they do so out of a self-interested "insurance" program, kin selection, generalized reciprocity, tolerated theft, or pure altruism.[7]

What, then, are the resources that people traditionally depend on to make their living? The Kalahari is a vast sandy semidesert, which is full of food, water, and shelter for those who know how to find it, but desperately inhospitable to anyone who does not have the knowledge and skills that suit the environment. The !Kung have these skills, and they live in groups of ten to fifty people (average twenty or so), with a mixture of workers and dependents, hunters and gatherers, men and women, old people, adults, and children, so that all their knowledge-based resources are likely to be present in every small group. People live in intimate contact with their kin, with virtually no privacy or independent individualistic ambitions, in a way that seems to be deeply satisfying to most people, most of the time.

Babies live in skin-to-skin contact with their mothers from the day of birth, carried much of the time, and take breast-milk whenever they wish, several times an hour, for years. !Kung babies seem orders-of-magnitude happier with their lives than any American babies I have known, despite the high infant mortality rate (20% of babies failed to survive the first

---

7. We will return to the question of motivation for sharing in the last section of this book.

year of life in the 1960s, and about 45% died by age 15). Konner (in Lee and DeVore, 1976: 245) describes the general rules of !Kung child rearing as "indulgence, stimulation, and nonrestriction."

We note that daily satisfactions of life are not necessarily correlated with the probability of death. Babies enjoy physical satisfaction of their needs; children enjoy that, plus freedom from constraint; adults enjoy the close social relationships that they live in, the mastery of their way of life that they exercise, and the gratification of seeing their children grow and thrive. I don't want to romanticize the life of the !Kung, but we need to recognize that there are a lot of benefits to their way of life in order to understand the adaptation as a whole.

At the same time, we need to be aware that people often work very hard under difficult circumstances of heat and thirst and hunger. Later we will attempt to quantify exactly how hard they work. People of all ages are forced into extreme exertion when they have to move long distances, carrying heavy loads, despite sickness, injury, and handicap. People are extremely thin (we will see just how thin they are) and they say that they are often hungry. The debates about "the affluent society" as applied to the !Kung have an element of truth but the phrase also misrepresents the reality as !Kung people live it. The !Kung I knew in the 1960s owned nothing or very little, worked hard, and by and large seemed to be enjoying their lives. Applying concepts of poverty from industrialized societies, as Wilmsen does (Wilmsen, 1989), has a certain value in understanding where the !Kung are, compared to others in international perspective, but also distorts the reality of how they see themselves, and how they manage to move toward their goals.

Social Change in the Kalahari

Our second preliminary question is whether the !Kung as described in 1968 still exist. The answer is both yes and no. To find "hunters in a world of hunters" uncontaminated by influences from people who live by other forms of economy, we would have to go back at least 1,000 years in the Kalahari, as there have been herders, agriculturalists, miners, and travelers through the desert over the past millennium and no doubt before that as well. Even so, it was probably true that 99% of the calories acquired by the Dobe !Kung came from hunting and gathering until 1920, more than 90% until 1950, and still the great majority of calories in 1967–1969 when this study was done. It wasn't until about 1980, when the Xangwa area was firmly incorporated into the structure of the Botswana state, that

the !Kung needed to be considered "ex-hunters," living now by garden-
ing, herding small animals, selling craft items, welfare payments, and
wage labor (Howell, 2000:1–16 and 370–377).

In 1967–1969, when the data of my study were collected, there were
or previously had been cattle at eight of the nine permanent waterholes
in the Xangwa-/ai/ai area, and about 30% of the !Kung population were
living in groups that Lee (1979) calls "client groups" rather than traditional living groups, dependent on Herero and Tswana cattle owners for
work, food, and income. The tallest, strongest, most cooperative young
men tended to be selected as employees by cattle keepers, and they
would be offered opportunities to live with the cattle owners, alone or
with their immediate families, in these special "non-!Kung" settlements,
which I often refer to here as "cattle posts." These individuals and
families are included in our study of the !Kung, which is the basis for
this work (although the Tswana and Herero cattle owners they lived
with were not included), and for some purposes we will want to identify exactly which people these were and how they differ from the rest
of the population.

In 1967–1969, therefore, the majority of the !Kung were still living
by hunting and gathering most of the time, and my study (and that of
Lee and the others on the Harvard expedition) focused on the portion
of the population that was living in the traditional way, most of the time
(Lee, 1979; Draper and Kranichfeld, 1990; Howell, 2000). Virtually all
!Kung would pay an occasional visit to relatives who live at a cattle post
in the 1967–1969 era, and would eat a few meals of domesticated meat
and milk while they were there, before returning to their bush diet and
workload. Some families, especially aging adults or families that include
a handicapped or sick member, who were finding it difficult or impossible to survive in the bush, deliberately moved to a cattle post to ease the
workload and reduce the need to walk so much, and of course, this
move changed the bush camps from which they came just as it changed
the cattle posts to which they went. We need to remain alert to the possibility that findings focused on bush camps are distorted by the absence
of people who would otherwise be there—especially people who are
particularly strong and productive, who are prime employees for the
cattle owners, and those who are sick, handicapped, or aged, or who
have many children to be supported, who go to the cattle posts in search
of an easier life.

As I reviewed in the concluding chapter of the second edition of my
previous book (Howell, 2000), there has been considerable social

change in the Dobe area after the collection phase of that study was completed. In the decades since the data for this study were collected, !Kung have encountered problems regarding jobs and welfare, animal husbandry, private property, alcohol consumption, shopping and currency, debt, taxes, and the dilemmas of improving as well as deteriorating health, especially AIDS. It would take us too far afield to review the many kinds of social change that have occurred in the Kalahari since 1969, but this work, harking back to the late 1960s as though that is the only time period that matters, should not be interpreted as a denial of contemporary changes in the lives of the Dobe !Kung.

In the subsequent chapters, we will draw on my previous database and its analysis by me and by the others who work on the !Kung, to reorganize our understanding of the demography of the Dobe !Kung, reconciling ages and stages, work and calories, fatness and well-being into what I hope is a better and clearer image of the functioning of the Dobe !Kung society in the twentieth century.

CHAPTER 2

Life History Stages

In my earlier account of the !Kung people (Howell, 1979, 2000), I organized the presentation around the standard demographic processes of death and birth, marriage, and migration, and presented the data in the framework of the ages that I estimated for individuals. In a comparable study (Hill and Hurtado, 1996) of the Ache hunter-gatherers of Paraguay, the authors organized the presentation of their data around life history stages. Not only was this approach compatible with the data already collected on the !Kung, but the theory of life history helped to organize our understanding of the importance of age (and sex) and put the data into the theoretical framework of evolutionary biology, within which the behavior and social structure of hunting and gathering people were most appropriately viewed. Hill and Hurtado suggested (citing J. T. Bonner, 1965) that "the life history of an organism can be thought of as a complete description of that organism" (Hill and Hurtado, 1996; Draper and Howell, 2006). As I aspire to "a complete description" of the life and culture of the !Kung, we will adopt the life history approach here and integrate it in this chapter with the framework of individual ages.

I will begin by defining the life history stages for the !Kung unambiguously, and relate them to the age of individuals when they reach and depart from these stages into the next (assuming that they live long enough). The methods are ethnographic observation and the results of interviewing, especially from the women's reproductive histories. In the discussions of each stage of life, I will bring the knowledge that we have developed on !Kung life into focus, and end by relating the boundaries of each stage of life to participants' ages and the proportion of the population expected to be in each stage at any point in time. When I say "we" in this context, I refer to my own work on the !Kung, as well as that of my colleagues (Lee and DeVore, 1976; Lee, 1979; Harpending and Wandsnider, 1982; Konner, 1991; Draper and Harpending, 1994; Shostak, 2000) and the other members of the 1967–1971 Harvard Research Group, and that of other scholars (Thomas, 1959; Marshall, 1976; Blurton Jones and Howell, 1984; Schrire, 1984; Cashdan, 1985; Wilmsen, 1989; Biesele, 1990) who have studied the !Kung.[1]

DEFINITIONS OF LIFE STAGES

Life stages are best defined as bounded by distinctive life events that can be easily observed and are significant to the individuals involved. In the case of people like the !Kung, we have advantages over biologists who study other species. We are able to discuss with the subjects of the research what events define the main stages of life and how those stages influence the life course. In addition, we have the second advantage that we can simultaneously use both the measuring rod of age and the associated social and biological definitions to discuss these stages of life.

For the !Kung, observation and discussions in the field suggest certain defining events and stages of life. In any life, the dramatic event of birth is the first event in the sequence. The first stage of life for !Kung people of both sexes is infancy, the time from birth until weaning.

The second stage of life is childhood, from weaning until the start of sexual maturation. Weaning is readily observed in this population, although it is a process that goes on a long time, from supplementation of lactation, which starts a few months after birth, to cessation of lactation, typically a few (2–4) years after birth. The boundary event of sexual maturation is somewhat different for the two sexes, in timing and in social recognition. The !Kung vaguely divide childhood into smaller segments (a "little little girl," a "big little girl," a "little big girl," etc.), but there are no clear-cut defining boundaries of these stages, so those culturally defined groupings will be ignored here. Menarche (the first menstruation), marking the start of ovulatory cycling for girls, is clearly

---

1. In other places in the manuscript, however, for example in the next paragraph, "we" includes the reader with the writer in proposing the work to be carried out. I hope that the meaning of "we" is clear from the context.

recognized and celebrated. Because "genarche" (the equivalent of menarche for males) is not celebrated or clearly recognized by !Kung, it is difficult to identify for individuals, and so the age distribution of the women's event, menarche, will be applied to the boys as well to define the end of their childhood and the beginning of the stage of adolescence.

The third stage of life is adolescence, from the onset to the completion of sexual maturity, timed for both sexes by the birth of their first child.

The fourth stage of life is the period of childbearing, from the first to the final birth of a child. Menopause (the cessation of menstrual periods that results from the cessation of ovulation) is frequently cited as the event that ends the reproductive period for women, but it is very difficult to date for any particular individual, and there is no comparable event for men. The last birth, however, is easy to date, and it can be observed in both sexes retrospectively, even if one cannot tell that it is the final birth at the time it occurs. Defining the end of the parenting stage of life by the birth of the final child allows us to distinguish between the time in life when children are being born and the time past that point. The final birth is the defining event that ends the childbearing stage, even if individuals may feel that they are at risk of pregnancy for some unknown period of time after the final birth.

The fifth stage of life is post-reproductive adulthood, the time of life when one continues to raise children already born but is no longer having new births. Menopause occurs (for women) during this period, although it is difficult to date precisely in this population, and women and men go on being strong and vigorous for many years, even decades after the end of childbearing. The "grandmother hypothesis" (Hawkes, O'Connell, et al., 1998; Hawkes, O'Connell, et al., 2000) convinces us that this is a crucially important stage of life for individuals and for theoretical models of the life span.

And finally, the sixth stage of life is frailty or disability, the time (usually even if not always in old age) when one becomes dependent on others, sometimes just because there are others who expect to provide for the elder, more often because one is too weak and handicapped to continue to work consistently to support oneself and provide for others. Some elderly people classified as frail are healthy and clear-minded, and a few live for long periods in this stage of life. For most !Kung, however, loss of the ability to work is followed quickly by death.

Each of these stages of life can be ended by death, or by arrival at the next stage, whichever occurs first. Except perhaps for the young men's arrival at adolescence, and some ambiguity about whether the most recent child born is the last born, any !Kung person or other knowledgeable observer could understand the stages and tell what stage any particular person is in, even though these stages are not part of the !Kung vocabulary.

The typical characteristics, activities, strategies, and concerns of individuals tend to vary strongly between these stages, which are very different from one another. Each person normally passes through all the stages of life (if he or she lives long enough); a person who does not reach a stage (such as parenthood) at the age-appropriate time is deviant, by definition, in this society. (Infertile people are treated as if they continue to be adolescents in this model until the last age of adolescence for their sex, and then they move directly to the post-reproductive stage of life.) Differences between stages are not merely a function of the characteristics of the people who happen to be in that stage of life at a particular point, but are more likely to be a function of the constraints and interactions of the "decisions" and the strategies of optimization of well-being and reproductive success that make sense at that time of life. There are only minor differences in life history stages for males and females during infancy and childhood, and so the sexes will be discussed together. At later stages of the life span, adolescence and beyond, the differences are sufficiently great that they need to be described separately.

PRENATAL LIFE AND BIRTH

!Kung women seem to menstruate at all phases of the moon, and knowing the cycle of one woman doesn't tell you the cycles of the others in the group. The !Kung live, however, in intimate connection with the night sky, and women (and men) use the cycles of the moon as a mnemonic device to keep track of their own menstrual cycles. Hence, they are usually aware of the possibility of a pregnancy at an early stage. One woman told me in 1968:

> "When you first expect a period and don't see it, you smile to yourself and say nothing. When the moon comes again and you don't see it, you know there is a baby growing, and your heart is happy."
>
> (Howell, 2000:117)

This quotation suggests that women are always happy about a pregnancy, and usually that is true. Women usually feel blessed to conceive a child, and they complain that their god is stingy in giving children and greedy in taking children back after they are born. Only under special circumstances is a pregnancy resented or regretted (Shostak, 1981).

The !Kung have several beliefs about behavior that they believe will likely terminate a pregnancy, such as having sex with a man other than the father or cooking food at someone else's fire during the pregnancy. In addition, women speak of certain herbs and roots that will "spoil" a pregnancy or produce sterility, temporarily or permanently. Attempts to follow up on these reports and have the substances analyzed have not produced concrete results, so the herbal "remedies" may be as magical as the behavioral prescriptions. The reasons for not wanting a particular pregnancy include extramarital conception when the woman wants to stay married to her husband (Shostak, 1981:186–199), a dislike of the father of the child, a fear that the mother will not be able to provide for the child, or the fear that the addition of the child will harm older children. Almost all conceptions occur within marriage (Harpending, 1976), and the typical long birth-spacing of the !Kung ensures that the parents are usually prepared for the birth of a new child when it occurs.

!Kung women do not change their behavior particularly during pregnancy. They recognize that it is important to have a good diet consisting of plenty of food and especially meat during pregnancy, but that is desirable at all stages of life. From the fetus's point of view, maximal growth and well-being require the mother to have a good diet and require that the mother not give away the needed nutrients to an older sibling in the form of lactation (Trivers, 1974). Hormones automatically suppress lactation at a relatively early stage of pregnancy, so that the mother has no choice but to wean the older child, resolving the conflict of interest between the fetus and the older sibling in favor of the fetus. Similarly, the fetus might be favored if the mother took it easy and did not work quite so hard during pregnancy, but no one in the family would benefit from the loss of the food that the mother regularly brings in to feed herself as well as the children, and so women do not noticeably change their schedule of gathering trips during pregnancy. Women gain about 7 to 9 kg from conception to live birth and lose about 5 kg at birth (the baby's weight is about 3 kg).

In the last stages of pregnancy, women may be anxious about the event, particularly if it is a first birth, and young women prefer to live near their mother or older sister when they experience their first birth. But most women are remarkably calm and courageous about facing birth, and most births occur relatively quickly (over a few hours) without complications. When complications occur, however, they are likely to be fatal, and both the mother and the child die. A half dozen cases of mothers dying in childbirth have been reported (mostly in the accounts of their own mothers). I know of only one case in which the mother died in childbirth and the child survived, raised by her maternal grandmother on cow's milk. Other maternal orphans in the population lost their mother at older ages, when they had a better chance of adjusting to a diet of cow's milk.

When labor pains start, women make no general announcement but quietly go to a spot in the bush out of sight of the village and off the main paths that lead in and out to give birth in privacy. Often, and especially with a first birth, one or several experienced women will accompany the mother to provide moral support and to make a fire and provide some protection from the dangers of animals during the birth. Perhaps the lifelong habit of squatting to sit helps the women give birth relatively quickly, with a minimum of suffering (Shostak, 1981). When the baby is born, the mother will inspect it carefully. She has the option of smothering it and burying it with the afterbirth, if she finds abnormalities or believes that the child will not survive. Most women, of course, have no wish to smother the child they have carried for nine months and have just given birth. They wait until the afterbirth is expelled and bury it. The mother then returns to the village with the baby to announce its name and receive admiration and affection from her spouse and others in the village.

INFANCY

From the !Kung point of view, infancy starts not at birth but an hour or so later, when the new baby enters the village and is announced by name.[2] With the naming, the child becomes a person in their eyes. Parents have the right to name their children, and often the parents and other people in the village will have engaged in many discussions during the pregnancy about which name should be given. It is an important decision, because the "young name" has a strong tie to the "old name"

---

2. The name given is sex specific, one of about thirty-five names that each sex has. The child cannot be given the name of the parent or of any sibling currently living, but is sometimes given the name of a sibling who has died, to "replace" that child in the family. Ideally, the first male child is given the name of the father's father, the next the mother's father, and then the family starts to use the names of the parents' brothers, more or less alternating naming children for the father's side and the mother's side. Similarly, girls are named for the father's mother, then the mother's mother, and then the sisters of the parents, alternating sides. There are many exceptions to this formula for choosing names seen in the population.

Figure 2.1. An infant boy, age
16 months.

Figure 2.2. An infant girl, age
18 months.

for the rest of his or her life, and the name forms the basis of most of the
fictive kinship connections that !Kung have.

It is believed that mother's milk is helped to come in by consuming the
broth of a freshly killed and cooked animal, so the husband and father will
often go hunting immediately after he has greeted his child to bring in this
meat. The !Kung, like many people around the world, consider the
colostrum (the clear fluid that fills the breasts before the milk arrives, which
is known to be filled with valuable antibodies that can protect the infant
from infectious disease) as a "bad thing" (Shostak, 1981), and mothers spill
it from the breast into the sand rather than allow the baby to drink it.
Within a day, most babies are taking their mother's milk frequently and in
sufficient amounts that some of them become fat as shown in Figures 2.1
and 2.2 (Howell, 2000).

Babies are carried naked in a leather sling tied on the mother's un-
clothed body, either on the hip or on the back. Babies are in skin-to-skin
contact with their mother almost constantly from birth, near the breast
when awake, on the back when asleep, and lying on the mother's *kaross*
(leather cape) with her at night while the mother sleeps, able to breastfeed as often as the child wants. For the first six months of life, babies
live almost entirely upon breast-milk, and mothers start to supplement
their child's diet around that time, with premasticated meat and sweet

vegetable foods, withholding nuts and sour and bitter vegetables until the child is older. Babies are talked to and stimulated by siblings and others in the living group regularly, and babies learn to sit and stand and walk at ages that are somewhat accelerated over the pace of development of the North American children that we are used to seeing, perhaps (as suggested by Konner in Lee and DeVore, 1976) as a consequence of the strengthening exercise babies get automatically in maintaining their upright position on the mother's hip or back, balancing on the items of food she is likely to be carrying.

Mothers do not spend a lot of time in face-to-face contact with their babies, preferring to communicate with the child by nonverbal means. Mothers express their affection for their children by attentive care, patience with the aggravations that babies necessarily generate, and decoration of the baby with beads and pretty clothing. Hewlett, Lamb, and their colleagues (2000) argue that forager children are typically treated with parental warmth and affection, and they build up a positive "internal working model" of the universe that affects their behavior throughout life. This description of early life seems to describe the !Kung well. Ivey (2000:57) asks "who cares for Efe infants?" referring to the Ituri Forest hunter-gatherers and answers that these Pygmy peoples seem to be extreme in their use of alloparenting of infants, such that "the percentage of time young infants spent in physical contact with individuals other than their mothers increased from 39% at 3 weeks to 60% at 18 weeks." The !Kung seem to be at the other extreme of this distribution: The mother's body is the normal location of !Kung babies almost all the time until they can walk, and even after that, the child will be held and carried during sleep, during feeding, and in the presence of any danger or threatening situation for infants. Perhaps we saw babies being carried more than the actual average, because, by definition, anthropologists may be considered threatening by infants (Ivey, 2000).

Babies establish sphincter control at a young age, as a result of the intimate communication between themselves and their mothers that is encouraged by their skin-to-skin contact. When a baby spontaneously urinates, the mother responds by taking the baby out of the sling and cleaning off the baby (and herself and her nonabsorbent leather clothing) with a handful of grass. As the mother develops the ability to reach the child before the stream of urine is finished, she will add a hissing sound to the urine stream. Gradually, without verbal instructions and without scolding, babies can be induced to release the stream of urine at the hissing signal while being held out from the mother's body. Many children of six months of age are trained in this way, before they can talk. Similarly mothers are aware of their children's movements and sounds and learn to anticipate defecation, and move the child off her body before it occurs, while the child is still very young. Succeeding in avoiding "accidents" of defecation is valuable to the mother, but it is not entirely clear whether it is the mother or the infant who has been "trained." The nonverbal communication between mother and infant seems to depend upon the lack of clothing, so it will be interesting to know whether "toilet training" is becoming more of a problem for !Kung mothers now that most of them wear cloth clothing most of the time and carry their babies outside their clothes.

Traditionally, mothers continue to carry their children much of the time for several years. They permit the children to breastfeed at will. Konner and Worthman (1980) show that the typical baby feeds several times an hour, day and night, for years. The effect of the frequency of feeding, each bout of which releases a burst of the hormone prolactin into the mother's body, which decays gradually over a period of several hours, is that the mother's return of ovulation is suppressed until lactation becomes less frequent. This sequence of events is called "the baby in the driving seat" (Lunn, 1985:41–64), envisioning the baby as having taken control of the mother's hormonal balance while he (or equally she) needs the supply of breast-milk to maximize his (or her) survival throughout infancy.

In my data (Howell, 2000:149–150), birth intervals average forty months to forty-one months when the first child survives, and less when the earlier child dies (depending upon the age at death) if we count only one interval per woman (and an average of thirty-five months if we count all of the intervals that occurred during the eleven-year period of observation, a group biased to include many short intervals). The birth interval includes the next pregnancy, so the average age of a child when the average mother becomes pregnant again and weans the older child in the second month of pregnancy is in the range of twenty-eight to thiry-five months. Lactation increases the duration of the birth interval, and it is relatively rare for a mother to actually wean her child and menstruate for some months before becoming pregnant again. Instead, most mothers wean after the next pregnancy is established and are both lactating and pregnant for a month or two.

Some children fight hard against being weaned (Shostak, 1981). The !Kung believe that a child who is weaned too early (in the second year of life) will be small and unhealthy and will have an angry heart not only

Figure 2.3. A boy, representing child-   Figure 2.4. A girl child, age 13 years.
hood, age 12 years.

as a child but perhaps even as an adult. Weaning is more difficult when
the child constantly sees the desirable breasts, and so others—father,
grandmother, aunts, and cousins—often step in to help the mother
wean the child by carrying and distracting him or her for some weeks.
About 30% of children born are not followed by another birth, and
these lucky children wean themselves from the breast when they are
ready, typically around forty-eight months, trailing off to sixty months.
Eventually children grow too large to be carried constantly as nursing
children typically are, and the mother cannot or is not willing to carry
her child on gathering expeditions. Occasionally one sees a "big baby"
run to his mother—in the extreme case as old as five or six—when the
women return from gathering, to throw himself into her lap and take
the breast, but the other children are likely to tease him about it, and
the breastfeeding eventually ends. Weaning marks the end of infancy.

CHILDHOOD

From the age of weaning, approximately age 3 to 5, to the age of sexual maturity for girls (menarche), approximately age 15 to 17, children's work
consists of play (see Figures 2.3 and 2.4). The youngsters usually stay in the
village, under the general supervision of the adults (their parents or others)
who choose to stay in the village that day. The children spend their time

playing, growing, and practicing the skills of adult life in an informal way. Since 1970, they have had the option of attending school, but none of them did during the years of this study. !Kung parents do not attempt to give systematic lessons in the knowledge and skills that their children will need in the future. They merely aspire to keep their children safe and healthy until they grow up and can learn the skills of adult life for themselves.

Children form multiage play groups and rarely have enough children in one place to engage in complex games with rules and teams. Competitive games are not practical when the village consists of only a few nuclear families, when one child may be 4, another 8, and the third 12 (Konner, 1976; Lee and DeVore, 1976; Hewlett, Lamb, et al., 2000). Generally they play games of "pretend," and they make up their play group including all the children present. Only in the largest groups is there likely to be any segregation by sex or by age group. There is very little privacy in a !Kung village. Children's play can usually be observed by others, just as adult activities can be casually observed by children.

Children are treated affectionately and indulgently by adults, both their own parents and others who live in the village (most of whom are likely to be relatives of the child in one way or another). Adults rarely join in children's games (see Biesele and Howell, 1981, for an exception) or make any attempt to influence the children in what kinds of games they play.

"Bad behavior" that children can engage in includes hurting others by hitting and biting, throwing sand or stones, and rude speech. Most adults take the attitude that "children have no wits" and so they cannot insult an adult and are not much danger to themselves and others. A child having an unusual temper tantrum might be picked up by an adult and held so that he cannot hurt himself or others, but there will be no punishment afterward. Sex play is common among children (Shostak, 1981) and is not taken very seriously, even if it would be classified as incestuous if adults did it. All children seem to have the opportunity to observe sexual intercourse between adults at night, when the children are supposed to be sleeping. Parents and children are in a "respect" relationship, which does not permit casual conversation or joking about sexual matters, so mostly parents ignore their children's sexual initiatives, just as children ignore their observation of parents' sexual intercourse. Children play at sexual intercourse so frequently and consistently that there is no sharp dividing line between a sexually experienced and inexperienced child, no "virginity" to be lost. Shostak's Nisa describes the way that children's sexual games gradually prepare young women for marriage (Shostak, 1981).

!Kung children will gather food when it is readily available to them (i.e., they will pick berries and eat them as they travel between villages with their parents, they will gather up mongongo nuts that are lying on the ground to help to fill their mother's backpack when they are in the mongongo groves, or they will gather an armload of large, velvety baobab fruit and carry it back to the village). Similarly they might pick up a tortoise if they see one on the path, and will be delighted if they occasionally knock down a duiker or other small animal with a toy arrow or a throwing stick in the bush near the village. But, compared to other hunter-gatherer children, !Kung children put little effort into acquiring food and provide a very small portion of their own diet while they are still children. Children are almost entirely dependent upon their parents and village adults for their food.

!Kung children do some useful tasks around the village. They learn to remove the inner shell off already roasted and cracked mongongo nuts that their mother has prepared for the family, and Lee says that children over age 8 shell about half of the nuts they consume each day (Lee, 1979). Children will watch and sometimes help adults who are carrying out tasks such as making tools, stretching and scraping a new hide that will be used to make clothing, or cooking food. Older children may, if asked, go to the well to collect water and carry it back to camp in a pot or in ostrich egg shells, and more often a group of children of mixed ages will accompany an adult to the waterhole and help to carry back a portion of the water that they can manage, or will go along on a firewood-collecting expedition (most of which are carried out within a few hundred yards of the village) and help to carry back some sticks and branches of firewood. Children are frequently asked to bring a coal from the fire to light a pipe of tobacco, or to carry a dish of food or some beads from one sitting adult to another, and usually they do so, but it is well under-stood that children do these chores only if they feel like it, and that children are not compelled to work.

Blurton Jones and his colleagues (Blurton Jones, Hawkes, et al., 1996) note that !Kung children are much less oriented to work and obtain much less food than Hadza children do. They suggest that the environment of the Kalahari is more dangerous to children than that of the open hilly areas of the Hadza terrain. !Kung parents worry that their children can easily become lost in the Kalahari, where it is difficult to get a long-distance perspective on the environment, and that the combi-nation of risks from animals, snakes, and being lost is too great to justify allowing children to roam the desert seeking food. Children are too noisy and too slow to accompany the hunters. They can be herded along with the women on gathering expeditions, and sometimes they do accompany the women, especially during the rainy season when the weather isn't too hot and there will likely be water to drink along the way. Depending on what kind of food is being sought, children can be helpful in collecting and can eat a substantial portion of the food right out in the field where it is collected, so that the food carried home can last the family longer. But during the hot and dry season, it is too difficult for the women and children to carry the water that the children will need to drink during the day, and so it is better for the mothers to leave the children in the village with a supply of water (and usually some cooked food for the children to snack on) where they can play safely until their mothers return.

Typically, mothers do not go gathering every day (Blurton Jones, 1986; Blurton Jones, 1987), and each day at least a few adults remain in the village to rest and carry out housekeeping tasks while keeping an eye on all the children. Mothers who stay behind in the village are not necessarily expected to feed all the children who are there, but when they feed their own children, they expect that their children will share part of their portion of food with their playmates. "Babysitting" is not a formally arranged activity, but children are never left alone either.

Growth is slow throughout childhood for !Kung children, especially for those in the age group of about 7 to 12. We will see later that these are the thinnest members of the !Kung population, and the most stunted in height and wasted in body size by international standards, although the children seem to be normal in vitality and activity. At ages when Western girls are expecting their menarche, !Kung girls may still have five years or more to wait.

In the later stages of childhood, growth accelerates, with both sexes gaining height and weight. The increase in weight for girls is largely made up of fat and for boys primarily muscle tissue, which produces the characteristic shape differences between the sexes in adolescence. During the "growth spurt," both boys and girls may be more motivated to collect as well as eat food. The girls sometimes start to accompany the older women on gathering expeditions voluntarily, driven by their hunger to eat earlier in the day and to bring back more food to the household than their mother could otherwise manage. This change in behavior is noted approvingly by adults, who start to think about which young man would make a good husband for this hardworking girl. Thus, a process starts that often continues throughout adolescence, of arranging marriages for young girls to older young men. The probability of menarche by age for young women can be seen in Table 9.3 in Howell (2000:178).

ADOLESCENCE

Adolescence is the time in life when the young men and young women diverge in their typical activities (Bogin, 2006). Let us focus on the young women first. Girls' bodies gradually change into those of young women, and they may be playing with the other children most of the day while beginning to interact with adults as a potential bride. Some young women are married when they are older children, but the marriage is more a matter of a promise than a reality at this stage, and it is not supposed to be consummated prepubertally. The event that marks the start of her adolescent stage of life is menarche, first menstruation.

When the first menstrual blood appears, the girl typically tells her mother or another close kinswoman. The girl is immediately secluded in a hut, and the women spread the word that they have a new adult in the group. Men may plan to go hunting the next day to bring in a fat animal to provide meat for a feast to celebrate the ceremony of first menstruation. Adults send messengers to nearby villages to invite residents to come and help celebrate the creation of a new woman. During the few days of menstruation, the girl is secluded so that sunshine doesn't touch her. When she needs to urinate, she is supposed to be carried on the back of a woman to the bush so that her feet don't touch the ground. When the menstrual flow is finished, her skin is rubbed with fat by her mother and other older women, and she is brought out of the hut with her grown-up *kaross* (leather cape) draped protectively over her head. She sits quietly at the fireside while the women enthusiastically hit ax-heads together, bare their breasts and rumps, and sing and dance in celebration of her maturation.

The next day the young woman may rejoin the children's play group, or she may join the women's gathering trip, depending on her inclination. There is no immediate demand to start producing food regularly or to start mastering the skills of gathering. But discussions by her parents with others about arranging a marriage for the young woman will certainly accelerate, and the young woman is likely to become more self-aware of her status as a sexually attractive woman, and perhaps more anxious about the implications of a marriage that threatens to take her away from her mother. Nisa (Shostak, 1981) helps us understand the conflicting motives of a pubescent girl, and Elizabeth Marshall Thomas illustrates the complexities of life in this stage with her tale of "Beautiful Uncka, the lily of the field" (Thomas, 1959:165).

When a potential husband for the girl is located, and he agrees to the plan, the young girl will be told by her parents that he is her husband-to-be. The girl may protest, especially if the proposed husband is much older than she, or if he is unattractive to her in some way. Generally, a girl wishes for a husband who is young, like the playmates with whom she has enjoyed sexual games, and one who will not take her away from her mother and nuclear family. The family will consider issues like the potential hunting success of the husband, his character and personality, his claim to n!ori (place) ownership, and the reputation and kin relationships of his relatives, whereas the girls are primarily concerned with the man's appearance and his attitude toward herself. If the parents agree, the groom and his family will come to visit the bride's village, and the two sets of parents of the couple will jointly construct a first home for them, just a grass shelter of the usual kind, near the girl's parents' hut.

Often the girl will run away when the young people come in the evening to take her to her marriage hut, but this display of reluctance is *pro forma* in most cases. The girl will be dragged back from the bush where she has run away and put in the hut with her new husband, and the couple will eventually go to sleep side-by-side. If she wants to generate more drama, the girl is likely to "run away" from her bridal hut again and again back to her mother (who is likely living "next door"). But, if she is really determined not to marry the man, she lets her parents know it, and eventually they have to relent and send the young man away. For a few days it may not be clear whether the new marriage has succeeded: One can tell only by listening carefully to the kinship terms that people are using for one another. As long as the girl's parents are calling the husband "son-in-law" and his parents "co-parents-in-law," the marriage is still on, but if they give up after a week or so, they will go back to using the kin terms to address one another that they used before the marriage was proposed. Young women may experience several brief "marriages" and "divorces" of this kind before they settle on a husband. The age-specific probability of first marriage for young women is shown in Table 9.2, Howell (2000:175).

Adolescence, then, is a time in a young woman's life when she is changing her appearance and her relationships to others in the group, when she is actively learning the skills of womanhood, when she is in the public eye as a potential wife for the young men, when she marries (and perhaps

Figure 2.5. A young man, age 18, in   Figure 2.6. A young woman, age 17,
the adolescent stage of life.   in the adolescent stage of life.

remarries), finally settling into a relationship with a husband and starting
her first pregnancy. This stage of life lasts from a mean age of 16.6 at
menarche, a mean age of 16.9 at first marriage, and ends at a mean age
of 21.4 at the birth of the first child. The oldest age of a woman at the
birth of a first child observed was 28: In the model of life stages we are
constructing, a young woman who has not produced a first child by 29
goes directly into the post-reproductive class (see Figures 2.5 and 2.6).

Adolescent girls typically wait several years after marriage before
their first conception. This long adolescent sub-fecundity is typical of
thin people and hunter-gatherers in general (Bentley, Paine, et al., 2001).
But if the first conception is delayed a long time, the girl begins to worry
that infertility may be her permanent fate, either because she has become
infected with a sexually transmitted disease (gonorrhea is common in
the area, and syphilis is known) or because she is simply unlucky.

The event that marks the entrance of young men into adolescence is
genarche, the production of viable sperm. This event is not announced
or celebrated in !Kung life, and so it is more difficult for us to determine
the age of entry into adolescence for the boys. To make things simple,
let's say it has the same age distribution as the girls' menarche, and that
boys remain in adolescence, like the girls, until they have their first child.
Men have a considerably longer adolescence than women, as even the

youngest husbands are at least 22 and the mean age at marriage for men is 26.7, with the birth of the first child a few years later. The probability of first marriage per year for men seems to be constant at about .17 per year from 22 to 30, and all men in the 1968 population who ever married were married by 39. The number of years spent as an adolescent by a man, then, might be as little as five (from 17 to 22) or as much as twenty-four (from age 15 to 39), a long time and a substantial portion of the life span. The average duration in this stage of life is eleven years for men, from 16 to 27; the median duration is more like nine years, from 16 to 25. The much greater length of adolescence for males than for females is a major source of the differences between the sexes in life history. Men go on growing longer, get bigger than women, and have many more experiences (such as employment and travel) outside the circle of family and kin ties.

Adolescent boys are not required to stay in the village like children, being supervised by any adults who are around. Instead they are free to go visit relatives, to accompany hunters on their rounds, to take jobs working for Bantu cattle owners, or to accept any other opportunities that arise, and to learn about anything that interests them. Some young men sign up for a term of employment with a labor recruiting firm that takes them to South Africa to work in mines or industry. Many travel widely during their adolescent years, and may visit and establish close ties with branches of the family that their parents hardly know. They are rarely asked to do any particular work by their families. Young men are smilingly referred to as "the owners of the shade" when they are at home, and they may be resented by the older generation when they come to pay long visits to relatives, as they compete with local men for the sexual favors of the women and eat the foods produced by the locals, typically without contributing much.

A young man starts to learn the serious business of hunting at the time during adolescence when he is ready to follow and act as an assistant to an experienced hunter, usually his father or another close relative. Hunting is difficult and complex work, requiring a lot of knowledge and practice in identifying spoor, learning the habits of the animal species that are hunted, learning to anticipate the behavior of the animals, tracking and following animals before and after they are shot, and learning how to butcher the meat, prepare hides for use, and prepare meat for drying and distribution. When the young man kills his first large animal, male and female, of each of the main species that the !Kung eat (kudu, eland, wildebeest), there is a ceremony and a celebration that involves tattooing the young man's face so that anyone who glances at him can see that he is an experienced hunter. In some ways, this event is parallel to the menarche ceremony for young women, but for the purpose of determining the stages of life, it seems more important to distinguish between the stage of life when children are confined in the village all day and when they are free to roam the Kalahari, so we will look at this "first meat" point as just another event that occurs during adolescence, like marriage.

When the young man has received his facial tattoos, he is eligible for marriage. It is likely that his parents would try to arrange a marriage for a young man as soon as he was eligible in the old days. During the 1967–1969 period, the young men were sometimes delayed in marriage by terms of work as "cowboys" for Bantu cattle owners, an opportunity that their parents welcomed for the chance to obtain store-bought gifts from their son, as well as access to milk and meat from the cattle herds he tended. At the same time, the young men were subject to competition from those Bantu cattle owners for sexual access to the young !Kung women, either as wives or as lovers. So I suspect that male adolescence was artificially lengthened by the arrival of the cattle in the Xangwa area, and we know that the reproductive success of the !Kung men has been reduced in comparison to that of !Kung women by the competition from men outside their ethnic group (Howell, 2000:177, 263, 274). The entry into first marriage for !Kung men can be seen in Table 13.2 in Howell (2000: 260).

Once the young man is married, he still has to face the difficulties of convincing a young girl to sustain the relationship. A young man who tries to force his child bride into a sexual relationship before she is ready is likely to find himself divorced and back at home, while his parents try to find another bride for him. The !Kung have an expression that a man has to "raise his wife up," feeding her and supplying meat for her and her family. He and his young wife typically live next door to her parents, under their scrutiny. He treats her with patience and respect, waiting for her to become sufficiently mature to conceive. She is likely to be still growing, developing breasts, and stabilizing her height and weight.

Finally, the couple conceives a child. The woman is likely to be between 19 and 21 by the time this occurs, and the man is likely to be somewhere between 24 and 30, average age 26. Both are likely to be skilled at the adult roles of hunting and gathering, hut construction, and social relations by the time the first child is conceived. The birth of that child, whether it survives or not, marks the end of the adolescent period for both males and females.

THE STAGE OF CHILDBEARING

The !Kung believe that the young couple should live in the village with the girls' parents, not just until the first birth but until several children have been born to the couple. The young woman will be, on the average, 21.4 at the birth of her first child, 24.9 at the birth of the second, and 27.5 at the birth of the third. Couples generally live with either the wife's family (especially the parents if they are alive) or the husband's family. Most often each party prefers to live with his or her own relatives, as they feel most comfortable there. The earliest phase of the childbearing stage of life is likely to be spent in the women's village, where a woman has her mother and other kin (especially sisters) to draw on for information and for concrete help with her tasks. So more than half of the reproductive period of a couple's life is likely to be spent living with the woman's parents. And if the man's parents are dead by the time the third child is born (which is likely, since the husband is likely to be about 35, and his parents are likely to be in their 60s by the birth of the third child), or if there are other advantages of staying with the wife's family, the couple may just decide to live permanently in the wife's family's village, even though the !Kung group as a whole is classified as patrilineal and patrilocal (see Figures 2.7 and 2.8).

Figure 2.7. A father, age 35, in the parental stage of life.

Figure 2.8. A woman, age 38, in the childbearing, or parental, stage of life.

One of the issues of the childbearing stage is how people use their time. Especially for the wife, the obligations of food collecting are increasing continually during the childbearing years (Lee, 1979; Blurton Jones, 1986; 1987). The woman starts this period of life at maximum health and strength (but probably not maximum skill). At first, she has only a small baby to carry and needs to collect enough food to supply her husband's and her own needs, including the caloric costs of lactation. But the child continually increases in weight, and by six months the mother needs to start providing vegetable foods for the growing child as well as for her and her husband. After six months, the child's need for calories exceeds the mother's ability to produce breast-milk. The nursing child is carried on the mother's back or hip, while she moves with the group, builds a new hut in the circle when the living group constructs a new village site, collects water and firewood daily to supply the household, gathers food every few days, bringing home a backload of vegetable food—roots, nuts, fruits, berries, leaves, and gums—for the family's consumption over the next few days. Lee (1979) has calculated that the average woman walks about 2400 km a year and carries the child, of increasing weight, with her, constantly over the first two years, and frequently over the next two. With the birth of subsequent children, the workload is continually increasing, as the requirements for providing food for the children overlap.

Women often go visiting, either with their husbands or with other women, to neighboring !Kung and Bantu villages where they have relatives living, to visit, to eat surplus meat that has been brought into the neighbor's village, to beg for tobacco or milk from the Bantu, or to engage in *hxaro* (gift giving). Other days they receive visitors at home and spend the day visiting and talking in their own village rather than working. One does not have the impression of a grim, never-ending round of work for people in this stage of life, but close observation indicates that they are doing a lot of work. We will examine the workload of adults in detail in Chapter 4, and since we have established the sequence of childbearing (in Howell, 2000), we won't spend a lot of time describing the daily routines of childbearing adults here. Suffice it to say that after two or three children are born, the parents are working at something close to their maximum, and they are glad to accept any help or labor saving they receive.

Women who are fully fertile are likely to be either pregnant or lactating at almost all times during their childbearing years. Only subfecund women spend long periods of time when they are menstruating, between births. One child follows another, with the crushing disappointment of an occasional child's death to punctuate the process. The problems of the childbearing years seem to be those of "packing"—packing or stacking the needs of a series of children who are dependent upon parents in overlapping cycles, and packing the tasks of the day so that all of the needs of the parents and children are met, without reaching total exhaustion.

Despite the burdens of childbearing, child care, and the work of feeding the family, many women have energy available for conducting extramarital love affairs and flirtations with style and flair. Some married couples are very devoted to one another, but in many others, one or both parties have lovers, whether serious and long-lasting or just occasional. Similarly, men have the ability to pursue alternative reproductive opportunities, to negotiate for a second wife, to learn the demanding efforts of ritual healing and trance-dancing, to experiment with growing crops and domesticated animals, and to test the sensations of drinking liquor and making home brew. The childbearing years are the focus of work over the lifetime, and reproductive age adults have less freedom and leisure than at any other period of life. But still, the demands on their time and energy are not constant and unrelenting.

This period of life ends when the parents give birth to their final child, which for the !Kung may be a birth order between first and ninth for women (Howell, 2000:141, 157) and first to twelfth for men (Howell, 2000: 269). The parent, of course, does not know at the time of the event that it is the final birth, and neither does the observer, so we have to obtain the estimates of age at final birth from people who are sufficiently old so that we can be quite sure they won't have another child. For women, this means past the age of 45, but men may have a child up to the age of 55 or so, which restricts the numbers of men who contribute to our distribution of age at final birth. Nevertheless, we conclude that the reproductive period ends from the early 20s to late 40s for women, with a mean age of 34.35 (and a standard deviation of 9.2 years) at the final birth. For men, both the start and the end of the reproductive years is later, as the men marry later than the women and their reproductive ability is more a function of the age of their wife or wives than of their own (Howell, 2000: 253–275). The mean age at birth of all children is about 35 for men, approximately equal to the average age of women at the birth of their final child and the mean age at final birth for men is about 50.

POST-REPRODUCTIVE LIFE

Post-reproductive life starts with the birth of the final child and includes raising that child and any older children who are still dependent. It is the stage of life in which one is contributing to the reproductive process as a grandparent as well as a parent. It includes menopause, for women, to the extent to which this is a distinguishable event. This stage of life starts with high workloads, for both sexes, as all the children who need to be supported are born, and that work increases in the early years as the final child grows and needs to be carried, nursed, and increasingly supplemented by his aging mother. A few years after the start of this stage of life, however, the work demands on women start to decline, as older children become capable of helping with the family workload and gradually become independent of the support of their parents. The work requirements generated by children shifts during this stage, as older children marry and produce grandchildren who may be supported in part by the grandparents (see Figures 2.9 and 2.10).

It is an interesting and important question whether the productivity of women in this stage of life declines in response to reduced demand, or whether they create surplus production to "invest" in their own children, in their grandchildren (the "grandmother hypothesis"), and in

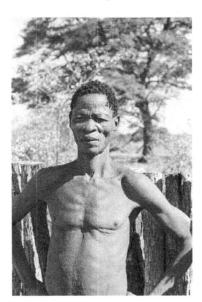

Figure 2.9. A man in the post-reproductive stage of life, age 51.

Figure 2.10. A woman in the post-reproductive stage of life, age 53.

other related or unrelated children or needy people (Hawkes, 1989; Hawkes, O'Connell, et al., 1998; 2000).

The post-reproductive adult stage of life, in fact, tends to be a time of high productivity for !Kung (and others), as the skills of the hunting and gathering life have been mastered and strength has not yet declined. If it were not for the contributions from the post-reproductive class, any short-falls in production by young adults would prove fatal to them and their families. Lee (1992) stresses that work demands decline for the woman who has finished childbearing, and that her sex life and role in public life improves. Eventually, however, the productivity of the post-reproductive women will decline, until the period ends with the "retirement" from active life into a more sedentary and specialized role of being what the !Kung call a *ju n!a*, a "big person" (which also means an old person).

Men may encounter more difficulties in maintaining productivity than women do in the post-reproductive stage of life. This occurs partly because men are older than women when they arrive at the post-reproductive stage, but it is also true that the requirements of hunting are more demanding of acuity and agility than the work of gathering. Men complain that "their eyes refuse them" in middle age and that they have difficulty seeing game and tracking it. They find that they no longer have the speed or endurance to chase an animal over long distances to help the poison work quickly. Many men specialize in snaring small game and digging animals out of their burrows as they get older, and many aging men increase the amount of gathered vegetable foods that they bring to the village.

Both sexes of post-reproductive adults may change their activities gradually as they get older, specializing in more sedentary activities such as tool making and bead work rather than hunting and gathering. Some specialize in healing and spiritual activities. Many take a special interest in passing on stories and knowledge to the younger generation (Biesele and Howell, 1981).

RETIREMENT: FRAILTY AND DEPENDENCE

If they live long enough, older !Kung eventually reach a stage at which they cease work and are dependent upon gifts of food and water from others, typically spouse, siblings, adult children, and sometimes grand-children. Draper and Buchanan (1992) noted that particular older people, those with admirable personal qualities and with numerous surviving younger relatives, were well treated and respected in old age, when Draper carried out a special study of old age in the 1980s, but that

Figure 2.11. A blind man in the frail   Figure 2.12. An old woman in the
elderly stage of life, age 72.   frail elderly stage of life, age 81.

other elders, without kin and an accumulation of social credits, fared poorly. Draper (in Keith, Fry, et al., 1994) noted that no !Kung person interviewed had anything good to say about old age.

Some elderly people and especially sick or injured people may be relatively neglected. Contemporary !Kung tell stories of such instances, but we also observed attempts to support handicapped and elderly people with food, shelter, medical care via the trance dance, and protection from animals and cold. In 1968, there were five totally blind people and eleven elders who needed to walk with crutches or canes who managed to live with assistance from spouse and kin. Pat Draper recalled two old widows living at Mahopa in 1968, when she was in residence there, totally dependent on their adult daughters. In general, however, people tend to die soon after they lose the ability to carry out what the gerontologists in our society call "activities of daily living," such as walking, dressing, eating, and toileting. Obviously the more the group is under stress to provide food for all, needing to move the village often to obtain a regular supply of food, for instance, the less ability it has to support dependent elderly. The !Kung do not engage in active senilicide, as the Inuit are reported to do, or leave old people behind on the path, as the Ache are reported to do (Hill and Hurtado, 1996). Figures 2.11 and 2.12 show some dependent elderly.

Rosenberg (1989) documented the "complaint discourse" of the frail elderly, who often kept up a running stream of commentary on their needs and problems and the shortcomings of those who should have been solving their problems. Rosenberg identified the "retired" people she interviewed and whose requirements and abilities were spelled out in detail. Their ages can be determined from her descriptions, as people in their mid-70s to late 80s. Draper commented (personal communication, 2003) that the "primitive communism" of the !Kung people seemed to require the kind of continual nagging that Rosenberg had pointed to. It was not altruism or saintliness that reinforced the sharing that !Kung depended upon, but an unending chorus of *na, na, na* ("gimme, gimme, gimme") that directed resources to the corner where they were needed. We will return to these questions in the final chapter of this book.

Life usually comes to an end for elderly !Kung in an episode of acute infectious illness, most often pneumonia (Howell, 2000: 47–71). Less often, the old die of what seem to be degenerative diseases like heart attacks and strokes (one case was described as "He wasn't sick, he just fell down"). But it is striking that old age is not particularly associated with death for the !Kung, because there is so much death at younger ages. Draper and Harpending (in Keith, Frye, et al., 1994:104–105) found that many !Kung express dislike and fear of old age, as a time of suffering and disability, but also found that many elderly !Kung express an enjoyment of life and satisfaction with the life that they have led. A few !Kung regularly live into their 80s, and there is no reason to believe that the maximum possible old age (life span) is any shorter for them than for people in any other human group.

LIFE STAGES FOR INDIVIDUALS AND FOR THE POPULATION

Having reviewed the ethnographic knowledge of each of the stages of life, we want to summarize this information into a population framework. We do this in three stages: first, we look at the proportion of people in each age and sex group who are in each of the life stages; second, we adjust that information to take into account the different numbers of persons at each age, resulting from death by each age; and third, we put that information into the format of an age-sex pyramid, which we are familiar with from population studies, so we can compare the information on age and on stages of life.

Assuming that people survive to the next event, the proportion of the life span spent in each life stage is simply a function of the ages of entry and exit from the stage as we have described them above. Think of the population at risk in this first stage of analysis as 100% of the people (of one sex) alive at that age. Figure 2.13 diagrams the age distribution for each of the boundary events that we have used to define the stages of life, and the proportion of females occupying each, by age, is indicated by the proportion of the population between those events. The more that the age distribution of the boundary events is straight up and down, the more closely the stages of life correspond to the ages of people in the group. For example, the first event, birth, occurs at age zero (by definition) and the line is straight up and down, while the second event, weaning, occurs between ages 3 and 6 and therefore has more variability and a somewhat broader slope. Events that have an even broader slope, such as the birth of the last child and the loss of independence, however, introduce wide variation in the ages of people in a life stage.

But, of course, people do not necessarily survive to reach the next event, so when we want to know what proportion of the population currently living at each age is in each of the stages, and what proportion of the life span is spent in each stage, we have to take mortality by age into the calculation, as we do in Figure 2.14.

Figure 2.14 includes the proportion of the population that survives to each age in the calculation, multiplying it by the proportion of the living population as seen in Figure 2.13. The first graph tells us what happens in the life of a group of women who are all alive and who all survive to the end of the life span, and the second set shows those same consequences among the survivors to each age in the living population at a point of time.

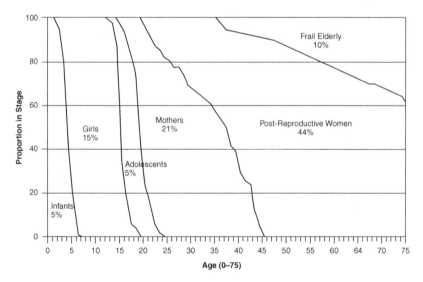

Figure 2.13. Transition probabilities for stages of life for !Kung women by age. (Source: http://hdl.handle.net/1807/17969.)

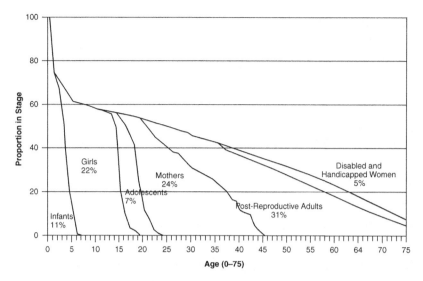

Figure 2.14. Proportions of living !Kung women in each stage of life. (Source: http://hdl.handle.net/1807/17969.)

The probabilities of both death and reaching each stage in life are somewhat different for the two sexes, and so we need to repeat the analysis for !Kung men. Figures 2.15 and 2.16 show the percentage of males who have reached each stage of life, and the proportion of the living population at each age.

In demography, we often show the proportion of people living at a point of time as a population pyramid rather than as a graph of survivors, as we did in Figures 2.14 and 2.16. The population pyramid is a rather eccentric form of data presentation, but students of population are used to reading the data in this way. The pyramid shows the percentage of an initial birth cohort of 100 males (on the left) and also of 100 females (on the right side), at each age, from age zero to a time in old age (in our case, 70). Think of them as bar graphs of the number of survivors to each age, around a central axis.

Figure 2.17 shows the outline of the population pyramid of the !Kung (Howell, 2000) with the stages of life overlaid on the age categories. Note that it simply takes the area graphs of Figures 2.14 and 2.16 and rotates them on the page to form the age pyramid.[3] This age pyramid

3. The age distribution incorporates a minor shortcut, by using the $l(x)$ (survivorship) column of the life table (rather than the $L(x)$ (age distribution column) to represent the proportion at each age. The difference is small for a single-year life table like this one. For details of calculation, see Barclay, G. (1958). *Techniques of Population Analysis*. New York: Wiley.

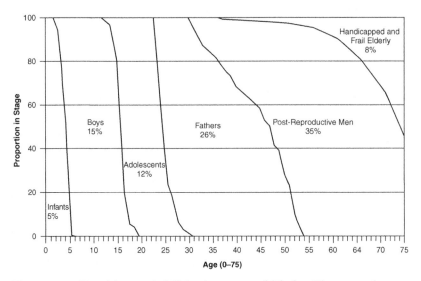

Figure 2.15. Transition probabilities for stages of life for !Kung men by age.
(Source: http://hdl.handle.net/1807/17969.)

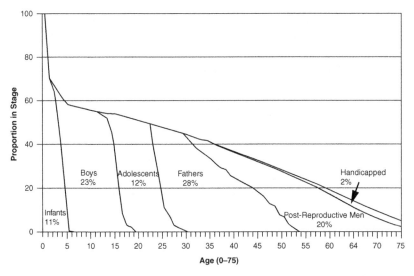

Figure 2.16. Proportions of living !Kung men in each stage of life. (Source:
http://hdl.handle.net/1807/17969.)

incorporates both the age distribution in years and the life stages as we
have defined them in this chapter.

Are there any surprises here? We note two kinds of insights from
Figure 2.17: methodological and substantive.

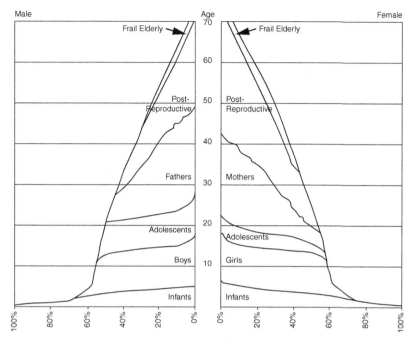

Figure 2.17. Stages of life as an age-sex pyramid. (Source: http://hdl.handle.net/1807/17969.)

Methodologically, we see that if we did not have age estimates of individuals, but only the stage of life that they are in, as variables that help us understand events such as maturation and reproduction, we would be very handicapped indeed. The problem is not so acute in infancy, childhood, and adolescence, where the age distribution of boundary events are quite flat, but for events in the reproductive, post-reproductive, and fraility stages of life the age ranges of entry and exit are extremely wide. Stages of life cannot satisfactorily substitute for age estimation studies, as time-consuming and exasperating as age estimation can be in a population like the !Kung, where people do not know their own ages or the dates of a calendar.

Substantively, we see that the stages of infancy, childhood, and to a lesser extent, adolescence make up a larger proportion of the total population than their average duration would lead you to expect, because a larger proportion of each cohort is alive at those young ages. The reproductive stage of life is perhaps shorter than one might have guessed, and a smaller proportion of the total is in it at any point in time. This stage of life is essential to the ongoing production of the whole group. People in the reproductive stage of life produce all the children, and later we will see in detail that they do much of the work of the society in addition, but if (like chimpanzees) adults died soon after their reproduction was finished, human life as we know it would not be possible (Robson, van Schail, et al., 2006). We also need the second half of the adult stage of life, after reproduction, to maintain our society and produce the work that must be done. In the !Kung, as in most human groups, the post-reproductive stage of life holds rewards of income and status, of power over others, and it is a time of decision making for the group as a whole. The post-reproductive stage of life is large and important. On the other hand, I am struck by the smallness and brevity for most people of the stage of frailty and dependence, which is a small proportion of the total population among the !Kung.

CONCLUSION: AGES AND STAGES OF LIFE, FOR !KUNG WOMEN AND MEN

In this chapter, we have seen that there are regular stages of life defined by events: birth, weaning, sexual maturation, birth of the first child, birth of the final child, and retirement into dependence on others in old age. These events define the boundaries of stages of life that are strongly age related, and only slightly different for the two sexes. Among the !Kung, people die at all stages of life, so that old age is not particularly associated with death, although all who enter that stage die in it. The requirements of food and support from others are closely associated with these stages of life, as are the ability to produce food and to provide for the needs of self and others. Later, we will look closely at the patterns of requirement for consumption and production of food as measured by calories per day, by age, for the purpose of better understanding the energy produced and consumed in each stage of life. In the next chapter, we will consider the body size of the !Kung people, and the pace of growth of !Kung to understand how their small size contributes to the overall adaptation they have evolved.

CHAPTER 3

Body Size and Growth

WHY ARE THE !KUNG SO SMALL?

One of the most distinctive features of the !Kung people is their small body size. They are short and slender and fine-boned. Many of the people are so thin that bones and muscles are readily seen through the skin, even though most of them seem to be healthy and vigorous.

There is considerable analysis and research currently underway on the dynamics of human body size, especially since the discovery of an extremely small-bodied fossil hominid population, the Flores people (Brown, Sutikaa, et al., 2004). Life history theory concentrates attention on the speed of growth (fast/slow), which has been investigated in a substantial cross-cultural study of contemporary small-scale societies (Walker and Hamilton, 2008) and in an intensive study of human pygmy populations (Migliano, Vinicius, et al., 2007), which concludes that pygmies stop growing at a younger age than non-pygmy populations, like the !Kung.

This small body size of the !Kung and all the Khoisan people does not seem to be an immediate reaction to the poor quality of the environment where they live. Biological anthropologist Susan Pfeiffer (personal communication, 2004), who studies the bones of the residents of southern Africa over the past 10,000 years, of people who are presumably the ancestors of the contemporary !Kung and other Khoisan people, notes that small bones are found uniformly across the wide territories of southern Africa and over many centuries, along with other distinctive skeletal features of contemporary Khoisans. Surely some of the environments in which these people lived must have been rich, she reasons, and some of the centuries must have been times of plenty, yet the bones are always small compared to other human groups, so she concludes that the determinant of small size must be other than simply immediate responses to local scarcity (Sealy, Pfeiffer, et al., 2000; Pfeiffer and Sealy, 2006).

We ask why the !Kung are small, and a number of hypotheses come to mind. Perhaps it is a matter of reproductive benefits: Small babies are born more easily, are easier for the mother to carry, and are easier to provide with sufficient breast-milk. Thus, small babies may have better survival rates than large babies, and small babies may grow to be small adults. But the birth weights of !Kung infants are not particularly low (Kurki, 2007), and physiologists tell us that larger babies generally have a higher probability of survival than small and low birth-weight babies (Bogin, 1988).

An alternative hypothesis is sexual selection: Perhaps small people are more attractive to the opposite sex. !Kung tell us that the tallest women are considered unattractive, but this designation was applied to only a few women, and women do not seem to have any difficulty finding mates at any time during their reproductive years, no matter what their height or assessment of beauty is. Sexual selection can operate on males more easily than females, as essentially all females are in sexual unions throughout their reproductive years, using their reproductive opportunities to the full, but males quite often fail to form a sexual union with a reproductive woman, at least at some period of time. Men's reproductive opportunities are limited by the women they are mated to, more than by their own limitations. Lee (1979) tells us that shorter men tend to have somewhat better hunting success than tall men, especially in the later years of the reproductive period when men might be making second marriages to younger women and hence inflating their reproductive success. Hunting success is attractive to women, and so to the extent to which the shortest men are the best hunters, they may succeed in getting a wife (or a second wife) more often than tall men.

A third possibility, suggested by Bergmann in 1847 (Nurse, Weiner, et al., 1985), is that small people can manage their body temperature in a hot climate better than large people, because they have more surface area in proportion to their body mass. Most of southern Africa is often very hot, and small people may well have evolved there. This is consistent with Pfeiffer's observation of shortness all over southern Africa for centuries.

Perhaps it is a matter of the "cost" of food in the Kalahari. Although there is no shortage of food species in the environment, perhaps it is so "expensive" for adults to go find and collect the food, carry it back, process it, and consume it that people aim to consume the minimum amount consistent with survival, not the amount that produces maximal growth and large body size. Or it may simply be that small size in childhood leads to small size in adulthood, so that that people require considerably less food over their whole life span, and thus they are "less expensive" to provision by themselves and by others (Martorell and Habicht, 1986; Ulijaszek, 1995). In another context (Howell, 1986), I have noted that the foods of the veldt are frequently bitter, fibrous, and difficult to process. Adults and children are unlikely to overeat such foods, and especially young children being weaned are likely to prefer sweet and warm breast-milk over the alternative of eating plenty of bush foods, hence setting their lifelong size by scarcity of calories during the weaning years.

The small size of the !Kung of all ages presents a puzzle for the analyst. It is associated with low fertility, as we would expect if it is an indicator of inadequate diet, but it is also associated with high vitality, generally good health, and low rates of degenerative disease. We would like to know what proportion of their genetic potential in body size the !Kung are achieving, but of course, we do not know what that potential is. The determinants of body size—diet, disease, and physical activity—can be explored but the implications of their consequences are not entirely clear.

Lee (1979) has shown that there is no shortage of food in the local environment and that the people work relatively short hours to acquire food, which seems to imply that food is not the limiting factor in body size. We know from physicians' examinations that there is a lot of infectious and parasitic disease in the population, but the doctors also concluded that the population is generally healthy and well nourished (Hansen et al., 1993). Adults and even children smoke tobacco as often as they can get it, which is likely to contribute to lower appetite and to health problems (maybe even stunted growth). And everyone walks long distances through the hot desert sands and generally shows a level of physical strength and endurance that others are hard pressed to match.

Lorna Marshall (in Lee and DeVore, 1968:94) summarizes the dilemma sharply:

> It has been suggested that because they (hunter-gatherers) do not have to work every day they can be said to have an "affluent society." This is a *bon mot* but does not add to the understanding of the reasons. I have pointed

out that the !Kung we worked with are all thin and that they constantly expressed concern and anxiety about food. There must be reasons why they do not gather and eat more. I think that energy for digging runs out and the daylight hours come to an end, for one thing. It has been suggested that that they cannot eat more roots, berries and seeds than they do, because the roughage is too much. And . . . if a woman gathered much more than her family needed at a given time, would it turn out that she was working for others?

Should we interpret the small size as an indication that children are stunted in their growth and are wasted in their bodies? Many analysts, especially the experts on international nutritional standards (National Research Council, 1989; Dwyer, 1991; Bogin, 1999), automatically do so, but Lee (1979) argues that we should not. Should we expect to see reduced immunity to disease at all ages and higher rates of mortality than we would otherwise expect? Epidemiologists and world health experts seem to do so (Food and Agriculture Organization, 1982; Falkner and Tanner, 1986). If people are marginally nourished and children are stunted and wasted, why do we see parents working relatively short hours in the traditional way of life, and why do we see efforts being put into activities such as trance dancing and artistic performance that do not immediately produce food? Should we view the small body size as a negative consequence of stunting and wasting, or as a positive consequence of a culture-wide adoption of a program of caloric restriction, which has been shown to increase health and longevity in modern human populations, and which is the only reliable method of reducing morbidity due to chronic disease and thus extending longevity into old age known to work in industrialized societies?

These questions are central to this book, and later we will explore the calories obtained and required by the whole population. In this chapter, we start our analysis by looking at the issue of the size of the individuals in the population, drawing upon the accounts of medical and physical anthropology studies of the !Kung (Trusswell and Hansen, 1968; Wilmsen, 1978; Harpending and Wandsnider, 1982; Nurse, Weiner, et al., 1985; Jenkins, Joffe, et al., 1987; Jenike, 2001) and also on the 3,081 observations of height and weight and skin-fold thickness that Richard Lee and I collected during 1967–1969, to review how big the !Kung people are at their various ages and stages of life, and to pose the questions that emerge from these observations. The results reported here are, in some ways, more detailed but do not differ in any striking way from our earlier reports on the !Kung (Lee, 1979; Howell, 2000).

COMPARISON TO INTERNATIONAL STANDARDS
OF HEIGHT AND WEIGHT

The U.S. Centers for Disease Control (CDC) provide standard graphs of normal childhood growth for infants and older children, based on measurements of tens of thousands of well-nourished children in the United States. These graphs are the successor to the National Institute of Child Health and Human Development (NICHHD) graphs (Dwyer, 1991) and also for the Harvard graphs, which are frequently cited (for instance, Truswell and Hansen, 1976:176). The standards provide a valuable framework with which to examine the variability of !Kung children's growth by age, in comparison, even though we do not expect that a normal !Kung child will be the same size as a normal U.S. child. Figure 3.1 shows the CDC standards of height and weight by age for boys (age 2 to 20), and Figure 3.2 shows the same standards for girls.[1] The lines show the percentiles of the normal U.S. (and generally Western industrialized countries) children who reach various levels of height and weight at each age. The graphs are commonly used by pediatricians to plot the height and weight at a number of points of time for an individual child, to show what percentile the child reaches at each age. The percentile level for a particular child is generally interpreted as expressing a combination of genetic and environmental determinants that are characteristic of that child. Crossing the percentile lines, up or down, might be a result of nutritional changes, sickness or recovery, or possibly the onset of a genetic problem, which may require medical care.

Over decades public health experts have found these standards to be relatively stable, although third-world countries have found that their children tend to move higher and higher on the North American standards as their health and nutrition improve, and the populations of the industrialized countries have discovered that they have had to raise the standards for the top percentiles on height and especially on weight as their children have moved from well nourished to super-nourished (and underexercised) in recent decades, as a part of what many public health physicians are calling "the epidemic of obesity" in industrialized societies.

We use these standards to help us interpret our look at the !Kung children in cross section, at the end of 1968, noting that the third percentile line, which corresponds to 2.5 standard deviations below the median, and

---

1. These forms are downloadable from the U.S. Centers of Disease Control website, at www.cdc.gov/growthcharts. Similar charts are available for infants (0 to 36 months old) and for "preschool" children, ages 2 to 5 years.

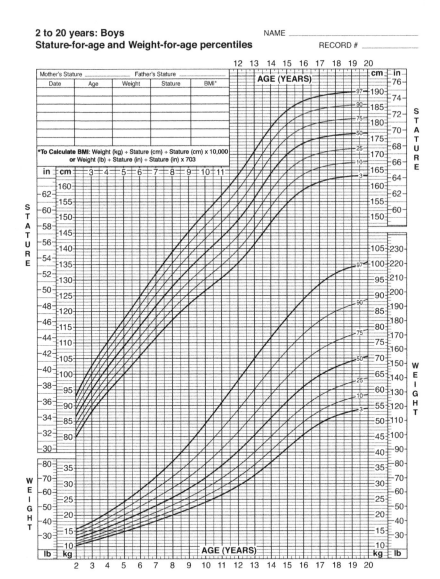

Figure 3.1. Stature-for-age and weight-for-age percentiles (boys 2 to 20 years) Centers for Disease Control (CDC) growth charts. Developed by the National Center for Health Statistics in collaboration with the National Center for Chronic Disease Prevention and Health Promotion (2000).

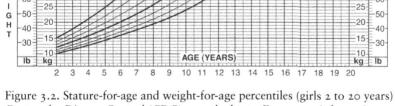

Figure 3.2. Stature-for-age and weight-for-age percentiles (girls 2 to 20 years) Centers for Disease Control (CDC) growth charts. For source information, see Figure 3.1.

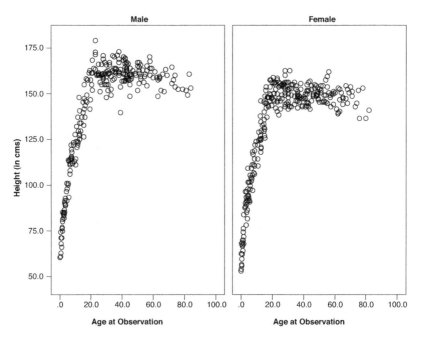

Figure 3.3. Heights (in cm) by age, for males and females. (Source: http://hdl
.handle.net/1807/10414.)

which is often used as the dividing line between normal and undernour-
ished in the U.S. population, is the best predictor of the !Kung median.
Fully 97% of North American children are taller and heavier than the average !Kung child at the same age. It is ironic that the level that approaches
the mean body size for !Kung is frequently used as the boundary of patho-
logical undernutrition in Western studies. We also see from these standards
that the lower levels of height and weight shown by the !Kung correspond
to a later pattern of achievement of the maximum height and weight.

We start our examination of the size of the !Kung by looking at the
distribution of height (measured in centimeters).[2] Height is somewhat
simpler to understand than weight, in that growing young people only
gain or fail to gain in height over time—they do not actually lose height
in response to poor environmental conditions. Full adult height is
reached in the early 20s for men, somewhat earlier for young women.
Figure 3.3 shows an overview of the height of all !Kung individuals
(counted once each) in cross section, by their age at the time of the
measurement, for all !Kung males and females. We note that height
increases steadily and in a narrow range until adulthood, when the boys

2. To convert height measures to inches, multiply centimetres by .3937.

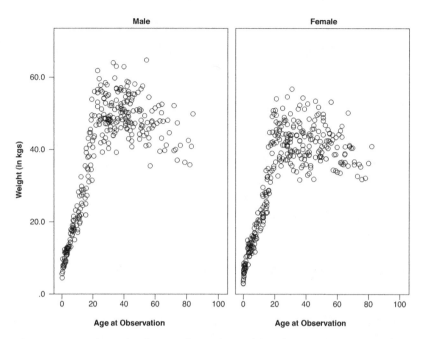

Figure 3.4. Weight (in kg) by age, for males and females. (Source: http://hdl
.handle.net/1807/10414.)

approach the adult mean height of a little more than 160 cm, and the
girls approach the adult female height of somewhat less than 150 cm.
The individual measures for both sexes then spread out into a cloud of
differences. When we check the extreme cases among adults, we generally find that the tallest have the nickname "tall" added to their name,
and the shortest are referred to as "short" by their peers.

We follow the study of height by looking at an overview of weight (in
kilograms)[3] in Figure 3.4. We have many more weight measures than
heights because weight changes are indicative of growth and well-being,
environmental fluctuations, and health. And !Kung as well as the inves-
tigators encouraged the collection of weight measures, because people
were usually rewarded with a choice of a handful of tobacco or a few
hard candies for their cooperation in weight measurements. !Kung suffering from "tobacco hunger" (most people, most of the time) urged and
reminded us not to forget to measure their weights. People were weighed
on a heavy-duty balance scale, wearing their usual clothing. The items
of clothing worn were noted, samples of clothing of each type were
weighed, and the typical weight for the items of clothing worn was

3. To convert weight measures to pounds, multiply kilograms by 2.2046.

subtracted to provide the measures reported here. Babies and small children were usually weighed by being held by an adult, subtracting the weight of the adult without the child.

We also combine height and weight into a measure of body mass index[4] to consider relative fatness or thinness of individuals in comparison to their fellows. The number of measures of body mass index (BMI) available for study is limited to those for whom we have both height and weight on a specific day, which usually was only done during our four focused "campaigns" of data collection, carried out in August 1968, October 1968, December 1968 (includes January 1969), and April 1969. Almost all body mass indices we will use here come from the end of 1968, when we made a major effort to collect heights as well as weights.

Body mass index has come to replace a number of measures (height-weight ratio, percentage of body fat, etc.) as the standard form of expression of body weight and height in a single number. In our weight-conscious society, many of us are acutely aware that a "normal" body mass index is considered to be in the range of 20 to 25, and the dividing line between "overweight" and "obese" is generally accepted to be 30. Figure 3.5 shows the BMI measures for all !Kung for whom we had measures of height and weight at the same time, showing the trends over the life span. The pattern over the life span seen in Figure 3.5 combines a quadratic curve in childhood, with the minimum BMI measures seen there, with increases in body mass index in adolescence for both sexes, and a wide range of measures in adulthood, although none exceed the top of the "normal" range of 25 and the vast majority of people of all ages are below the lower limit of the so-called normal range of 20. We will look at these patterns in more detail below.

When we compare the !Kung as a group with other hunter-gatherer populations (Jenike, 2001), we see that the !Kung are not the shortest people (the Efe, Mbuti, and Aka pygmy peoples of central Africa, the Batak and Agta of the Philippines, and the Hiwi of Venezuela are all (slightly) shorter as adults on the average). Many (but not all!)[5] hunter-gatherers are short: The !Kung are not included in the group classified as pygmies as adult male height exceeds the boundary of 155 cm, and they do not terminate growth at very young ages, as pygmies are said to do (Migliano, Vinicius, et al., 2007).

4. Body mass index is defined as weight (in kilograms)/height (in meters) squared.
5. The Colusa hunter-gatherer people of southwest Florida, for example, are noted for having been unusually tall.

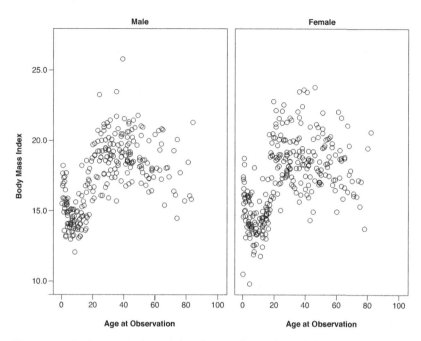

Figure 3.5. Body mass index (wt/ht²) by age, for males and females. (Source: http://hdl.handle.net/1807/10414.)

The !Kung are closer to the extreme in weight: Only a few populations (the Efe and Agta) are lighter. Combining these measures into body mass index shows that the !Kung have the lowest body mass index among the hunter-gatherers overall: The average body mass index for adult females (including pregnant and lactating women) is below 18.5, a level that Jenike calls "a recognized indicator of chronic energy deficiency" (Jenike, 2001). Jenike further notes that Dobe !Kung women, along with Agta (Philippines) and Australian Aborigine women, stand out as having the lowest body mass indices of the hunter-gatherer women. The !Kung men (mean body mass index 19.1) are the lowest of the hunter-gatherer men, who otherwise range from 19.2 to 24.5.

Body mass indices for individual adults and children are shown in Figure 3.5 (and see also Figures 3.17 and 3.20 later in this chapter), with one indicator for each person. Note that the level that Jenike felt posed a real problem, 18.5, is about the mean for the adults in the reproductive age groups, and many individuals are substantially below this level. In a book on the relationship of fatness and fertility, Frisch (2002) refers to the range from 17.5 to 20 as "underweight" and the range below 17.5 as "very underweight." She tells women who want to become pregnant that it is advisable to have a body mass index of more than 18 and adds that the hormonal environment for a successful pregnancy outcome will be improved by a body mass index of 19 and over. Women who are pregnant and lactating are apparently heavy and, hence, well nourished by this criterion, but may actually be physically stressed by the combination of low fat reserves and high biological activity levels during pregnancy. We note that the !Kung women can reproduce successfully despite low fat reserves and low body mass index, but we also note that the !Kung have low fertility and long birth intervals, compared to other populations.

Figures 3.3 and 3.4 show that there is a great deal of regularity in height and weight by age, but no single standard distribution such as a normal or binomial distribution fitting the data over the whole life span. In order to see the regularities of changes over the life span more clearly, we need to subdivide the measures of size into life history stages corresponding to the portions of the curve with predictable patterns: In this chapter, we will examine body size by age: infants (0 to 36 months); children and adolescents (ages 2 to 19 years); the reproductive age group along with some of the younger post-reproductive adults (ages 20 to 44); and the post-reproductive and frail adults (45+).

It is very interesting to note that the average body mass index is about the same for men and women in the same population, despite the clear pattern of men being taller and having more muscle, while women are shorter and have more fat. These variables tend to cancel each other (as fat is lighter than muscle), and access to the same diet by men and women tends to produce similar BMI measures. Because there is an age pattern to body mass index, we really need to know the age distribution of a population before we can interpret the mean body mass index for the population.

In the following sections, we will look more closely at body size for age groups in the population. We start by looking at the infants and young children.

BODY SIZE IN INFANCY AND EARLY CHILDHOOD

The CDC standards separate out the youngest group for study of their height (or rather length, for those who cannot yet stand) and provide reference standards in months of age (0 to 36). This decision directs our attention to the crucially important issue of the growth of nursing children. Bogin (1999) points out that maximal growth velocity is achieved *in utero*, and postnatal growth rates actually decelerate during infancy. Infancy is a particularly vulnerable time for survival and also for growth. We need to keep in mind that about 20% of the !Kung infants born alive die by their first birthday, and about 35% die by age 3, so we need to think of these infants as fragile. Nutritionists tell us that the prenatal period and the first several years of postnatal life are critical for growth and health over the whole life span.

Figure 3.6 shows one measure of height for each of some fifty infants measured during the first three years of life, plotted on the CDC standard percentile lines for comparison. Small children frequently did not want to stand on our equipment and allow height measurements to be taken, and they were never coaxed or forced to do so, so our coverage of infants is poorer than that of older children and adults. (We have many more observations of weight of babies, because children did not object to being weighed in their mothers' arms, and then being handed to another family member while we obtained the mother's weight, which was subtracted to learn the baby's weight.)

We wonder whether there might be a bias for children who were weaned early (who might be shorter than others at the same age) to be more likely to have "volunteered" to allow their height measurements to be taken, but that hypothesis is difficult to test, because we cannot compare those babies with the ones who refused to be measured. Because of these several factors of measurement error, possible bias in participation and low rates of participation, we are more hesitant about the quality of the infant measurements than that of any other age group.

During the first year of life, only one !Kung boy and four girls were below the third percentile on the CDC height standards in this body of data, but growth seems to falter around the point when mothers first start to supplement the diet of infants (4 to 6 months) and it continues to fall below the standards as they wean them. Physicians Truswell and Hansen found that about 50% of the infants in the first year of life were under the third percentile in height, whereas 80% of the children age 1 to 5 were similarly under that crucial third percentile (Trusswell, 1977). We note that the defining characteristic of the syndrome that pediatricians call "failure to thrive" is stature and weight below the third percentile for age, without obvious organic cause (Bogin, 1988). Overall the !Kung infants are on the small side compared with the CDC standards, and they seem to fall further behind the standards through early childhood, but we would not go so far as to say that they are failing to thrive.

Figure 3.7 shows the weight for age of !Kung infants, plotted on the CDC standards for U.S. infants. We notice that, in the first year of life, most of the children are above the third percentile line, indicating that

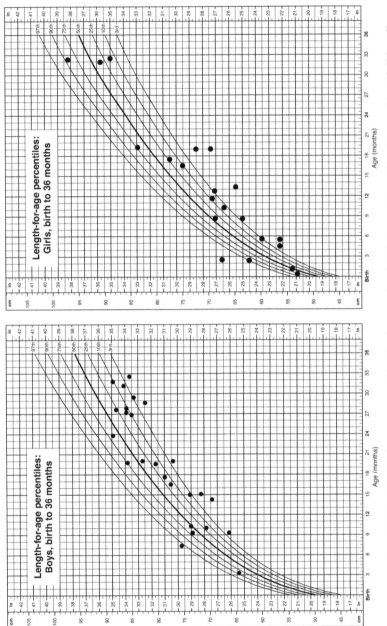

Figure 3.6. Infant heights: length-for-age percentiles, for boys and girls, birth to 36 months. (Source: http://hdl.handle
.net/1807/10396 and http://hdl.handle.net/1807/10401.)

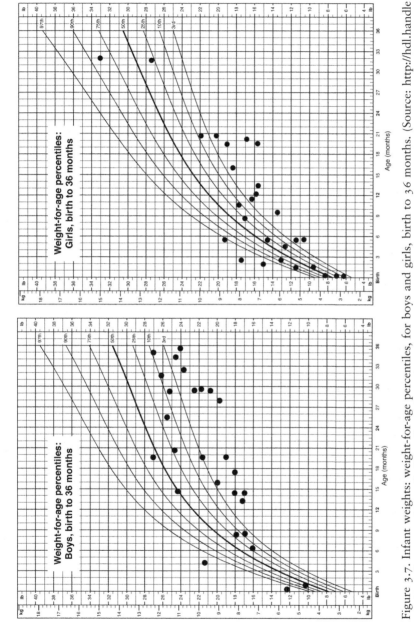

Figure 3-7. Infant weights: weight-for-age percentiles, for boys and girls, birth to 36 months. (Source: http://hdl.handle .net/1807/10396 and http://hdl.handle.net/1807/10401.)

their weights are substantial, considering the size of their mothers and their genetic heritage. But during the second year of life, the time between 12 and 24 months, most of the boys and all but one of the girls fall below the third percentile line. Truswell and Hansen (1976), in their sample (much smaller than the sample used here), show that 40% of the infants and 60% of the children age 1 to 5 fell below the third percentile of the reference standards they used (slightly different from the CDC standards). The reduction in weight below that expected is striking, and it seems to be related to the failure to adequately supplement the generous amounts of breast-milk these babies are offered. Mothers premasticate and pound samples of the foods that the whole family is eating, but these tend not to be very satisfactory for babies.

Figure 3.8 shows us that the weight and length measurements are coordinated for infants, in the sense that it is generally the short infants who are light and the tall ones who are heavy. Some !Kung babies have Bantu fathers, and these children tend to be larger than others. Only five of the boys and one of the girls fall below the third percentile of weight for length. The body mass index, our usual measure of the relationship of height and weight, is not considered an ideal index for infants, and we will look at their scores on this measure only as a part of measures for all the children.

CHILDHOOD MEASURES CONTINUED: BODY SIZE FOR OLDER CHILDREN AND ADOLESCENTS

The measurements for children, birth through 19 years, are the crucial ones, as they set the overall body size that remains for the rest of life. Shortages of nutrients and calories in childhood will surely produce a slowing or reversal of gains in weight and may slow or stop growth in height (Wooton and Jackson, 1996). Later a resumption of good nutrition may produce "catch-up growth" (growth exceeding the amount expected at that stage), compensating fully or partially for growth that did not occur at any earlier stage. Much seasonal growth halting is of this kind, made up in the season of plenty. When deprivation is extreme, as in famines and wars, catch-up growth is associated with health problems in later life (Lucas and Fewtress, et al., 1999).

Figure 3.9 shows the stature of boys and girls through their childhood, and Figure 3.10 shows the increases in weight with age. We note that the majority of !Kung children at all ages are below the third percentile of growth of U.S. children, and we note too from the graphs that the markers of growth, the points where growth slows down and

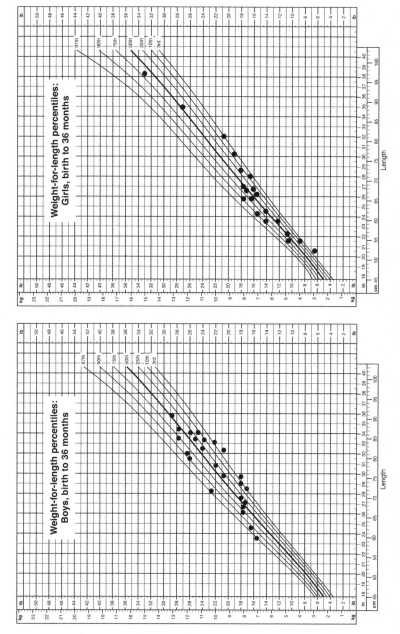

Figure 3.8. Weight-for-length percentiles, for boys and girls, birth to 36 months. (Source: http://hdl.handle.net/1807/10396 and http://hdl.handle.net/1807/10401.)

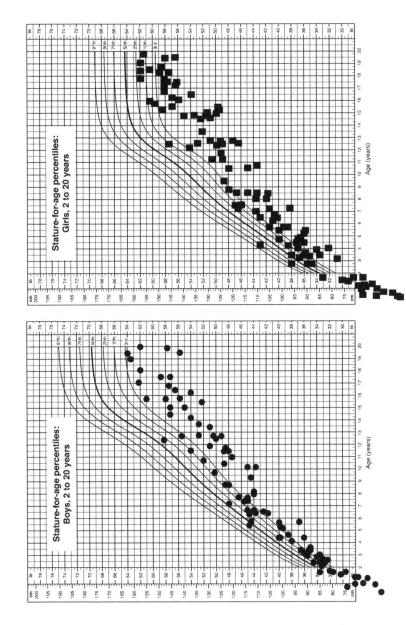

Figure 3.9. Stature-for-age percentiles, for boys and girls, 0 to 20 years. (Source: http://hdl.handle.net/1807/10396 and http://hdl.handle.net/1807/10401.)

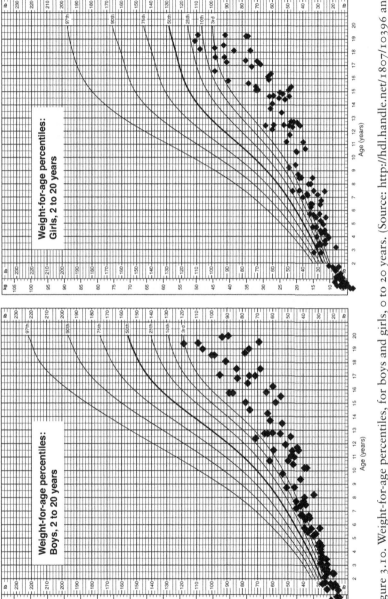

Figure 3.10. Weight-for-age percentiles, for boys and girls, 0 to 20 years. (Source: http://hdl.handle.net/1807/10396 and http://hdl.handle.net/1807/10401.)

speeds up, seem to occur at somewhat later ages in !Kung children than in the U.S. standards.

Weight was measured frequently for children because it is a sensitive indicator of physical state, but it is also a somewhat unreliable indicator, as weight can change during the course of a day in response to eating and drinking, perspiration, and elimination. The interval between measurements is variable, depending on how often we saw the child in question when our scale was nearby. We note that unlike height, weight can go down as well as up. When we go to the collection of multiple measures of weight per child, we can calculate the change in weight between measures and convert that into a change in weight per year (by dividing the change in weight (in kg) by the length of the time between measurements, in decimal years). Figures 3.11 and 3.12 show the measures of height and weight changes by age.

The line on Figure 3.11 (and subsequent figures) is a product of a statistical technique called a lag and latency smoother line, available in the SPSS statistical analysis package. It differs from the percentile lines provided by the CDC standards, by being based entirely on the raw data rather than the experience of large numbers of other people, but it serves a similar function for the reader as a guide to the eye. Lag and latency smoothers help in recognizing the patterns of the running average of the variable on the vertical axis at each point on the horizontal axis.

Figure 3.11 shows the pattern of growth in height for boys and girls. We note that growth is rapid in infancy and declines sharply through

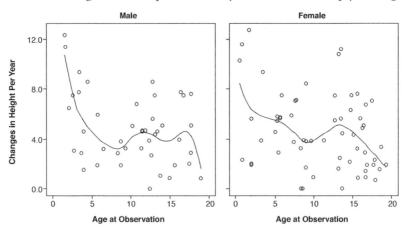

Figure 3.11. Changes in height per year, by age of child, for boys and girls, o to 20 years; age measured at start of observation period; with LLR smoother line. (Source: http://hdl.handle.net/1807/17983.)

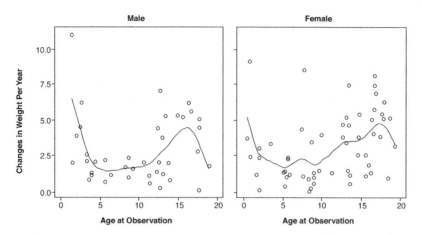

Figure 3.12. Changes in weight per year, by age of child at start of observation, for boys and girls, 0 to 20 years. (Source: http://hdl.handle.net/1807/17983.)

early childhood, reaching a low point around 7 or 8 years of age. Then growth in height accelerates, starting around 9, reaching a maximum rate around 14 or 15, and slowing in the teenage years but continuing to be positive past the age of 20. The shape of the curve of height by age is similar for the two sexes in mean and standard deviation, and it is slightly convex in shape, curving above a straight line, but clearly strongly related to age. A linear regression line of height by age (not shown) fits well for the boys and girls age 2 to 20, accounting for about 93% of the variance in height by age (for each sex).

The calculated variable "weight change per year" (based on the weight change between adjacent measurements, divided by the length of the interval to estimate the effect over a year) can be negative as well as positive. It is impossibly large in some cases from extrapolating gains or losses made in a short time to a whole year. In general, however, these measures point out that increases in weight accelerate during the teenage years, consisting of increases in muscle mass as well as increases in height for boys, and much more of the gains for girls are increases in fatness, contributing to their adult body type of breast and buttocks fat (Pawlowski, 2001).[6] Even though the girls are thin and are typically increasing their activity level at this age as they join the adult women in

6. Pawlowski suggests that the function of the fat deposits on the buttocks and thighs of maturing girls is to lower the center of gravity in women with frontal breasts and abdomens to maintain balance in walking, especially during pregnancy.

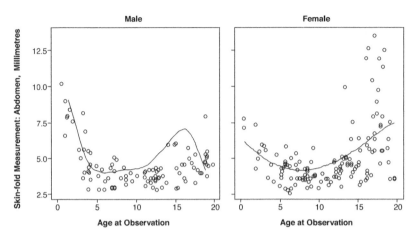

Figure 3.13. Abdominal skin-fold measures by age, for boys and girls, 0 to 20 years. (Source: http://hdl.handle.net/1807/10413.)

the work of gathering, they manage to deposit substantial amounts of fat, and they typically continue to deposit fat until their first pregnancy.

Growth in weight starts high in infancy, declines to a minimum around 4 or 5 years of age, remains relatively flat until 11 or 12, and accelerates in the adolescent growth spurt, reaching a maximum rate of increase around 16 or 17, slowing gradually afterward and still positive at age 20 for both sexes. The shape of the growth curve for males in Figure 3.12 is smooth and classic, seen in many countries around the world (Tanner, 1960). The curve for the girls is less clear, probably distorted by idiosyncratic events in the lives of the small numbers of girls we measured. Figure 3.12 shows that both sexes experience a slowdown in weight increases during the final teenage years.

We see these regular changes in degrees of fat storage in children by age more clearly in the measurements of skin-fold thickness.[7] Figure 3.13 shows the results of pinching the skin on the abdomen of children. The measure tells us the thickness of two layers of skin and the associated layer of fat that clings to the skin on the belly of the children, pinched not so tightly that it hurts but so that nothing else is included in the measurement. We see that the girls tend to have thicker layers of fat than the boys at all ages after infancy and that the teenage girls have a much wider range of fatness, according to this measure. All of these girls would be considered "thin" in an obesity clinic, but !Kung girls are fatter than the boys in

7. For simplicity, only the first of three measurements taken is reported here.

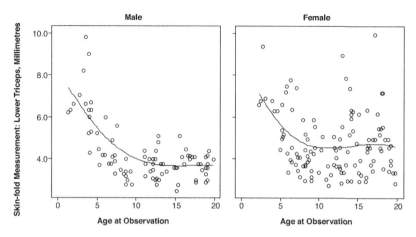

Figure 3.14. Lower triceps skin-fold measures by age, for boys and girls, 0 to 20 years. (Source: http://hdl.handle.net/1807/10413.)

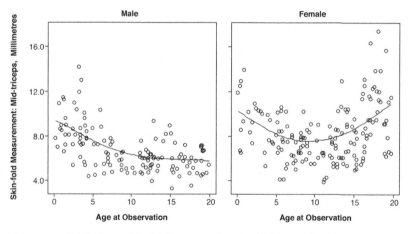

Figure 3.15. Mid-triceps skin-fold measures by age, for boys and girls, 0 to 20 years. (Source: http://hdl.handle.net/1807/10413.)

adolescence. Figure 3.14 shows the same measure for the lower triceps (just above the elbow) (Hansen et al., 1993). Fat deposits are highest in infancy and early childhood at this site, and they decline to a flat distribution by age 9 or 10, after which the mean doesn't increase but the variance for the girls increases strikingly in the later teenage years.

Figure 3.15 shows the mid-triceps skin-fold measure for the children, the place over the muscle of the upper arm. We note again that the girls have considerably thicker skin-folds than boys the same age, and much

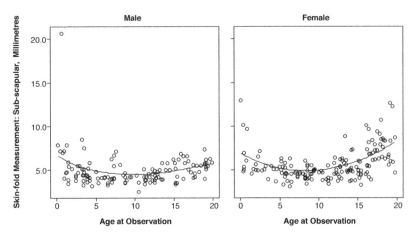

Figure 3.16. Subscapular skin-fold measures by age, for boys and girls, 0 to 20 years. (Source: http://hdl.handle.net/1807/10413.)

more variance, especially in the teenage years. And finally, Figure 3.16 shows the subscapular measures (on the back, just under the shoulder blades). Aside from one very fat baby boy, the boys tend to have somewhat thinner subscapular skin-folds than the girls, and the girls' fat deposits in this area increase in adolescence considerably more than the boys' do. With these features of the typical patterns of fatness in mind, let us look more closely at the BMI measures of !Kung children.

Figure 3.17 shows the body mass index for !Kung children plotted on the CDC standards. Note that measures for children in the first two years of life have been added to this graph, to emphasize the drop in BMI early in life. There is a distinct quadratic curve shape to the BMI distributions of the !Kung children, more symmetrical than the CDC standards for children in the United States. As we also saw in Figure 3.5, we note that the BMI indices are relatively high at the beginning and end of childhood, with a minimum in mid-childhood, say from ages 7 to 13. At this middle-childhood age, virtually all of the boys and most of the girls are in the BMI range of 12 to 16, levels of thinness that are seen in North America only at the minimum for U.S. children, which occurs much earlier in childhood, at the ages of 4 to 8. Only 3% of U.S. children ever get below body mass index of 13, and that only at ages 6 to 8, whereas a substantial group of !Kung children from infancy to age 17 are found to be below that level, which is very thin. The thinnest !Kung boy observed, an 8-year-old with a body mass index of 12 had been ill, but recovered and survived into adulthood. The

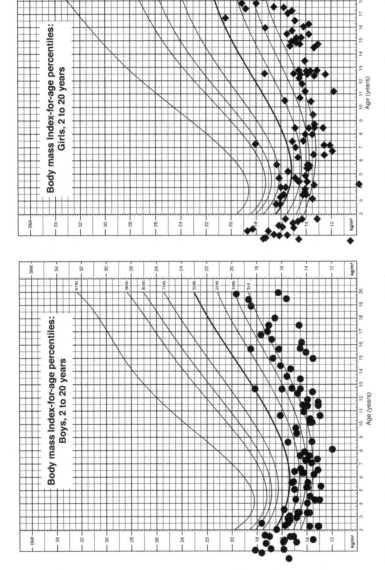

Figure 3.17. Body mass index by age, for boys and girls, 0 to 20 years. (Source: http://hdl.handle.net/1807/10396 and http://hdl.handle.net/1807/10401.)

41/2-year-old girl with a body mass index of about 10 had rheumatic heart disease, diagnosed by physicians Truswell and Hansen (Truswell, 1977; Lee and DeVore, 1976). She died soon after these measurements were taken, despite the antibiotic treatment they provided.

Others (Lee, 1979; Wilmsen, 1978, 1982) have shown that there is some seasonality to patterns of weight in !Kung, with considerable differences in seasonality from one year to another. Although my data are not ideal for exploring seasonality,[8] I find only a minor effect (Howell, 2000), and I am much more impressed by the persistence of patterns of thinness over years of childhood. Several studies (Tobias, 1962; Hansen et al., 1993) have reported some increased stature of Bushmen when they live with an improved diet, leading Nurse (1985) to conclude that the small size of the San may be due less to any inherited factors than to an overall energy deficit during the growing period. The unhealthy pattern of "catch-up growth" is associated with acute shortages such as seasonal shortages and plenty. In this context, the argument that I have made elsewhere (Howell, 1986) that !Kung cultural practices concerning food and food preparation discourage eating beyond the amount needed in any given day is relevant. Children stay thin even in periods of plenty in part because their mothers do not encourage them to eat beyond the minimum needed to satisfy their appetite and do not prepare particularly delectable meals. Nurse (1985) goes on to conclude that "though spare in build, they are generally remarkably healthy."

Attempts to assess the effects of seasonality on changes in height are frustrating, as the measurements were taken mostly in the so-called height-weight campaigns so that the observations are clustered at a few points in the year rather than spread out throughout the year. The differences between gains in various seasons seem to be small, slightly greater in the first half of the year (January to June, the rainy season) and slightly less in the second half (the dry season). Lee (1979) shows that seasonal weight changes differ rather sharply by age. Old people lose the most weight in the second half of the year when food becomes scarcer, while children gain less than in the first half of the year, but usually do not actually lose weight (Lee, 1979). Wilmsen (1978) found the seasonal changes to be much greater in 1973, when the !Kung were incorporating a number of new sources of income into their lives, but the seasonal changes were minimal in 1967–1969, when Lee and I measured them (Lee, 1979), and are not shown here.

8. The data presented here are only one observation per person, taken at the end of 1968. I have multiple measures per person, but they are not evenly spread across the years of observation, so coverage is quite uneven in some seasons.

Adolescence is a time of dramatic changes in body size, both in height and in weight. Girls slow and then stop their growth in height after menarche, and they gain fat deposits to form their characteristic adult female bodies during the years of 15 through 20, when their body mass index goes from about 15 to about 19, on the average. Photos of young women (found in Howell, 1979:168–171) illustrate this process on the individual level.

Young men continue to gain height to later ages, and end up about 10 cm taller than the women. During the adolescent growth spurt, the young men are gaining muscle mass while their sisters are gaining fat deposits, and both sexes increase their body mass index significantly in the late teens, in preparation for full adult status.

BODY SIZE DURING THE REPRODUCTIVE AGES

During the ages 20 through 44, !Kung women do all of the reproductive work of the society and a great deal of the productive work of food procurement and processing, shelter construction, and so on. Men get a somewhat slower start on adult work, but they too are intensely engaged in the productive activities of adult life. Adults are at their maximum strength and activity levels during this stage of life.

Figure 3.18 shows the height of adult !Kung (ages 20 through 44). Fully grown, !Kung men are about 160 cm tall on average; women are about 150 cm.[9] Variability in height for adults is in part a product of their childhood experience, and nutritional changes make no further impact on height. Lee (1979) has shown that stature is associated with somewhat better hunting success in short adult men than those of taller stature. An attempt to find a correlation between height of women and their gathering success or their reproductive success (measured as number of children ever born, number surviving, and number coresident with mother) among women over the age of 45 showed no significant pattern.

Variability in weight in adults may be a product of their physical activity level, health, and reproductive status as well as their access to supplies of food. During the childbearing years, workloads and responsibility for others become heavy for many of the people, as we will see in detail later, and these pressures may be reflected in their weight.

9. It is striking that skeletal biologists report that the estimated height of the adult female skeletons from prehistoric contexts over the past ten thousand years average 149.9 cm. Sealy, J., and S. Pfeiffer (2000). "Diet, body size and landscape use among Holocene people in the Southern Cape, South Africa." *Current Anthropology* 41: 642–655.

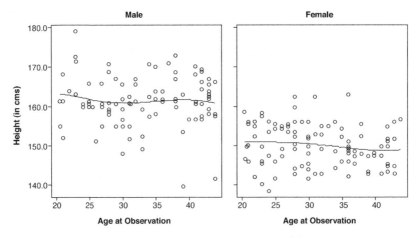

Figure 3.18. Height (in cm) by age, for male and female adults, age 20 to 45.
(Source: http://hdl.handle.net/1807/10408 and http://hdl.handle.net/1807/10403.)

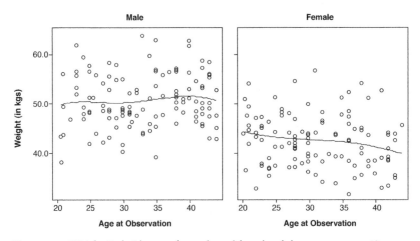

Figure 3.19. Weight (in kg) by age, for male and female adults, age 20 to 45. (Source:
http://hdl.handle.net/1807/10408.)

Looking at the BMI indices of the young adults in Figure 3.18, we see
that about 25% of each sex has an index over 20, while the majority are
in the range of 16 to 20, labeled by most public health analysts as "un-
dernourished." Note that the body mass indices of the women include
the bodily effects of pregnancy and lactation, so that they are actually
somewhat thinner than these BMI measures make them appear.

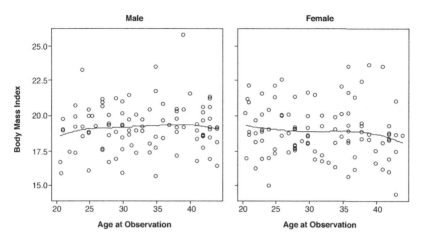

Figure 3.20. Body mass index by age, for male and female adults, age 20 to 45. (Source: http://hdl.handle.net/1807/10403 and http://hdl.handle.net/1807/10408.)

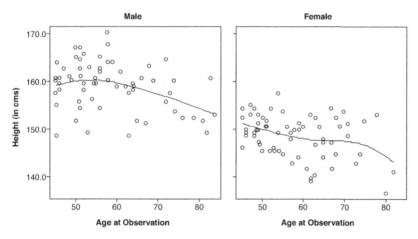

Figure 3.21. Height (in cm) by age, for male and female post-reproductive age adults. (Source: http://hdl.handle.net/1807/10410.)

BODY SIZE OF POST-REPRODUCTIVE ADULTS (45+)

Figure 3.21 shows that the mean heights by age have a slightly declining slope as people get older, probably because of osteoporotic skeletal changes associated with aging, which are known to occur in all populations, but perhaps also because of secular changes in height over the lifetimes of living people. If the consumption of cow's milk, for example, in childhood is making people taller in adulthood, then the people born before the 1930s, when the Herero moved cattle into the Xangwa area for year-round pasturage, are likely to be shorter, on the average. In any case, the difference in height is not large.

We note too, in Figure 3.22, that mean weights tend to decline along with mean heights, and so we see in Figure 3.23 that the body mass index for the older people declines moderately through what we might call the "middle-aged years" (the 40s and 50s). There is a downturn in weight and consequently in body mass index at the oldest ages, and we recall that the proportion of the population who are no longer able to

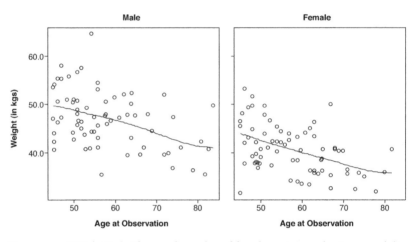

Figure 3.22. Weight (in kg) by age, for male and female post-reproductive age adults. (Source: http://hdl.handle.net/1807/10410.)

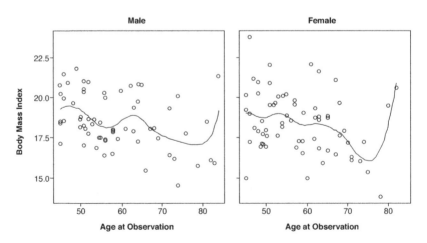

Figure 3.23. Body mass index by age, for male and female post-reproductive age adults. (Source: http://hdl.handle.net/1807/10410.)

work and provide for themselves increases in this age group, and that such people tend not to live very long. It may well be that the loss of weight in extreme old age is a precursor and indeed a contributor to the short remaining span of life of the frail elderly, not because they are deliberately starved by their relatives but because the physiological demands of coping with illness and accidents reduce fat deposits, and the probability of death increases in the absence of sufficient fatness. It is probably true that the support system is not adequate to provide fully for adults who cannot provide for themselves at all, even when there are highly motivated relatives anxious to help.

SUMMARIZING BODY SIZE: THE BODY MASS INDEX DIFFERENCE MEASURE

To conclude this section, we start by looking back at the information on body mass index by age for the whole population, which we saw in Figure 3.5. Then we partition the information in the body mass index into two components: that associated with age and sex (the Expected BMI, found in Figure 3.24) and the residual, the "BMI difference"

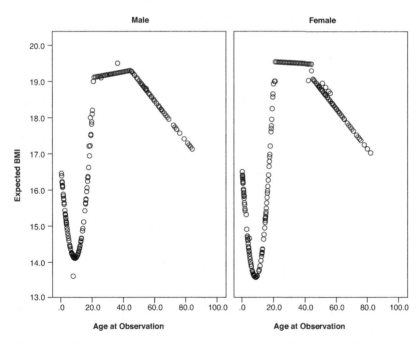

Figure 3.24. Expected body mass index by age and sex. (Source: http://hdl.handle .net/1807/10414.)

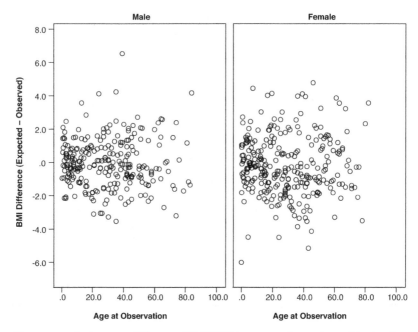

Figure 3.25. Body mass difference (BMIDiff) by age and sex: the residuals when Expected body mass index (Fig. 3.24) is subtracted from Observed body mass index (Fig. 3.5). (Source: http://hdl.handle.net/1807/10414.)

(Figure 3.25). Both of these variables are expressed in units of body mass index (weight divided by height squared).

First, the Expected BMI: We have seen that body mass index is a sensitive indicator of the relation between height and weight for individuals, and that it differs sharply by age and sex in predictable ways. Expected BMI, seen in Figure 3.24, expresses the central tendency of the pattern of the complex relationship of body mass index to age. The causal variables that contribute to the part of an individual's body mass index that remain in the Expected BMI measure are all those that have a strong age and sex component, such as growth, the role in the household as child or parent, marital status, and the stage of reproductive career that one is in.

These distributions of Expected BMI for males and females show the pattern shown in Figure 3.24. We note the features we have seen before for the age segments: the distinctive quadratic relationship of body mass index and age in childhood, with a higher body mass index in infancy and a lower body mass index in mid-childhood for girls than for boys. We see a flat linear relationship of body mass index and age during the reproductive stage of life, higher for women than men. We note that reproductive-age men's body mass index is sloped gently upward, so that they experience a peak of Expected BMI around age 45 through 50. We see that the highest Expected BMIs in the population are for reproductive-age women, a group that Lee (1979) and Blurton Jones (1986; 1987) have led us to worry about, because their workload is so hard and their resources for producing enough food for themselves and their families are so limited. These authors see the long length of birth intervals as an adaptation to the scarcity of resources the mothers live with, and that formulation seems to be a significant insight into the overall !Kung adaptation. Our finding that reproductive-age women have the highest Expected BMI of any age and sex group in the population does not contradict their models. Even so, the high level of body mass index for this group is exaggerated because we count the extra weight of pregnancy and lactation in their calculation, so that body mass index is not measuring only fatness, in this case, but also reproductive status. No doubt the small gap at the boundary of the reproductive-age women's BMI measures is caused by this average increment of the extra weight of pregnancy and lactation. And we see a declining linear relationship in Expected BMI in post-reproductive adults, a somewhat steeper decline for women than for men, despite the higher mortality rates for men.

Finally we create a new variable, "BMIDiff," which represents the difference in body mass index that an individual shows at a point in time from that expected for the age and sex group he or she is in. This variable is calculated by subtracting the Expected BMI score that we have just examined from the actual BMI measurement that we made for each person. The difference is an indication of the idiosyncratic fatness (and thinness) of individuals, above and beyond that associated with their age and sex. It might reflect the consequences of an individual's specific genetic constitution, a run of hard work, of good luck, or the results of illness in oneself or in one's providers. BMIDiff scores can provide information on the consequences for well-being of the birth order of children, or the presence of a grandmother to help the parents feed the children. In adults, it might reflect the number of dependents one is trying to support. BMIDiff is a valuable variable, because we feel we understand the causal connections between Expected BMI and age and sex, and all the unexplained variations that we wish to explain have been isolated in this measure of BMI Difference (or BMIDiff, as we will call it in the rest of this book).

Look at Figure 3.25. This constructed variable, "BMIDiff," has a range of +4.5 to −4.5 (in units of body mass index), a mean close to zero (−0.125) and a standard deviation of about 1.5. It is our best indicator of well-being in individuals that can be attributed to their individual characteristics and their place in the social structure. It will be our task, in Chapters 6 and 7 that follow, to account for variation in BMIDiff by social structural variables (such as kinship resources and residential group composition).

Before we proceed to that task, however, we will first use the data on body size to estimate the number of calories that individuals require in order to sustain their life and growth, and then the number of calories that individuals typically produce by age and sex. We want to be clear about the relationship of body size to the number of calories produced and required to help us understand the !Kung adaptation.

CHAPTER 4

Calories Required

Our task in this chapter is to estimate, for each age and sex group, how many calories are needed to support its members, so that we can consider the relationship between calories produced and consumed.[1] We are constructing a framework to understand the production and consumption of calories over the life span, so it will be helpful to have an idea of how much food is needed by individual people at all ages, in order to understand the ties between them. This exercise will allow us to describe the reality of !Kung life in a clearer and more compact way (Lee, 1979) and to make comparisons between the !Kung and several other populations that have been studied in this way, notably the G/wi Bushmen of the central Kalahari (Tanaka 1980), Ache hunter-gatherers of Paraguay (Kaplan, Lancaster, et al., 2000), and the Maya of Mexico (Lee and Kramer, 2002).

Note that this task is not based on an empirical survey of how many calories individual !Kung actually put in their mouths and consumed per day. That would be very difficult, perhaps impossible. Lee attempted to measure exact intake for a few people in 1964 (Lee, 1969), but it is almost necessary to be with someone 24 hours a day to measure intake accurately, as people eat out in the bush as well as in the village, and eat

---

1. When we refer to a calorie, we mean a kilocalorie, as the term is used in nutrition rather than in chemistry. Nutritionists measure the energy of food as calories or as Joules. Here we use calories = kcals = 4.180 Joules.

between meals as well as during them, in amounts that aren't easily measured. Instead of annoying the !Kung by a serious attempt to carry out an impossible task, Lee reasoned that if he measured the weights of people of all ages, he could infer that people who were gaining weight were consuming more than they required for their activity levels, and people who lost weight were consuming less than needed.

Here we will take another approach to the problem. We can calculate the amount of calories a !Kung person requires from formulas designed by nutritionists and physiologists to describe all human populations. We combine information on !Kung size and observed activity levels with these standard formulas to obtain estimates of the calories required for each age and sex group. Note that we are constructing the expected value of a variable here, rather than measuring that variable on individuals, so we will end up with measures of central tendency but we will not have the information that we would ordinarily expect to find on the variability of calories required from person to person.

Jasienska (2001) provides a diagram of the flows from energy intake that will help us carry out the calculation. Figure 4.1 is taken from her work, showing the flow of energy intake (measured in calories or Joules) to the energetic requirements of an individual: the basal metabolism rate (BMR), the physical activity level (PAL), and reproduction. Surplus energy taken in is stored as fat, and if there is a shortfall of energy, fat can be mobilized to support these caloric requirements.

We will use this framework to estimate the caloric requirements for each age group by following the arrows in Figure 4.1 in the opposite direction. We do not know how much food people in each age group eat, but we know how much they weigh, what activities they take part in, and how often they have children, which are the facts

Estimating Caloric Requirements

Figure 4.1. Allocation of energy by individuals. (Source: Jasienska, 2001.)

we need to estimate each of the components of the energy requirement. The calculation has several stages, and we will consider each of them, to be explicit about where this variable comes from. First, we will estimate the individual basal metabolism rate (as a function of body weight) according to formulas produced by nutritionists for the FAO, applied to the mean weights by age that we explored in Chapter 3.

Second, we will construct time budgets of activities for !Kung age-sex groups, as best we can from data that were not collected for quite that purpose. We will use the data on hours of activity over the 24 hours in a typical day to calculate the PAL (physical activity level) for the average individual in each age and sex category. We compare our results with the efforts of a number of scholars (Leslie, Bindon, et al., 1984; Sackett, 1996) who have used the quantified !Kung data to form examples in their work. Lee has made estimates of calories required for broad age groups (Lee, 1969; Lee, 1979), which we can also use to assess the plausibility of our results. Here we will estimate requirements for finer age groups than he did, so that we can apply these estimates to individual !Kung. It is gratifying to see at the end of this process that our estimates of calories required roughly agree with those of these other scholars of the !Kung.

Third, we will estimate the energy requirements for the level of reproduction that we actually observe in this population: these requirements apply to the women of reproductive age (15 to 44).

To put these components together, we multiply the basal metabolism rate by the physical activity level and add the allowance for reproduction, to obtain our best estimate of daily caloric requirements per person.

CALORIC REQUIREMENTS FOR BASAL METABOLISM

The basal metabolism rate is the caloric cost of maintaining the body over a 24-hour period if the person is maximally resting, as in sleep (Ulijaszek, 1995). It includes the costs of maintenance of the body and the autonomous activity of heart, brain, circulation, breathing, and liver and kidney function. It also includes allowances for the growth of children, the costs of increases and decreases in fat deposits, healing of wounds, and response to infectious and parasitic disease processes. There is an attempt to eliminate the effects of digestion of food by requiring the test to be performed at least 12 hours after the last meal. The concept is closely related to resting metabolic rate (RMR), or resting energy expenditure (REE)

TABLE 4.1. EQUATIONS FOR ESTIMATING BASAL METABOLIC RATE
FROM BODY WEIGHT FOR AGE AND SEX GROUPS

Age Range	Kcal/Day	Correlation	SD
Female			
0–3	61.0W −51	0.97	53
3–10	22.5W + 499	0.85	63
10–18	12.2W + 746	0.75	117
18–30	4.7W + 496	0.72	121
30–60	8.7W + 829	0.70	108
60+	10.5W + 596	0.74	108
Male			
0–3	60.9W − 54	0.97	53
3–10	22.7W + 495	0.86	62
10–18	17.5W + 651	0.90	100
18–30	15.3W + 679	0.65	151
30–60	11.6W + 879	0.60	164
60+	13.5W + 487	0.79	148

NOTE: W=weight in kgs. The equations are derived from individual weights and BMR measured by respiration in resting and fasting subjects in a range of developed and underdeveloped countries. The correlation coefficients relate weight and "actual" BMR for people in that age group in a range of societies, and the standard deviations are of differences between actual BMRs and predicted estimates. For details, see Table 5, from FAO, 1982: 71.

(Sackett, 1996), which includes the thermic effect of food (National Research Council, 1989), and a related concept, energy expenditure rates (Sackett, 1996). These different measures are more loosely defined than basal metabolism rate, including the thermogenic costs of processing food. For our purposes, these measures, which are within 10% of one another when measured carefully, can be used interchangeably. We will call it basal metabolism rate because that is the term most widely used.

Basal metabolism rate can be measured directly by tests that capture oxygen discharge from the resting body, or by double-labeled isotopes of water. These accurate measures of basal metabolism rate on large populations have allowed the construction of prediction equations as seen in Table 4.1, based merely on age, sex, and body mass as estimated by weight.[2] Column two of Table 4.1 (Food and Agriculture

2. Recently, an alternative set of equations for people who live in tropical areas of the world, like the !Kung, has been proposed (Henry and Rees, 1991), suggesting that the standard equations overestimate BMR by as much as 8% for tropical people. These new formulas will not be used here, but might be worth further investigation by !Kung scholars in the future.

TABLE 4.2. ESTIMATED BASAL METABOLISM
REQUIREMENTS BY SEX AND AGE GROUPS

Ages	Female	Male	Female Smoothed	Male Smoothed
0–4	466	506	466	466
5–9	834	1126	834	1080
10–14	1033	1131	1033	1140
15–19	1141	1309	1141	1300
20–24	1128	1440	1160	1390
25–29	1135	1452	1180	1452
30–34	1203	1465	1203	1465
35–39	1203	1465	1203	1465
40–44	1203	1459	1203	1459
45–49	1194	1459	1194	1459
50–54	1189	1445	1190	1400
55–59	1177	1427	1140	1340
60–64	1003	1119	1020	1220
65–69	992	1097	1000	1190
70–74	984	1084	984	1090
75–79	974	1051	974	1051
80+	971	1041	971	1041
Total	17835	21074	17900	21007
Average	1052	1240	1053	1236

SOURCE: Calculated from equations in Table 4.1 and mean weight of individuals.

Organization, 1982) shows the prediction equation for each age and sex group. The correlations found in column three refer to the association between the predicted basal metabolism rate for a population of persons of various age and sex categories with the measured basal metabolism rate by O^2 intake or double-labeled water. These prediction equations allow us to estimate the basal metabolism rate for age and sex groups of !Kung.

We start with the observed weights for each age and sex group, as found in Chapter 3, based on the people at single years of age. Figure 4.2 shows the raw and smoothed mean Kcalories required per day for basal metabolism for the two sexes. As there are only a few individuals at each age, we have to smooth the results before going on to the next step, which is to apply the formulas shown in Table 4.1 for estimating the basal metabolism rate by age and sex. Applying the formulas to the smoothed mean weights for single years of age gives us a rather jagged result at the boundaries of the age classes, so the results are again smoothed and then grouped into five-year age groups, for the men and women separately, as seen in Table 4.2.

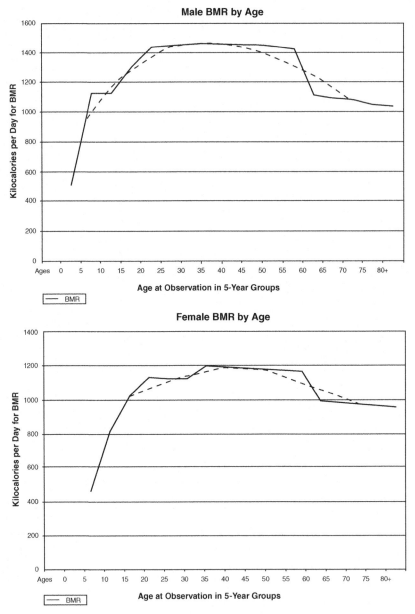

Figure 4.2. Calories required for basal metabolism rates, raw and smoothed. (Source: Table 4.2, this volume.)

TIME BUDGETS OF MEAN DAILY ACTIVITIES

We don't really know what all the !Kung people were doing with their time on any one day, never mind every day, but Lee invested a great deal of time and effort to document all the activities of one living group, the people at Dobe, for twenty-eight days in July 1964. Similarly Draper (Lee and DeVore, 1976) collected detailed time budgets based on samples of children's behavior in a wider group of villages and over a longer period of time. We cannot give precise figures on the average and standard deviation of how much time people of various age and sex groups spent carrying out various activities at any one time, but we can make plausible estimates of the central tendency, acknowledging that there must be differences between one person and another, one season and another, and even one day to another for a single person in a particular season. We are trying to estimate the use of time for the mean of age and sex groups so that we can use those expected distributions of calories required as a characteristic of individuals later in this work, when we try to understand the flow of resources between individuals and groups in the society.

The next step in estimating calories required is to figure out the average level of physical activity for each age and sex group in the population. This task requires that we estimate how many hours per day the average person spends in each of a number of activities, accounting for the 24 hours of time available to people in all age and sex groups. This kind of research is called "time budgets," and detailed studies have been done in a wide range of populations, from foragers to horticultural and agricultural societies, to place beside the studies of time budgets in industrialized societies. These activities can in turn be rated by the degree of energy they require, and combined to produce an estimate of calories required for 24 hours for the "average person on the average day."

Lee (1979) started by maintaining a census of residents and visitors to the Dobe camp each day during the four weeks of his observation, to enumerate the "person-days" of consumption and of work. He counted each day as spent either hunting, gathering, out visiting, in camp, or "other," and only hunting and gathering are counted as "work days" in his preliminary analysis. Overall, the surprising conclusion is the shortness of the work week: 3 days a week of hunting and gathering for adult men when they are staying at home (1.7 days/week when they are away from home, visiting others) and 2.2 days a week for adult women at home (1.7 for visitors) (Lee, 1979).

Visiting other groups is frequent: the Dobe residents were out visiting others 58 out of the 662 person-days observed in July 1964, and they
entertained visitors 204 person-days during the observation period. It is
the custom that visitors are fed for a day or so when they come, given
the same food that the family is eating, but after that they are expected
to pitch in and go hunting and gathering with their hosts. Note that
adult women go out gathering about as often when they are visiting as
when they stay at home. The custom of frequent visiting serves several
purposes: people enjoy seeing their relatives, news and information are
exchanged, gifts are given, and people tend to flow toward the places in
the environment where food is most plentiful. A visit may be triggered
by news from another visitor that a hunter has killed a large animal, or
that a certain vegetable resource known to be plentiful in an area has
ripened. Lee (1979) notes that Dobe received many more visitors from
other waterholes in July 1964 than its residents paid to others, and he
speculates that his presence at Dobe may have increased visits, because
of the curiosity of those who wanted to observe the strange antics of the
anthropologist. In the long run, he speculates, visiting reciprocity balances out between groups, or perhaps more prosperous groups entertain
somewhat more than average.

Hunting and gathering is the only form of work counted in the tabulation, but it is not the only form of activity engaged in. Lee (1979) notes
that many kinds of tools need to be manufactured and maintained, food
needs to be processed and cooked, and hides need to be scraped and
tanned for sleeping mats and clothing. Water has to be obtained from
the well each day, firewood has to be collected from the bush, and fires
have to be tended, hearths cleaned, and pots scrubbed with sand.
Villages are abandoned and moved to a new location occasionally; then
brush has to be removed from the center of the village so that people can
feel secure that there are no snakes near their children, new houses
have to be constructed, new hearths for the fire established, new nut-
cracking stones found and brought to the hearth, and fires restarted.

Lee (1979) counted the duration of the activities he observed and
summarized the activities of the adults in his Table 9.12. Subsistence
work includes both hunting and gathering: an average of 21.6 hours per
week for men and 12.6 hours per week for women were recorded.
Toolmaking, repairing, and maintenance takes up 7.5 hours for men,
and 5.1 for women. And what Lee calls "housework" (food processing,
cooking, fire tending, water collecting) takes up about 22.4 hours per
week for women, and 15.4 hours per week for men, making a total of

an average of 44.5 hours per week for men's work and 40.1 hours per week for adult women. Note that Lee is not counting pregnancy, lactation, or childcare as work, but just as something that women do continuously along with their other activities.

And life is not only work, either for adults or for children. A lot of time in camp is spent sitting around, talking, eating, doing beadwork, cutting each other's hair and searching for and removing head lice, making or listening to music, telling and listening to stories. Lee doesn't quantify this activity, or that of sleep, but we must quantify them in order to account for activities over the 24 hours.

To supplement Lee's findings, we need to take a closer look at the activities of children. Blurton Jones and his colleagues have alerted us to the striking absence of subsistence work among !Kung children (Blurton Jones, Hawkes, et al., 1994). In general, we assign none of the time of children to the most demanding activities, in accordance with Lee's observation that boys don't begin to hunt until they are full grown (around age 20), and girls only begin to gather food in their mid-teenage years. Infants divide their time between riding on their mother's back awake and asleep. Children crack some nuts, tend some fires, and collect a little water along with adults, but do little strenuous activity that could be described as work during the course of a day, and none of it under compulsion. Young people seem to enter into adult tasks remarkably late and remarkably slowly. This is one of the indicators that Lee used to conclude that the !Kung have a secure and leisurely life.

Children's activities were systematically explored by Patricia Draper in her dissertation research in 1968–1969 (Lee and DeVore, 1976). She took time samples of children's activities in the camp in which she was observing, with studies on time samples an hour long, 10 minutes, or just a "spot observation." At randomly determined intervals, she reached into her pocket to draw a button from a collection, each marked with the name of one of the children in the local village, and she would go find that child and record the observation, noting what the child was doing and in whose company he or she was for the activity, adults and children. In this way Draper can provide numerical data on the percentage of time (between roughly 8 a.m. to 8 p.m.) that children of different ages and sexes are with their mothers, fathers, siblings, grandparents, and other relatives, or are with unrelated children or adults, or are alone. She describes their activities and rates the vigor of it, and notes whether children are touching others, playing with objects, eating, and so on. And fortunately for me, Draper studied many of the same

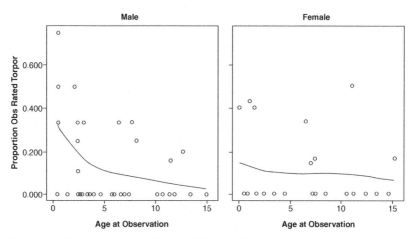

Figure 4.3. Proportion of activities of !Kung children rated as sleep or torpor (Draper). (Source: http://hdl.handle.net/1807/18217.)

children that I was studying at nearly the same time, so her results can be linked to the other characteristics of children that I know.

Draper (1976) finds that children's activities include some vigorous play and some accompanying of adults on long walks and visits to other camps, but most of their time is spent playing informally with other children within the village. She codes each spot observation (she has approximately five to ten per child) as at one of five levels of activity: (1) "torpor," which is sleep or complete inactivity, either on the mother's body or lying down; (2) sitting activity, often leaning on someone else, often grooming or being groomed, or just sitting, talking, daydreaming, etc.; (3) standing activity, which may including talking, watching, listening; (4) walking activity, moving around, whether or not the child seems to have a specific destination; and finally (5) running and other high-energy activities, such as dancing or climbing trees. Figures 4.3 through 4.6 show the percentage of child observations at each age that could be coded at one of these levels. The most striking difference between the sexes is seen in the percentage of children engaged in high activity (running), which increases with age for both sexes. The boys have much higher rates of high activity than girls, especially as they approach adolescence. Unfortunately for my purposes, Draper did not include children over age 15 in her study,[3] but her systematic observations on

3. It would have been hard for Draper to include adolescents (15 to 19) as they are so often away from the village during the day.

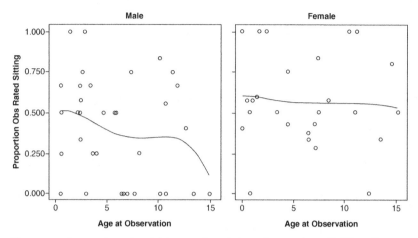

Figure 4.4. Proportion of activities rated as sitting. (Source: http://hdl.handle.net/ 1807/18217.)

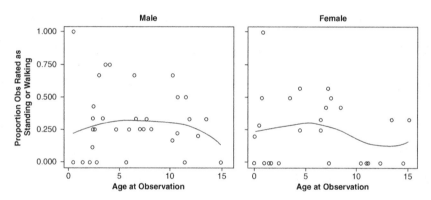

Figure 4.5. Proportion of activities rated as standing or walking. (Source: http:// hdl.handle.net/1807/18217.)

frequency and intensity of activities allows us to extend the analysis of caloric costs of activity from adults to include children.

Draper has many fascinating observations in her data. Little children (0 to 4) are almost always with their mothers. This closeness declines steadily throughout childhood (5 to 14), except that girls increase their association with their mothers again as they approach adolescence. Children are with their fathers much less often than with mothers, but we also note that girls increase their association with their fathers as they approach adolescence. Little children are very often found in the village space, but this location declines to about 50% of the time for girls by the

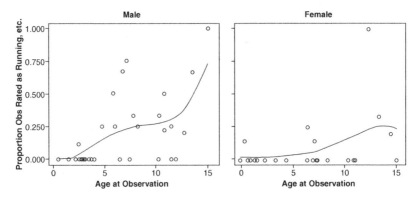

Figure 4.6. Proportion of activities rated as running (or very vigorous). (Source: http://hdl.handle.net/1807/18217.)

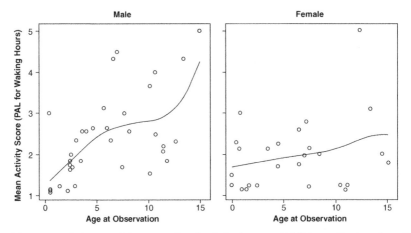

Figure 4.7. Mean activity score for daylight hours of children. (Source: http://hdl.handle.net/1807/18217.)

time they reach age 15, and to almost zero percent for the boys at the same age. The percentage of activities not rated by Draper, because when the child's number was drawn he or she couldn't be found, increases to about 20% for both boys and girls in the 10 to 15 age group. Draper points out that all children play much more vigorously in the cool portion of the year than when the temperatures are high.

Lee (1979) tells us in his Table 9.5 how many days and hours men and women engaged in hunting and gathering during the month he closely observed them, divided into young (ages 20 to 39 years), middle-aged (40 to 59), and old (60+). In addition, he gives us the names of identifiable hunters in Tables 9.6 and 9.8, telling us the details of the animals obtained, their species and weight of their meat, the hunter's success rates, and caloric and protein returns per day, so that we can place the hunters into their known age groups. He goes on in Table 9.10 to provide details, in minutes per day, of times spent manufacturing and maintaining tools, and doing housework (in Tables 9.11 and 9.12), such as cooking, food preparation, collecting water and firewood, house construction and maintenance, and so on.

And finally, people spend part of each day sleeping, around 8 hours for adults, and 9 to 12 hours for infants and children. People sleep at night on the ground next to their fires, depending on the direction the smoke is blowing, typically on an animal hide mat, with the family baby closest to the fire at the mother's breast, then the father, then other children, sharing whatever blankets or animal skins they have and their communal body heat. Someone has to adjust the fire several times an hour throughout the night, and sleepers must often accommodate to the moves of others, so sleep may be relatively disturbed. Sometimes a person is sleepless in the village and may play a musical instrument or sing during the night, but usually the village is silent, except for the crackling of fires and the noises of birds and animals in the bush. Before dawn, the early risers start to build up the fires and sit up around the fires, and quiet conversation and movements gradually wake everyone and the day begins early, often before dawn, especially in the warm times of the year. When it is hot, people like to get their vigorous work done early in the morning and late in the afternoon, staying in the shade during the hottest hours. Conversely, during the winter, the sun doesn't warm the village until late in the morning, and people prefer to huddle in their blankets around the fire as long as possible and do the heavy work in the midday.

Adding time spent in sleep to Lee's work time budgets, we are left with a margin for leisure and recreation, such as talking, artistic composition, making and asking for *hxaro* gifts, and so on. Some of these kinds of activities may be essential to life but they have a quality of ease and relaxation about them, and I classify them as "leisure and rest." Actually a lot of important activities in !Kung life are incorporated into this category of activity—items like religion and healing, education and entertainment, gift giving, gift making, and maintenance of ties of kinship and friendship.

Table 4.3 integrates the data from Draper and from Lee, which are 12-hour accounts, into the 24-hour-a-day time budget of people in each age and sex group of the !Kung. After making an allowance for sleep and adding up the activities that Lee and Draper quantify, we subtract them from 24 hours to produce an estimate of time per day spent in leisure and

TABLE 4.3. TIME BUDGETS IN HOURS PER DAY ON
TYPICAL DAY BY AGE AND SEX

Activities	Sleeping	Leisure/ Resting	Tool Making/ Playing	Housework	Gathering/ Walking	Dancing/ Hunting/ Running	TOTAL
Multiplier	*1*	*1.25*	*2*	*2.5*	*4*	*6*	
MALES **Age Groups**							
0–4	12.00	11.50	0.00	0.00	0.50	0.00	24.00
5–9	10.00	7.5	4.00	1.00	1.50	0.00	24.00
10–14	9.00	8.00	2.00	1.00	1.00	3.00	24.00
15–19	9.00	7.50	1.00	1.00	2.00	3.50	24.00
20–24	8.00	10.50	1.00	1.00	1.50	2.00	24.00
25–29	8.00	9.85	1.00	2.15	1.00	2.00	24.00
30–34	8.00	9.75	1.00	2.25	1.00	2.00	24.00
35–39	8.00	9.75	1.00	2.25	1.00	2.00	24.00
40–44	8.00	9.75	1.00	2.25	1.00	2.00	24.00
45–49	8.00	9.75	1.00	2.25	1.00	2.00	24.00
50–55	8.00	9.75	1.00	2.25	1.00	2.00	24.00
60–64	8.00	9.55	1.20	2.25	1.00	2.00	24.00
65–69	8.00	9.55	1.20	2.25	1.00	2.00	24.00
70–74	8.00	9.55	1.20	2.25	1.00	2.00	24.00
75–79	8.00	10.00	1.00	2.00	1.00	2.00	24.00
80+	8.00	16.00	0.00	0.00	0.00	0.00	24.00
Total	136.00	158.25	18.60	26.15	16.50	28.50	384.00
Average	8.50	9.89	1.16	1.63	1.03	1.78	24.00
FEMALES **Age Groups**							
0–4	12.00	11.50	0.00	0.00	0.50	0.00	24.00
5–9	10.00	8.00	4.00	1.00	1.00	0.00	24.00
10–14	9.00	9.00	3.00	1.00	2.00	0.00	24.00
15–19	9.00	9.70	1.50	2.00	1.80	0.00	24.00
20–24	8.00	10.20	0.75	3.25	1.80	0.00	24.00
25–29	8.00	10.00	0.75	3.25	2.00	0.00	24.00
30–34	8.00	10.00	0.75	3.25	2.00	0.00	24.00
35–39	8.00	10.00	0.75	3.25	2.00	0.00	24.00
40–44	8.00	10.00	0.75	3.25	2.00	0.00	24.00
45–49	8.00	10.00	0.75	3.25	2.00	0.00	24.00
50–55	8.00	10.00	0.75	3.25	2.00	0.00	24.00
60–64	8.00	10.00	0.75	3.25	2.00	0.00	24.00
65–69	8.00	10.00	0.75	3.25	2.00	0.00	24.00
70–74	8.00	10.00	0.75	3.25	2.00	0.00	24.00
75–79	8.00	11.00	0.75	3.25	1.00	0.00	24.00
80+	9.00	14.25	0.75	0.00	0.00	0.00	24.00
Total	137.00	163.65	17.50	39.75	26.10	0.00	384.00
Average	8.56	10.23	1.09	2.48	1.63	0.00	24.00

SOURCE: Lee 1979, Draper 1973, and Figures 4.3 to 4.7, this volume.

rest. The resulting total is surprisingly high, about 10 hours per day of rest
and leisure throughout adulthood, even for these hard-working people.
On the average about 4 hours of that leisure would be experienced after
dark, and 6 hours in the day, interspersed between more high activity
tasks. During the hottest time of the year, most people rest in midday.

PHYSICAL ACTIVITY LEVELS

The next task is to convert the time budgets of Table 4.3 into physical activity levels (PAL), the multipliers of the basal metabolism rate[4] that tell us how many calories are required by people for their activities (Black, Jebb, et al., 1991).

Sleep is the lowest level of physical activity, given an index of 1. Leisure and rest ordinarily have a multiplier of 1.25. The rest of the activities listed in Table 4.3 are called "work" (Sackett, 1996): These activities have been studied in many populations and there is considerable agreement (Durnin and Passmore, 1967; Leslie, Bindon, et al., 1984; Jenike, 2001; Draper and Howell, 2005) about the PAL measure associated with each activity: Toolmaking has an index of about 2; and housework is 2.5.

The physical activity levels of hunting and gathering activities are somewhat harder to estimate, but Leslie, Bindon, and their colleagues (1984) and Jenike (2001) have independently investigated the !Kung case. They agreed on an index of 4 for gathering, as it is similar to walking with heavy loads, and they give an index of 6 for hunting, the maximally vigorous activity of !Kung that includes running, digging, climbing trees, butchering, and carrying heavy loads of meat. Only adult men engage in hunting, and I have added the energetically expensive activity of trance dancing to hunting, as maximally expensive, with an index of 6. No deduction from the allowance has been made for the intervals of simple walking during hunting expeditions.

Now we have the mechanical task of converting the time budgets of Table 4.3 into a measure of physical activity level for each age and sex group. Table 4.4 shows the activity hours multiplied by their physical activity level to provide an estimate of energy requirements for each age and sex group. The averages shown for men and women in Table 4.4 are somewhat lower than some estimates (Leslie, Bindon, et al., 1984) but are closely comparable to others (Jenike, 2001). It is not clear to what extent this is due to the lifelong perspective and the finer categories of age and sex that we are using here. When the physical activity level is multiplied by the individual's basal metabolism rate, as we do in Table 4.4, we have an estimate of the caloric costs of each of the kinds of activities discussed above for each person.

---

4. Black, Jebb, and their colleagues (1991) refer to this multiplier of BMR as EI, the Energy Intake indicator.

TABLE 4.4. CALORIC COSTS OF ACTIVITIES IN TIME BUDGETS
PER DAY, BY GENDER AND AGE

Activities	Sleeping	Leisure/ Resting	Tool Making/ Playing	Housework	Gathering/ Walking	Dancing/ Hunting/ Running	TOTAL	Mean PAL
Multiplier	*1*	*1.25*	*2*	*2.5*	*4*	*6*		
MALES **Age Groups**								
0–4	12.0	14.4	0.0	0.0	2.0	0.0	28.4	1.2
5–9	10.0	9.4	8.0	2.5	6.0	0.0	35.9	1.5
10–14	9.0	10.0	4.0	2.5	4.0	18.0	47.5	2.0
15–19	9.0	9.4	2.0	2.5	8.0	21.0	51.9	2.2
20–24	8.0	13.1	2.0	2.5	6.0	12.0	43.6	1.8
25–29	8.0	12.3	2.0	5.4	4.0	12.0	43.7	1.8
30–34	8.0	12.2	2.0	5.6	4.0	12.0	43.8	1.8
35–39	8.0	12.2	2.0	5.6	4.0	12.0	43.8	1.8
40–44	8.0	12.2	2.0	5.6	4.0	12.0	43.8	1.8
45–49	8.0	12.2	2.0	5.6	4.0	12.0	43.8	1.8
50–54	8.0	12.2	2.0	5.6	4.0	12.0	43.8	1.8
55–59	8.0	12.2	2.0	5.6	4.0	12.0	44.0	1.8
60–64	8.0	11.9	2.4	5.6	4.0	12.0	44.0	1.8
65–69	8.0	11.9	2.4	5.6	4.0	12.0	44.0	1.8
70–74	8.0	11.9	2.4	5.6	4.0	12.0	44.0	1.8
75–79	8.0	12.5	2.0	5.0	4.0	12.0	43.5	1.8
80+	8.0	20.0	0.0	0.0	0.0	0.0	28.3	1.2
Totals	136.0	204.6	37.2	65.4	66.0	171.0	673.4	24.2
Averages	8.5	12.8	1.6	2.7	2.8	7.1	42.1	1.5
FEMALES **Age Groups**								
0–4	12.0	14.4	0.0	0.0	2.0	0.0	28.4	1.2
5–9	10.0	10.0	8.0	2.5	4.0	0.0	34.5	1.4
10–14	9.0	11.3	6.0	2.5	8.0	0.0	36.8	1.5
15–19	9.0	12.1	3.0	5.0	7.2	0.0	36.3	1.5
20–24	8.0	12.8	1.5	8.1	7.2	0.0	37.6	1.6
25–29	8.0	12.5	1.5	8.1	8.0	0.0	38.1	1.6
30–34	8.0	12.5	1.5	8.1	8.0	0.0	38.1	1.6
35–39	8.0	12.5	1.5	8.1	8.0	0.0	38.1	1.6
40–44	8.0	12.5	1.5	8.1	8.0	0.0	38.1	1.6
45–49	8.0	12.5	1.5	8.1	8.0	0.0	38.1	1.6
50–54	8.0	12.5	1.5	8.1	8.0	0.0	38.1	1.6
55–59	8.0	12.5	1.5	8.1	8.0	0.0	38.1	1.6
60–64	8.0	12.5	1.5	8.1	8.0	0.0	38.1	1.6
65–69	8.0	12.5	1.5	8.1	8.0	0.0	38.1	1.6
70–74	8.0	12.5	1.5	8.1	8.0	0.0	38.1	1.6
75–79	8.0	13.8	1.5	8.1	4.0	0.0	35.4	1.5
80+	9.0	17.8	1.5	0.0	0.0	0.0	28.3	1.2
Totals	137.0	204.6	35.0	99.4	104.4	0.0	580.3	24.2
Averages	8.6	12.8	2.2	6.2	6.5	0.0	36.3	1.5

SOURCE: Table 4.3 times Activity Multipliers found in column heads.

CALORIC REQUIREMENTS FOR REPRODUCTION

Table 4.5 shows the detailed calculations of the caloric costs of reproduction for !Kung women. The seventh column shows the percentage of women in the age range who are neither pregnant nor lactating on any given day, which includes all the girls less than 15 and all the women past 45.

To find the percentage who are pregnant, we start with the age-specific fertility (ASF) rates (the probability of giving birth during a year for each woman in the age group) for the 1963–1969 period (Howell, 2000). We calculate the expected percentage of women pregnant at a point in time in each age category as their ASF * .75 (because a pregnancy lasts 9 months out of the 12). And we multiply that number by an average 250 daily calories as the cost of pregnancy (Durnin, 1991). The average cost of pregnancy per woman is less than 20 calories per day even in the peak childbearing years (25 to 29).

Lactation is more expensive to the mother, and a greater proportion of the women in the childbearing years are lactating than are pregnant. Column five shows the percentage of each age group who are lactating, assuming that each surviving child is breastfed for 30 months, and column six multiplies that figure by 500 calories per day, the average cost to the mother of providing about 450 calories in the form of milk to the infant. Note that this food source is sufficient to meet the baby's needs for only approximately five to six months. After this, the baby's diet must be supplemented while mothers go on providing approximately the same amount of milk per day for several additional years. Note too that women can go on paying costs of lactation into their 50s, if they happen to have a very late final child and nurse that child maximally long.

The per-average-woman caloric cost of reproduction is seen in column five of Table 4.6, summing the average costs of pregnancy and lactation. Jasienska (2001) mentions that the monthly production of the endometrial lining of the uterus has a caloric cost, which can be seen by a 6% increase in basal metabolism during the luteal phase of the menstrual cycle of nonpregnant women. This extra expense lasts only for several days and amounts to a very small requirement per day per average woman, so small that I am disregarding it here. The maximum burden of reproductive costs on women falls on the 25- to 29-year-old women and continues as a substantial cost into their 40s.

The final stage of calculation of the costs of reproduction to women is to take the estimated caloric cost for each individual woman and apply

TABLE 4.5. CALORIC COSTS OF REPRODUCTION TO !KUNG WOMEN

Age Groups	ASFR	ASF*.75 P. of Pregnancy	N. of Pregnancies	Daily Caloric Cost	Probability of Lactation	Daily Cost of Lactation	% Neither Preg. Nor Lactating	Per Woman Cal. Cost of Reproduction	% in Age Group	Per Group Cost of Pregnancy	Per Group Cost of Lactation
0–4	0	0	0	0	0	0	100.0	0	11.8	0	0
5–9	0	0	0	0	0	0	100	0	10.1	0	0
10–14	0	0	0	0	0	0	100	0	9.6	0	0
15–19	0.063	0.047	0.4277	4.7	0.071	35.0	88.2	39.7	9.1	42.8	318.5
20–24	0.208	0.156	1.3416	15.6	0.382	191.0	46.2	206.6	8.6	134.2	1642.6
25–29	0.238	0.179	1.4320	17.9	0.669	334.5	15.2	352.4	8.0	143.2	2676.0
30–34	0.183	0.137	1.0138	13.7	0.632	316.0	23.1	329.7	7.4	101.4	2338.4
35–39	0.107	0.080	0.5360	8.0	0.436	218.0	48.4	226.0	6.7	53.6	1460.6
40–44	0.043	0.032	0.1952	3.2	0.225	112.5	74.3	115.7	6.1	19.5	686.3
45–49	0.013	0.01	0.0550	0.1	0.084	42.0	90.6	42.1	5.5	0.6	30.3
50–54	0	0	0	0	0.019	10.0	98.1	10	4.8	0	48
55–59	0	0	0	0	0	0	100	0	4.1	0	0
60–64	0	0	0	0	0	0	100	0	3.3	0	0
65–59	0	0	0	0	0	0	100	0	2.4	0	0
70–74	0	0	0	0	0	0	100	0	1.5	0	0
75–79	0	0	0	0	0	0	100	0	0.8	0	0
80+	0	0	0	0	0	0	100	0	0.4	0	0
Totals		5.0013	63.2	1259	1322.2	100.2	495.2	9200.6			

SOURCE: Howell (2000:139) for ASFR and % in Age Group. Daily caloric cost of pregnancy from Durnin, 1991. Daily caloric cost of lactation from Wood (1994:19).

that estimate to the age group. In column nine, we give the percentage of the entire population of women in the age group, and multiply that by the per-person costs of pregnancy (column ten) and of lactation (column eleven) to produce the entire population caloric costs of reproduction.

The reproductive costs of reproduction to men are negligible, as spermatogenesis is very efficient. Note that we do not count the costs of attracting a spouse or supplying food for the spouse, their children, or the group as a whole under this heading, as these activities have been included in the activity time budgets above, for both sexes, even if the activity of hunting or other work might rightly be considered mating or reproductive effort.

ADJUSTMENT FOR TEMPERATURE

The Kalahari can be very hot, and extreme environments have been known to increase metabolism in the laboratory, both for cold climates and for hot, as the body attempts to conserve or dissipate heat (Leslie, Bindon, et al., 1984). Some sources (Food and Agriculture Organization, 1982), however, do not consider that temperature has a significant effect on caloric requirements because people tend to compensate for extremes of temperature by modifying their behavior. Adjustment formulas are based on mean daytime temperatures, and we realize that there are not many days in the Kalahari when the mean daytime temperature would go over 25°C, the level at which adjustment is needed. It is often over that level for some hours per day, but the !Kung tend to compensate by reducing their activity at that time, resting in the shade until it cools off. So, on balance, no adjustment for temperature has been made in this cross-sectional analysis, although it is possible that if one were combining measurements taken at different seasons of the year, it would be necessary to do so (Henry and Rees, 1991).

COMBINING THE COMPONENTS OF THE NECESSARY CALORIC COSTS TO THE POPULATION

Finally, we arrive at Table 4.6, which shows the calories required for basal metabolism, the PAL multiplier to account for the caloric costs of activity, and (in the case of the women only) those for reproduction, combining these for individuals at each age. We see in Table 4.6 that average caloric requirements range from 559 per day for female babies, and go as high as 2,880 calories a day for males in the 15- to 19-year-old

TABLE 4.6. CALCULATION OF TOTAL CALORIES REQUIRED BY !KUNG FOR AGE AND SEX GROUPS

MALES

Ages	(kgs) Mean Wt	Cals/Person BMR[a]	Mean PAL	Calories Required per Person[b]
0–4	9.2	506	1.2	608
5–9	17.3	1126	1.5	1689
10–14	27.4	1131	2.0	2261
15–19	37.6	1309	2.2	2880
20–24	50.0	1440	1.8	2592
25–29	50.5	1452	1.8	2613
30–34	50.5	1465	1.8	2637
35–39	50.5	1465	1.8	2637
40–44	50.0	1459	1.8	2626
45–49	50.0	1459	1.8	2626
50–54	48.8	1445	1.8	2601
55–59	47.2	1427	1.8	2568
60–64	46.8	1119	1.8	2014
65–69	45.2	1097	1.8	1975
70–74	44.2	1084	1.8	1951
75–79	41.8	1051	1.8	1892
80+	41.0	1041	1.2	1249
Total		21,074		37,417
Average		1240		2339

FEMALES

Ages	(kgs) Mean Wt	BMR	Mean PAL	Cost of Reproduct	Calories Required per Person
0–4	7.7	466	1.2	0	559
5–9	15.1	834.8	1.4	0	1169
10–14	23.6	1033.9	1.5	0	1551
15–19	37.5	1141.0	1.5	39.7	1751
20–24	43.0	1128.1	1.6	206.6	2012
25–29	43.5	1135.5	1.6	352.4	2169
30–34	43.0	1203.1	1.6	329.7	2255
35–39	43.0	1203.1	1.6	226.0	2151
40–44	43.0	1203.1	1.6	115.7	2041
45–49	42.0	1194.4	1.6	42.1	1953
50–54	41.4	1189.2	1.6	10	1913
55–59	40.0	1177.0	1.6	0	1883
60–64	38.8	1003.4	1.6	0	1605
65–69	37.8	992.9	1.6	0	1589
70–74	37.0	984.5	1.6	0	1575
75–79	36.0	974.0	1.5	0	1461
80+	35.8	971.9	1.2	0	1166
Total		17,835.9			28,803
Average		1052.2			1800
Total both sexes					66,220
Average both sexes					2069.4

[a]Basal metabolism rate.
[b]Calories Required Per Person = BMR times Mean PAL + Cost of Reproduction.

age group, boys who combine the caloric costs of growth and who are both almost full grown and very active (even though they are not working yet). The average for women of all ages is 1,828 calories per day and that for men of all ages is 2,462, according to these estimates. Men require about 33% more calories than women, because of both their larger body size and their generally higher level of activity. These age-specific estimates are clearly approximate rather than precise in all of their components, and they have no variability from one person in an age and sex category to another, but they seem to me more useful than estimates based simply on "an average man" or "an average woman." Individuals who are handicapped, or ill, or temporarily very active may have substantially different caloric requirements.

We conclude this analysis by reminding ourselves that the population has an age distribution, and we multiply each "calories required" index by the proportion of the population in that age group. Table 4.7 presents the proportion in each age group and the calories required for that age group and the whole population.

Table 4.7 shows a kind of irreducible minimum amount of food needed by the population. If there were any less, we would expect that some people would lose weight, and in this already very slender and marginally nourished population, we would expect to soon see increases in the mortality rates of the most vulnerable segments of the population (especially infants and old people) if the shortfall persisted. And if the population has more calories than this level, we would expect to see increases in fat deposits, and relatively soon (within a year or so, if the surpluses persist) we might see increases in fertility (as mothers regain ovulation more quickly after some period of lactation) and/or decreases in mortality, especially in infants and children. We would look too for decreases in the workload of heavily stressed providers. The !Kung adaptation helps us visualize the mechanics of the Malthusian models of population dynamics, as they are living so close to the minimum amount of food needed for survival.

ARE THE !KUNG HARD-WORKING PEOPLE?

Looking at these detailed estimates of the calories that !Kung require to carry on their metabolism and activity levels, we can return to the question that has been raised in passing before. Are the !Kung hard-working people, whose strength and endurance should fill us with respect for the rigors of the hunting and gathering way of life, as many observers have

TABLE 4.7. CALCULATION OF CALORIES REQUIRED BY TOTAL
!KUNG POPULATION

MALES

Ages	Calories Required per Person	Percent of Population	Calories Required Age Group
0–4	608	11.9	7230
5–9	1689	10.2	17226
10–14	2261	9.8	22158
15–19	2880	9.4	27070
20–24	2592	8.9	23069
25–29	2613	8.3	21688
30–34	2637	7.6	20038
35–39	2637	7.0	18456
40–44	2626	6.2	16282
45–49	2626	5.4	14181
50–54	2601	4.6	11965
55–59	2568	3.7	9500
60–64	2014	2.9	5840
65–69	1975	2.0	3950
70–74	1951	1.2	2341
75–79	1892	0.6	1135
80+	1249	0.3	375
Total	37,417		
Average	2339		

FEMALES

Ages	Calories Required per Person	Percent of Population	Calories Required Age Group
0–4	559	11.5	6431
5–9	1169	10.0	11687
10–14	1551	9.5	14733
15–19	1751	9.7	16987
20–24	2012	8.6	17299
25–29	2169	8.0	17354
30–34	2255	7.4	16684
35–39	2151	6.8	14627
40–44	2041	6.1	12448
45–49	1953	5.5	10742
50–54	1913	4.9	9372
55–59	1883	4.2	7909
60–64	1605	3.3	5298
65–69	1589	2.5	3972
70–74	1575	1.6	2520
75–79	1461	0.8	1169
80+	1166	0.4	467
Total	28,803		
Average	1800		

SOURCE: Table 4.6 and Howell (2000).

suggested (Tanaka, 1980), or are they rather lazy people, as Draper tells me the Herero commonly say of their !Kung neighbors? The answer is perhaps some of both.

When we learn from quantification of activity that the !Kung men spend only an average of 2 hours a day hunting, it doesn't sound like much. But Lee has shown that a typical day of hunting may consist of a swift walk of 10 or 20 km starting at dawn, stalking and killing an animal, butchering it at the site, and carrying a heavy load of meat back to the village. The strength and endurance required by this sequence of tasks are impressive, and the events have been found to exceed the ability of some of the observers who have studied them. But a hard and long day of hunting may be followed by several days of sitting around in the village, working a much shorter day, perhaps preparing a hide, drying meat, or making tools. The average work over the seven days of the week was found to be 44 hours for !Kung adult men and 40 hours for !Kung women. This level is relatively low even by the standards of foragers (Sackett, 1996), who in turn have lower numbers of work hours than agriculturalists and even industrial workers.

We need to keep in mind that there are wide variations between individuals in how much work they do in each stage of life, and that the group as a whole is producing enough food by their labor to meet the needs of the entire population. How the food is produced by various members of the population will be the topic of the next chapter.

CHAPTER 5

Caloric Productivity and Caloric Balance

PRODUCTION OF FOOD

The !Kung traditionally eat the fruits of nature, hunting and gathering the wild foods of the environment without planting, weeding, or tending crops or animals. As we saw in the last chapter, they do a lot of work to get that food, and many aspects of that work influence their overall way of life. The amount of food that a worker produces per day depends on the species of food available in the environment, the worker's choice of strategies for harvesting that food, and the degree to which the worker is willing and able to exert himself (and herself) to obtain the food and either consume it where it is found or bring it back to camp. The "cost" of food in this situation is not monetary, but it is very real. Every bit of food represents the caloric cost of the work of obtaining it, and also the "opportunity cost" to the worker of performing this work rather than some alternative activity that might contribute to the same or different goals (such as investments in childcare or elder care, investments in building a reputation or attracting a sexual partner, seeking pleasure or self-expression, or rest and recuperation from exertion).

Evolutionary theory urges us to consider the fitness consequences of any strategy of activity, and we can look at any program as the result of trade-offs between investments in self-maintenance, investments in already existing children, in potential future children, in more distant kin such as grandchildren, in opportunities for mating, and in opportunities for influencing social standing in the group (which can have consequences for one's own and one's descendants' fitness). These concerns are at the fore during the reproductive stage of life history, but are operative in various forms at all stages of life, even that of infancy or the frail elderly. And we can account for many of the forms of social structure constructed by hunter-gatherers living in simple societies as merely the consequences that flow from the activities of individuals maximizing their fitness at their respective stages of life history.

Let us start by looking at the daily caloric production of an "average" person as he or she goes through the life cycle, using the average production of a group of people to indicate that of an individual where we have group data. We will not worry, for the moment, about individuals who cannot carry out the normal activities of their age and sex, and we will not worry either about the proportion of the total population who are in those age and sex categories, but just look at food production per person over the life span among those who are living by hunting and gathering.

Productivity of Children and Youth

Babies and children produce no food among the !Kung, or so little that it can be disregarded, until they are nearly grown to full size.[1] The !Kung seem to be more resigned to the absence of economic value of children than some people, even hunter-gatherer people, are. Hadza children, for example, seem to feed themselves and even bring food home for sharing with the group from very young ages (Blurton Jones, Hawkes, et al., 1994; Blurton Jones, Hawkes, and O'Connell, 1997), while the !Kung children are routinely fed by adults. No one expects them to do their childish best to help in the food quest or even urges them to play at mastering the skills of hunting and gathering, until they are nearly full grown, in their late teens. Blurton Jones, Hawkes, and their colleagues (1994) suggest that that the Kalahari must be a more dangerous environment for children than the Hadza territory, so the risks that children would experience by moving around the area to look for opportunities to produce food would exceed the value of any work they could do. The Kalahari is flat and featureless, and it is easy to become disoriented or lost in the bush. There are many dangerous animals and snakes that a child might encounter if he or she were ranging widely, so parents feel better when their children stay together and play in the relative

---

1. But see Lee (1979:71).

security of the village space. As we saw in the last chapter from Draper's observations, children are usually found in the village until they are about 12 years or so, and after that time boys in particular are often out of sight and sound of the village.

Small children are carried by their mothers on gathering expeditions even after they are able to walk a little while they are nursing, but the mothers are relieved when the children wean themselves or are weaned by the mother at the start of the next pregnancy, and the child can be left behind in the village while the mother walks long distances (average of 6.5 km per day on the days she goes gathering) to get food. As Lee (1979) has demonstrated and Blurton Jones (1986) has further explored, carrying children adds a great deal to the women's workload. After weaning, children stay behind in the village to play with the other children when women go gathering, under the informal supervision of whichever adults have decided to stay behind that day. Children under the age of 10 of both sexes bring in so few calories per day that zero is the best estimate, and children in the age group 10 to 14 collect only a few calories in the course of their play. Between the ages of 15 and 19, the amount of food production increases sharply for both girls and boys, but they continue to produce considerably less than adults, and it continues to be true that adults don't spend much time urging them to produce more.

Women's Production of Calories

We need to look at the sexes separately as they approach adulthood, because their work patterns become different. Let's start with the women. Between age 10 and 14, girls may sometimes accompany their mothers and other women to collect food, and will eat what they can in the bush and collect and carry some food home when they go, but there is no pressure on them to do so. Around this age, girls get their first *kaross*,[2] which allows them to carry larger loads than they can manage without one. It seemed to me in the field that, as the girls approached their "adolescent growth spurt," they were more likely to choose to go along with the women, perhaps because hunger drove them to want to get some food earlier in the day than they could otherwise do, and perhaps also because they wanted to help carry back larger loads to provide for the family for the next day or so. Girls who wear the *kaross* and who volunteer to go on collecting trips may be perceived as "growing

2. The *kaross* is a cape made from the hide of a single animal that women use to carry back loads.

up," and this behavior leads people to consider such an enthusiastic worker as a good candidate to be a bride to a young man in their family (Howell, 2000:167–172).

During the older adolescent ages, 15 to 19, young women bring in increasing amounts of food on collecting trips, as they learn the skills of food collecting in an informal way by accompanying their mothers and other women, and as the frequency of trips goes up as their motivation to act as adult women increases. They have a lot of activity in their lives at this age: during the 1963–1973 observations (Howell, 2000), menarche came at an average age of 16.6; first marriage at 16.9; first birth at average 21.4 (median age 19.6).

After age 20, the amount of food produced by women seems to depend on the handicaps she has in collecting food, primarily pregnancy, the need to carry a child, and lactation, on the one hand; and the level of motivation she has to go out collecting often and to work long hours, on the other hand, which is related to the same events. Infertile women are less motivated to produce a lot of food than mothers with children depending on them, but it is also true that a strong young woman who has no child to carry can produce more and carry more than an equally strong but heavily burdened mother.

Lee (1969:250–280) quantified the production of calories by women by following individual women as they joined groups of women to go on collecting trips. He observed the foods identified, collected, and consumed by the women and children on the trip, as well as weighing and measuring foods collected and carried home to share with the group. His observations show that women's work consists not only of picking leaves, nuts, fruits, and berries and the harder work of digging roots (Hawkes, 1989), but also the work of walking to the food sites and back to the village, carrying loads on the way back that consist of quantities of food and firewood as well as the children, who are carried in both directions, and often ostrich eggshells of water too. For our purposes in this chapter, we are interested in the food produced for consumption, both in the bush and in the village. The average number of calories harvested per adult woman in a day of gathering depends largely on the species collected. It ranges from 16,920 calories for a 12-kg backload of mongongo nuts (Lee, 1979:187) to perhaps 6,000 for a full backload of melons or other foods that are heavy in weight but light in calories. The women seldom or never fail to find food, but the food found differs over seasons and areas in caloric value, in attractiveness and taste, and in ease of collection, processing, and cooking.

TABLE 5.1. CALORIES PRODUCED BY AN AVERAGE !KUNG WOMAN

Age Groups	Gathered Food Calories/Day	Lactation Cals/Day	Total Cals/Day
0–4	0	0	0
5–9	0	0	0
10–14	107	0	107
15–19	1111	35	1146
20–24	2300	191	2491
25–29	2500	335	2835
30–34	2995	316	3311
35–39	2995	218	3213
40–44	3274	113	3387
45–49	3274	42	3316
50–54	3302	10	3312
55–59	3302	0	3302
60–64	2452	0	2452
65–69	2452	0	2452
70–74	1465	0	1465
75–79	1465	0	1465
80+	0	0	0
Total	32,994	1260	34,308

As shown in Table 5.1, averaging several gathering days (2.2 per week according to Lee, 1979: 260), women in the reproductive years (15 to 44) bring in an average of approximately 1,000 calories per day for the 15- to 19-year-olds to over 3,000 calories per day of gathered food for experienced middle-aged women. Note that Table 5.1 has no measure of individual variation, no standard deviation of the averages, and there is just a smooth curve of productivity by age, guided but not actually averaged from Lee's data on productivity of individual women of various ages.

Women in the reproductive years are producing two forms of food: the vegetable foods (including fruits, melons, berries, and gums as well as roots, nuts, leaves, and stalks), and the milk they produce for their babies.[3] The babies receive several hundred calories of milk per day at birth, and this output increases to a maximum of about 500 calories a day, which continues until the mother has to start supplementing the baby's diet with other foods in order to provide the energy the baby

3. Readers of an early draft have raised the question of whether we are "double-counting" calories when we count lactation as a form of food produced, as the mothers produce it out of their own bodies and have to eat to provide it. A moment's thought will show that the same is true of food produced by hunting and by gathering. Lactation needs to be counted on both sides of the production-consumption equation.

needs for growth and activity. The amount of milk a mother can produce is insufficient to meet all of the baby's caloric requirements after about 6 months, but !Kung mothers continue to feed their babies approximately the same amount of breast-milk per day, feeding the baby often and for a long time, averaging around this same 500 calories a day for about 32 months from birth to the start of the next pregnancy for people whose inter-birth intervals average some 40 months (Howell, 2000:209). In the extreme case, a mother may continue to breastfeed a final child for as much as five years (or 60 months). The majority of the women age 20 to 35 are lactating at any one time; the rest are pregnant, infertile, or awaiting conception.

Table 5.1 gives the age pattern of production by women of calories in the form of breast-milk and in the form of gathered vegetable foods. Note that the first columns of Table 5.3 repeat the estimated average calories produced per woman who survives to the end of the life span from Table 5.1: These data describe the average per living woman. The second set of columns (marked "per group") discounts the production per person by the probability of surviving to that age, to make the estimated contribution to the food supply by the women in each age group.

The median age at final birth is about 35 (Howell, 2000). After that age, the increasing proportion of post-reproductive women continue to gather bush foods regularly for decades while they are raising the children born earlier, even after their children become adults. Efficiency in gathering no doubt increases for the women in their 40s when they have no infants to carry while they gather. And we see in Table 5.1 that the post-reproductive women, those in the age groups 45 to 74, are clearly not just elderly dependents of the young adults (although there are a few we called "handicapped and frail elderly" in Chapter 2); the vast majority of older women are still productive workers, even if their work capacity declines somewhat at older ages, especially over age 60.

By the time the women reach age 50, they are very unlikely to have a child who needs to be carried, and while they may still have a child or two at home that they are raising, they are also likely to have adult sons and daughters who may have produced grandchildren by that time. If the first child was born when the mother was 20, that child is going to be 30 when the mother reaches 50, and a daughter might have as many as three children, age 10 and younger. Even a son is likely to have a child by that age. Recall the cultural rule that young women and their husbands should live with the wife's family until three children are born. The first-born daughter might live near her mother when the mother is

40 to 50. A late-born daughter might live with her mother's group when the mother is 55 to 65, a time for women when productivity is still typically high. In addition, even if the young couple are not living with their parents for some reason, either couple, the maternal or paternal grandparents, may go visiting to the group of their adult child for part of the year to stay at times when their help can make an important difference to the children or grandchildren, such as the time of weaning of an older child (typically during the pregnancy of the next sibling), and during the time of birth when the daughter may like to have her mother nearby for moral support, and when the older children may need some extra care and supplementation of their diet.

Post-reproductive women regularly continue to provide food for themselves and their husbands, and if they produce a surplus, they can contribute to the food supply of their closest relatives and neighbors as well. The proportion of women who are living as widows gradually increases over the age of 50 (although widowed women may remarry if they wish and if an opportunity arises). In many cases, it is difficult to judge whether adult children are living with (and dependent on) their parents or whether the elders are living with (and dependent on) their adult offspring. There must be a time when these relationships shift. But we note that the pattern of older adults, especially widowed women, living nearby their adult children, especially daughters, is frequently seen.

Post-reproductive women are often skilled and knowledgeable gatherers and are usually still strong and vigorous (Biesele and Howell, 1981:82) until late in life. They are at least as productive per day of gathering as the reproductive-age women, and the amount of gathering they do may depend upon whether they have adult daughters (or daughter-in-laws) who need some help supporting their families, and whether the grandmother can be more help by collecting food or by staying in the village to watch the older children while the mother goes collecting. The mother and grandmother may take turns producing food and providing childcare. When weakness and the fragility of age occur, !Kung attempt to support and provide for the aged, but typically death occurs shortly after the point when older adults can no longer gather food and firewood. The "burden" of care of the aged is light on their children in this society, and would probably have been even lighter in the days when there were no cattle-posts to provide stable residential accommodations and supplements to the hunting and gathering diet (Howell, 2000:366–369; see also Kaplan, 1994).

Table 5.1 shows that maximal productivity in gathering occurs during a woman's 50s and that productivity remains substantial through the 70s, only declining (on average) to near zero by the age of 80, when there are few people of either gender alive.

Men's Production of Calories

When young men become hunters, others may offer the hope that "his heart will burn hot for meat" and that he will be highly motivated to go hunting early and often. Indeed, young men greatly increase their attractiveness to women and to the families of potential brides by successes in hunting. When marriage is arranged, typically around age 25 for young men, to a girl around the age of menarche, he is expected to do a period of approximately 10 years of "bride service," living nearby his in-laws and hunting for his bride, her parents, and their group. The bride's parents will be watching carefully to see if the young man is an enthusiastic hunter. Young wives are often reluctant to marry or to stay married while they are young, and any laziness on the husband's part about hunting will increase the probability that the marriage will dissolve at an early stage.

After the birth of the first child, the young man may begin to urge his wife to take the baby and move back to live with his people, but the cultural guideline says that the couple should stay near her family until the third child is born, which usually keeps the young couple living matrilocally until the wife is in her late 20s (Howell, 2000). Throughout life, most couples seem to have a low-level struggle about which side of the family to live with, each preferring to live with their own relatives. A couple who happens to have no living parents or older siblings on either side to go to would be considered very unlucky.

The rates of success in hunting for men vary widely, not only by age but also by skill, motivation, and luck. The solution to the phenomenon of the inequality of meat production by individuals for the !Kung (and for many or most hunter-gatherer societies) is that the meat brought in by a hunter will be divided among everyone in the living group, not just consumed by the nuclear family of the hunter. Indeed, when hunters are successful in obtaining large amounts of meat, nearby groups will be invited to come and share the bounty. Lee (1979) dates the start of a hunting career from the age of 25, and describes it as continuing for 50 years, or until the hunter dies, reaching a peak between the ages of 45 and 60. Men in their 50s or 60s may exceed younger hunters in knowledge and judgment but usually not in speed or stamina. The hunting-success score starts to decline around age 55, but may continue to be substantial into the 70s. Older hunters often take a young man, perhaps a son or son-in-law, as a frequent partner in hunting, and older hunters gradually shift their focus toward snares, capture of burrowing animals underground, and methods of hunting (like spearing) that don't require the chase. Older men also increase the amount of gathered food, especially nuts, that they bring in.

Lee (1979:231) found that hunters tend to go out hunting about 2.4 days a week (about 40% of the time), but only bring in a catch of their important big-game animals (gemsbok, kudu, or wildebeest) occasionally, perhaps a few times a year. Medium-sized animals, such as warthog, are more often caught. And often they bring back small game (birds, duikers, hares, porcupines), small packages of meat that do not need to be widely shared with others. If the hunters have been otherwise unsuccessful in the hunt on a particular day, they often bring back some vegetable foods or at least get a load of firewood before they return to the village.

It is difficult to calculate a hunting success rate per day, as many hunts require more than one day to bring down a large animal, and many hunts involve more than one hunter. Lee calculated in his detailed observation that men brought back a slightly lower mean amount of calories per day than the average woman, but that the variance of the return rate is much higher for men. His estimates of productivity per average day per hunter are found in Table 5.2. Note that there are also contributions to productivity per man from gathering in Table 5.2, reflecting the regular but small investments (overall 17% of men's work productivity) (Lee, 1979) that men make in collecting nuts, vegetable palm, and other vegetable foods. Note that the proportion of the total calories produced that come from gathered foods increases as men move into old age. Occasionally, !Kung men of all ages make a substantial effort to bring in vegetable foods, accompanying women and children to the mongongo nut groves where they may stay for weeks, eating and processing nuts before carrying back the largest loads that they as well as the women can manage to carry; or by harvesting ivory palm hearts or palm seeds (Lee, 1979) in large amounts. This vegetable food may be shared widely, in the usual male pattern for sharing meat, although women do not share their vegetable produce so widely or so formally.

Men's average production by age is somewhat different from women's. Boys bring in no measurable food before age 20, and even after they start their careers as hunters, they increase their productivity more slowly than

TABLE 5.2. CALORIES PRODUCED BY AN AVERAGE !KUNG MAN

Age Groups	Gathered Food Calories/Day	Hunted Cals/Day	Total Cals/Day
0–4	0	0	0
5–9	0	0	0
10–14	100	0	100
15–19	200	0	200
20–24	400	1600	2000
25–29	450	2600	3050
30–34	525	3000	3525
35–39	600	3200	3800
40–44	775	3000	3775
45–49	800	3000	3800
50–54	850	3000	3850
55–59	900	3000	3900
60–64	1000	2250	3520
65–69	1000	1500	2500
70–74	600	500	1100
75–79	200	250	450
80+	0	0	0
Total	8400	26,900	35,300

the women do as gatherers. Full growth in height is not achieved until about age 22, and it is very rare for men either to do much hunting or to marry before that time.

Calories by Men and Women for the Whole Population

Table 5.3 shows the summary columns of Tables 5.1 and 5.2 for a typical individual in each age group. According to my calculations, men produce about 20% more calories than women do, although Lee (1979) found that men worked somewhat more hours than !Kung women but brought in somewhat fewer calories.[4] Lee (1979:261) reports that men do somewhat more subsistence work than women, bringing in 30% of all the calories consumed by the population in the form of meat hunted, and another 13% in the form of gathered foods, while women brought in 55% of the calories in the form of gathered foods plus the 4% of food needed by the infants in the form of breast-milk. Table 5.3 also adjusts the amount of calories produced by the age distribution of the population. This table

4. This deficit of production by men no doubt comes from not counting the work of the younger men employed by Hereros in cattle-keeping. See the discussion of the "cowboy correction" in association with Figure 5.1.

TABLE 5.3. CALORIES PRODUCED AND CALORIC BALANCE

Age Group	Total Cals/Day	Proportion in Age Group	Cals Produced by Age Group	Cals Required by Age Group	Caloric Balance
MALES					
0–4	0	11.8	0	8536	–8536
5–9	0	10.1	–	15710	–15710
10–14	100	9.6	960	17568	–16608
15–19	200	9.1	1820	18778	–16958
20–24	2000	8.6	17200	20158	–2958
25–29	3050	8.0	24400	18582	5818
30–34	3525	7.4	26085	17343	8742
35–39	3800	6.7	25460	15703	9757
40–44	3775	6.1	23028	14240	8788
45–49	3800	5.5	20900	12839	8061
50–54	3850	4.8	18480	10405	8075
55–59	3900	4.1	15990	8773	7217
60–64	3250	3.3	10725	5538	5187
65–69	2500	2.4	6000	3950	2050
70–74	1100	1.5	1650	2438	–788
75–79	450	0.8	360	1262	–902
80+	0	0.4	–	624	–624
Total	35,300	100.2	193,058	192,447	610
FEMALES					
0–4	0	11.8	–	7903	–7903
5–9	0	10.1	–	11719	–11719
10–14	107	9.6	1027	13921	–12894
15–19	1200	9.1	10920	15939	–5019
20–24	2491	8.6	21423	15844	5579
25–29	2835	8.0	22680	15991	6689
30–34	3311	7.4	24501	15349	9152
35–39	3213	6.7	21527	13202	8325
40–44	3387	6.1	20661	11347	9314
45–49	3316	5.5	18238	9757	8481
50–54	3312	4.8	15898	8325	7573
55–59	3302	4.1	13538	6997	6541
60–64	2452	3.3	8092	4801	3291
65–69	2452	2.4	5885	3455	2430
70–74	1465	1.5	2198	2141	57
75–79	1465	0.8	1172	1130	42
80+	0	0.4	–	564	–564
Total	34,308	100.2	187,758	158,385	29,374
Total both sexes			380,816	350,832	29,984

corresponds to Table 4.7, which shows calories required by the total population, adjusted for age and sex. It is reassuring to note that the totals of the two tables are close to being equal, but given the large number of steps of estimation of quantities that we have made in the process of deriving these totals, the absolute numbers cannot be taken too seriously. The small surplus of calories produced over those required (estimated as 150 per day per person) leads us to conclude that, at this particular time of year (early in the rainy season), the population has a small surplus of food.

Similarly if we had found a small deficit, we might expect it to be made up at another time of year when either productivity or requirements were somewhat different.

Calories Produced in Comparative Perspective

Figure 5.1 shows the men's and women's daily energy production of the !Kung plotted on a graph from Kaplan, Lancaster, and their associates (2000:159), a study that did not include the !Kung, but focused on energy production of other hunter-gatherer groups. We see that the !Kung men get a slower start to productivity than the Ache and Hiwi men and never reach the level of daily productivity in hunting that the others do. This graph is consistent with our ethnographic understanding. The Ache are formidable hunters, constantly on the move, and they spend a great deal of time hunting. The !Kung's hunting investments and successes are more modest, and the !Kung men supplement hunting with some steady gathering as well. The !Kung men go on being productive much longer, crossing the production curve for the Ache men around age 50, and they continue to bring in substantial amounts of food between 50 and 70, when the Ache men's productivity has declined sharply.[5]

The initial plot of men's productivity showed a rather striking gap in the youngest ages (20 to 29), when Lee's data show very little hunting success for young !Kung men. A close look at the population at risk reminds us that many of the young men are employed by Hereros to work with cattle, work that wasn't included in the initial tabulation of production. The food produced by these workers needs to be estimated and added to men's productivity, a procedure that I have been calling "the cowboy correction," which can be seen in the shaded area on Figure 5.1. The correction is calculated by assuming that each "cowboy" has the mean productivity of older !Kung men in hunting, since there is no easy way of converting the pay of the "cowboys" into its food equivalent.

The !Kung women do not require this kind of correction, as they were rarely employed in 1968. The striking observation in Figure 5.1 is that !Kung women are more productive than women in other groups at all ages. They also go on being productive later in life than the Ache

5. According to Hawkes and Blurton Jones, the rough indication of the Hadza data plotted in Figure 5.1 is premature and should not be taken seriously (personal communication, 2002).

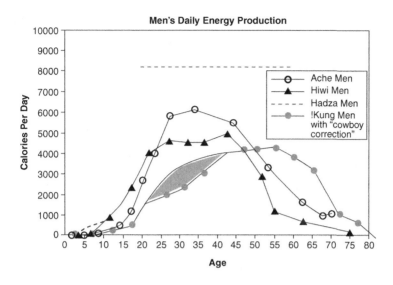

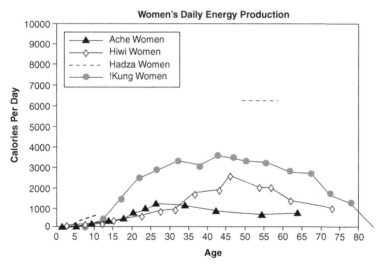

Figure 5.1. Daily energy production for men and women, for Ache, Hiwi, and !Kung (from Kaplan, et al., 2000: 159).

women, and they produce far more food than the Ache women do at all ages. This too is ethnographically sensible. Having to move their whole camp daily, when they are living the traditional way of life, the Ache women are constantly carrying their possessions and children and hence cannot produce foods as effectively as the !Kung women do. Hawkes (personal communication, 2003) sees the lowered productivity of Ache women as a cost that is paid for the increased productivity of Ache men. The burden of subsistence is more equally divided between the men and women among the !Kung, and at the same time it seems clear from body measurements and from direct observation that Ache get much more to eat than !Kung do.

CALORIC BALANCE

Figures 5.2 and 5.3 show the calories produced and consumed by all of the age groups of !Kung women and !Kung men. We see in Figures 5.2 and 5.3 that the women are not so productive that they could support themselves and all of the children if the men disappeared at adulthood, at least by the current economic arrangements, but neither are the men so productive that the women could afford to devote all their time and attention to reproduction while the men take care of production. The well-known sexual egalitarianism of the !Kung (Lee, 1979; Draper, 1975) has a solid economic basis.

If we subtract the calories required from those consumed at each age to obtain a measure of net production, as we see in Figures 5.4 and 5.5,

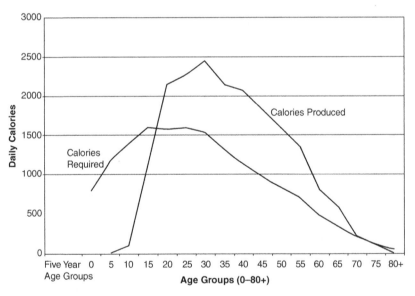

Figure 5.2. Calories produced and required by women. (Source: http://hdl.handle .net/1807/18218.)

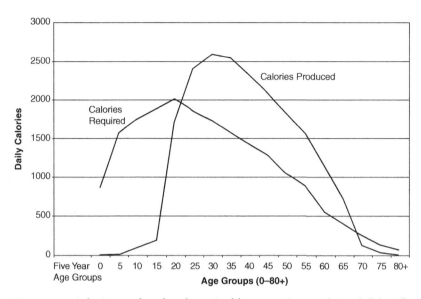

Figure 5.3. Calories produced and required by men. (Source: http://hdl.handle
.net/1807/18218.)

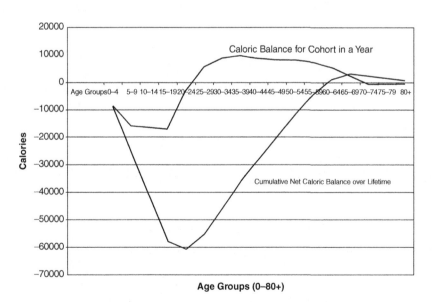

Figure 5.4. Net Caloric Balance for a cohort, over a year and cumulated over a
lifetime, men only. (Source: http://hdl.handle.net/1807/18218.)

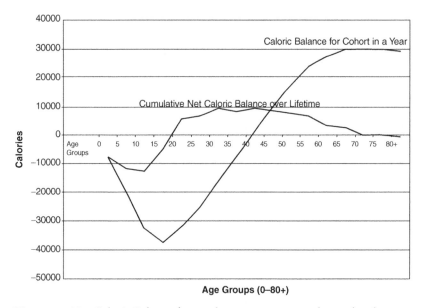

Figure 5.5. Net Caloric Balance for a cohort, over a year and cumulated over a lifetime, women only. (Source: http://hdl.handle.net/1807/18218.)

we see the age patterns of net production and consumption. Note that there are two lines for the males in Figure 5.4: the one closer to the zero line shows the Caloric Balance for individuals currently in that age, while the wider line shows the accumulation of Caloric Balance over the life span, summed from birth to each age. We see that males do not produce as much as they consume among the !Kung until they are in their early 20s, and they "owe" such a large amount for their feeding and that of other members of their cohort who die early that the "debt" is not entirely paid off until age 60 or so! Of course, the !Kung do not consciously consider the sum of net caloric balance for individuals or for groups, but there has to be some balance in the population over the life span or they could not continue to live the way they do.

Figure 5.5 shows the same calculations for women. We note that women "repay" the investment in their childhood earlier in life: They are on balance net contributors to the society by age 20, and have paid off the debt incurred by all women in their cohort by age 40 or so. Notice that we are not counting the dependents of the food producers in creating this "debt" but only the birth cohort, consisting of the producers themselves and their age-mates who survived and who failed to survive to the present. According to this analysis, it is clearly women

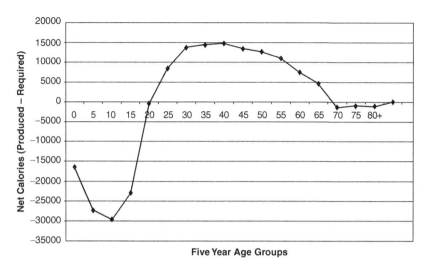

Figure 5.6. Balance of production and consumption over age groups, sexes combined. (Source: http://hdl.handle.net/1807/18218.)

over 40 who produce the net surplus that allows the society to meet emergencies and provide for those who cannot provide for themselves on a secure basis. The men engage in the dramatic distributions of meat in the villages, but they could not do so if the women were not producing so much food on a regular basis.

Figure 5.6 combines the Caloric Balance scores of males and females and shows that there is a nice smooth curve over the life span. Children are expensive for the society, but their cost starts to decrease around age 15, and the adults can afford to produce enough food for themselves and for dependent children, and the small amount of dependent elderly.

Figure 5.7 shows the variable "CalBal," or Caloric Balance, for each individual in the 1968 population, calculated by subtracting the mean daily calories required at ego's current age (and sex) from the mean daily calories produced by their age-sex group. It is purely a function of age and sex (and not effort or skill) so it is more a "theoretical variable" (like the Expected Body Mass Index variable that we created) than most of our observations about individuals. We can use it as an individual variable but it will be the same for all persons with the same age and sex. We see in Figure 5.7 that the distribution is much more smooth and regular than any of our "empirical variables," which show variability from one person to another, and only roughly smooth curves when averaged.

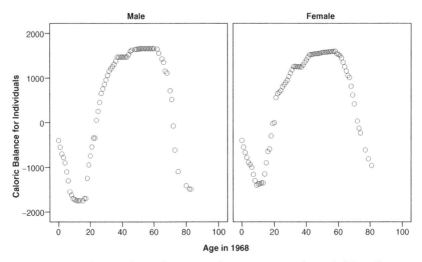

Figure 5.7. Caloric Balance by age and sex. (Source: http://hdl.handle.net/ 1807/18071.)

This theoretical variable reminds us of the main findings we have produced on the production and requirements of calories. We see in Figure 5.7 that children are a heavy caloric cost to the population, increasingly so throughout childhood from infancy to a maximum in the early teenage years, and decreasingly thereafter as the children learn to contribute to the supply of calories. Boys are more calorically expensive than girls, as they are larger at all ages and start to contribute calories later in their lives. Children are not self-supporting, on the average, until well into their 20s. Adults contribute to the surplus of calories, increasingly so from 20 to 35, decreasingly so after age 40 as death removes larger proportions of the cohort. Adults do not lose their self-sufficiency, on the average, until around age 70, and the cost of the dependent elderly is very small compared to the cost of the dependent children in this society.

If we look at the transfers from the point of view of the calories, we can say that "the average calorie" produced is a product of a 44-year-old female or a 41.6-year-old male, while the average calorie consumed is eaten by a 31-year-old woman or a 34-year-old man.

The obvious question that remains is whether the CalBal variable explains the differences in fatness that we have seen (in Chapter 3) in our variable BMIDiff (deviations of BMI from the expected pattern of BMI based on age and sex). Figure 5.8 shows the scattergram of CalBal by BMIDiff for people of all ages. We note that the relationship of these two variables is a distinctly odd one, with many cases falling at the

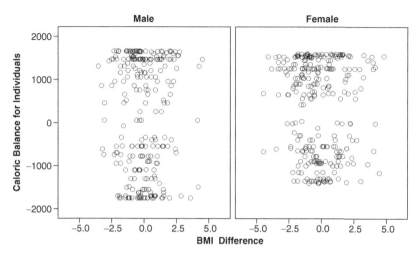

Figure 5.8. Caloric Balance by BMIDiff. (Source: http://hdl.handle.net/1807/18071.)

extremes of CalBal, and few in the middle. This corresponds to the finding that there are many expensive children, and many highly productive adults, and that people move rather quickly from one category to the other in their 20s, so there aren't very many in the middle of the range. The correlation coefficient of the variables is insignificant. What these relations tell us is that somehow the !Kung are managing to share calories between adults and children so that one's fatness is not simply a function of one's ability to feed oneself. It doesn't tell us how they do this, but only that they succeed in the task of sharing.

This analysis is based on a model created by economic demographer Ron Lee and anthropologist Karen Kramer for their study of the Maya (Lee, 2000; Lee and Kramer, 2002). The model focuses on the need to transfer calories across sex and age groups as an inevitable and insistent generator of human social structure. In the next two chapters, we will look at some aspects of !Kung social structure from the point of view of the transfer of calories from haves to have-nots. Before we turn to this task, we end this chapter noting some of the implications of this analysis.

Caldwell's question (1982) of whether intergenerational transfers are typically upward or downward from one generation to another is clearly answered for the !Kung as well as for the Ache (Kaplan, 1996): the transfers are downward. Each generation finances the growth of the next through the period of life in which they cannot support themselves, and post-reproductive adults finance the shortfalls when parents cannot fully provide for their children. We will look at the details of these food transfers in more detail in the following chapters.

Note that men have somewhat less variance in the ages at which they produce and consume food than women, as they start producing later and end somewhat earlier, in part because they die younger. We are not examining here how calories are transferred from one age group to another and we are not committed by this observation about averages to have confidence that there is a communistic distribution system among the !Kung permitting wealth to flow from where it is generated to where it is needed. These are empirical questions that we will tackle in the next group of chapters. We are not saying anything about variance between individuals in production and consumption, or about the justice of the process. This analysis is merely an early stage of an answer to the question of whether the crucial participants in sharing food with children are their parents, their grandparents, or whether "it takes a village to raise a child." We will return to these questions in the final chapter.

In the next chapter, we will begin to look at the actual relationships of those who share food and work, looking first at the residential social units of those who share a waterhole, a living group, and a household.

CHAPTER 6

Caloric Balance and Residential Units

Waterholes, Living Groups, Households

The first section of this book has been spent constructing a framework of life history of the !Kung, focusing on body size and the production and requirements of calories. The units of analysis have been individuals over the life span, on the one hand, and the total population, weighing the individuals in each age segment by their probability of survival to that age. In the past chapter, we constructed a variable of Caloric Balance, a measure of the net calories expected from someone of the age and sex of the individual, in our efforts to relate production and consumption of calories. In the section that begins here, we will start to apply the framework of calories and body size that we have been constructing to the observations we made of !Kung life in 1967–1969. We will try to account for observed variations in body mass index by group memberships that might produce individual differences, such as the geographical location, the composition of the village, the place of the person in the household, the kin resources of the person, and the investments they receive and make in others, kin and neighbors.

In this chapter, we will concentrate on the geographically organized groups of people that we saw living together and sharing their resources in 1967–1969. We are looking for substantial differences between residential units in the well-being of their members, and for significant correlations between characteristics of the units and the BMIDiff scores of residents. Where we find these, we attribute causal strength to the characteristics of the unit and sharing of resources within the unit. When we do not find much difference between the units and unity within them, we conclude that the unit is not important for that purpose, and look for other factors than residential propinquity (such as kinship ties that cross residential units) and mechanisms (such as migration and visiting between units) to explain the uniformity in BMIDiff between groups.

These units are nested into one another: Individuals are grouped into households, households are gathered into living groups (villages), and living groups live in particular places (*n!oris*) organized around a waterhole. The "magic numbers" that have been discussed for hunter-gatherer social structures (Lee and DeVore, 1968: 245–248) apply to these units: five hundred is a pretty good estimate of the average number of !Kung residents alive in the Dobe-/ai/ai area at any one point of time; fifty is a pretty good estimate of the number of people found at the average waterhole; twenty is close to the average for the typical living group; and the size of households varies regularly over the life cycle of nuclear families with an overall average of less than three (Kelly, 1995).

The task of this chapter is to consider each of these types of units, in turn, to explore empirically whether the characteristics of the units have causal importance for the individual's body mass index (or BMIDiff, the individual deviations around the mean for the age and sex group), which we are using as an indicator of relative fatness, and hence, in this thin population, of relative well-being. In the process of exploring these relations, starting with the larger units and going toward the smaller, we will review some !Kung ethnography.

We begin by looking at the distribution of the average Caloric Balance of all the people who are at the residential units at the end of 1968, the "Mean CalBal." Figure 6.1 shows the relationship of the Mean CalBal for the ten waterholes occupied at the end of 1968 to the number of people living at the waterhole: We note that the average CalBal goes generally down for the larger waterholes.[1] We see that Mean CalBal is a positive number in all cases: negative scores of individuals and small groups are averaged out in these relatively large groups. The smallest waterholes (with fifteen to twenty-five residents) have the highest mean CalBal, and these decrease through a rather narrow margin to about size 100, and then there is an increase to the largest waterhole, which is /Xai/Xai, which has cattle and an unusually large

---

1. Largest in the sense of !Kung population, not territory or amount of water.

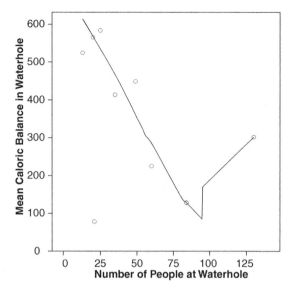

Figure 6.1. Mean Caloric Balance in waterhole, by number of people living there. (Source: http://hdl.handle.net/1807/10412.)

area of exploitation around it. The other "outlier" (mean CalBal about 100, number of people about twenty) is a group of descendants of a very old man, who went out for a few days to his ex-home, a small water-hole, which has an unexpectedly low score on mean CalBal. This rela-tively small group would need to recruit more food producers to balance its youthful profile, if it were to be viable in the long run, but the group was more like a holiday expedition than a real village.

Figure 6.2 shows the same variables on the level of the living group, or village. We note that the distribution of mean CalBal is almost flat: In other words, it is not related to size of the group on this level of analy-sis. Three of the groups have a mean CalBal less than zero: We hypoth-esize that these groups are unstable and will likely be gaining or losing some members in the near future. And we note that there is a cluster of three small groups with substantially higher mean CalBal than others: Again, these are probably temporary small groups of !Kung adults.

And finally we look at Figure 6.3, the same variables on the level of the household. The trend line decreases with size of the unit for house-holds, reflecting the composition of one or two adult workers (parents) with their dependent children. Note that a large proportion of units is below the zero line on the graph: Households are not large enough to fully average out the differences between individuals.

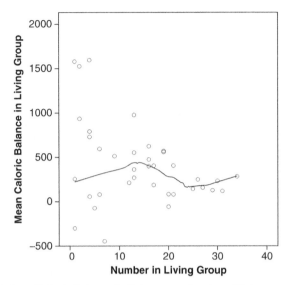

Figure 6.2. Mean Caloric Balance in living group by size of living group. (Source: http://hdl.handle.net/1807/10412.)

Figures 6.1, 6.2, and 6.3 are based on the same 468 individuals who were alive and resident in the Dobe-/Xai/Xai area in 1968. They differ only on how the individuals are gathered into groups. What these figures do not show us is the effect of group composition on the well-being of its members. We saw in the last chapter, in Figure 5.7, that Caloric Balance is heavily related to age and sex of individuals (although not linearly related), and we saw in Figure 5.8 that when we correlate Caloric Balance (a function of age and sex) with BMIDiff (which has had the effects of age and sex removed from the distribution of body mass index), there is no correlation and no meaningful pattern of distribution for individuals. What we want to know now is whether Caloric Balance acts on the level of the residential units to explain the differences in BMIDiff that we observe. To explore this question, we will take a closer look at the units on each level.

WATERHOLES AND N!ORIS

The Dobe region includes some 11,000 km² around ten permanent and four semipermanent water sources (Yellen, 1976), plus another fifty or so named seasonal water sources. It makes sense to think that some of the well-being of individuals may depend upon which waterhole area the person is living in, as some areas have many more patches of vegetable foods naturally occurring or are located near the border fence

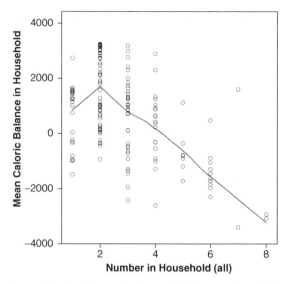

Figure 6.3. Mean Caloric Balance in household by the size of the household. (Source: http://hdl.handle.net/1807/10412.)

that interferes with the movements of wild animals and makes it easier (or in some cases more difficult) to hunt them successfully.

Some of the waterholes have much more water exposed near the surface of the land than others, and this feature tends to attract cattle owners to want to live at that waterhole. When cattle are watered, other changes in the environment soon follow. Wild animals find it more difficult to get to those sources of water and go elsewhere, and the grass and other vegetation that attracts animals may be eaten down by the cattle (and the accompanying goats and sheep). In fact, the areas where there are a lot of domesticated animals rather quickly become dominated by thorny plants, which is the only form of vegetation that isn't eaten down to the ground by the goats, in particular. So we would not be surprised to find differences in mean BMIDiff, our indicator of nutritional well-being, at the various waterholes.

Most of the temporary water sources in the Dobe area were uninhabited in 1967–1969, with an average of about forty (resident !Kung) persons at each of the ten named places that had any residents at the end of 1968. Figure 6.4 shows a map of the area of our study area and the neighboring regions (Yellen, 1976:29; Lee, 1979) with the main waterholes marked on them.

The !Kung organize their perception of the environment around a water source (a well or a pond) because water is scarce and essential to life

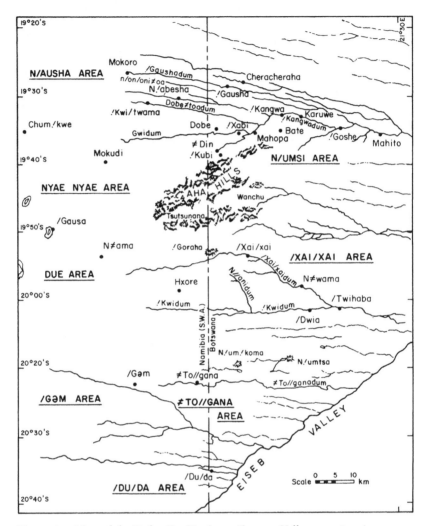

Figure 6.4. Map of the Dobe-/Du/Da Area. (Source: Yellen, 1976:29.)

for humans and animals in the Kalahari. Each !Kung person has a claim, inherited from their parents, to one or more named places that they call a *n!ori* (or *n!ore*), which is a territory around a water source that is large enough to support one or more living groups of people (for at least part of the annual cycle). Villages are built somewhere within the *n!ori*, located for convenience for minimizing the distance between the water and the vegetable resources that are currently being exploited. Traditional villages are never located right at the water source, because animals other than humans, including dangerous ones, need to have access to the water too.

The village is moved as frequently as necessary (typically multiple times per year) (Lee and DeVore, 1976) to harvest vegetable foods most efficiently, which allows them to leave behind their accumulated garbage and insect infestations and start a fresh site. Groups also move when any member of the living group dies, to avoid the place of death and burial. Moving and rebuilding the village takes only a day or so.

The main owners (k"xausi) of the area around the waterhole (n!ori) are a few middle-aged or older siblings or cousins who have lived there a long time, and who are acknowledged by others (who may also be owners by inheritance) as having the leading position. If there is more than one village in a n!ori, there will be some owners in each village. There is no competition for the claim to ownership, as there is little in the way of benefit or privilege that flows from being even one of the main owners of even the largest and most reliable water sources. Others must ask permission of the main owners to use the resources of the n!ori, but permission is rarely refused or even debated when the seekers are !Kung.

When the seekers are Bantu and/or cattle owners, the n!ori k"xausi (owners of the waterhole) may be hesitant to give permission to use the water, because cattle drink large amounts of water and the need to water them often leads to a muddy, trampled area around the well that will discourage other animals from using the water, but they will have a hard time refusing outright. The petitioners may negotiate for permission by promising employment to the n!ori k"xau or some of his relatives or may agree to share milk with the owners. Once the cattle are established and the Bantu are residents at the waterhole, the !Kung lose any bargaining power they might have had.[2] Indeed, under the laws of Botswana in the 1970s, there was a danger that if the new residents improve the well (by digging it deeper, for example), they may gain legal title to all the land around it.

There is reason to think that the !Kung have changed their pattern of land use considerably in recent decades before this study, as !Kung adults in 1967–1969 reported that they were "owners" of fifty-two places, only thirteen of which are found in the Dobe area. Only ten of those fifty-two n!oris were occupied in 1968, the places we see in the map in Figure 6.4 and see listed in Table 6.1. Traditionally, Lee has speculated, people might have spent a substantial part of the year at a seasonal waterhole that they owned, and only spent the dry season at one of the permanent or semipermanent water sources, moving around to maintain their ties with kin living in these places as well as maximizing their access to rich

---

2. Lee asked Herero why they provided meals to !Kung visitors in 1968, and was told "after all, they were here first."

sources of food in season (Lee and DeVore, 1976). In 1967–1969, however, most of the permanent water sources had multiple living groups at them, and people tended to maintain year-around residence at one of these waterholes, moving out into the territory of the temporary water sources to hunt and gather for short visits (typically a few days or a few weeks), carrying some food back with them when they return to the permanent water sources.[3] In late 1968, at the time of the census, which occurred at the beginning of the rainy season, there was one group of twenty-one people that had gone out to live at a small seasonal waterhole (near N!abesha on the map, Fig. 6.4), which is the traditional *n!ori* of the oldest man in the group, to take advantage of seasonal vegetation and the improvements in hunting chances that comes from moving away from the settled groups.[4] All the rest of our residents were found at one of the nine main waterholes in the !Numsi and /Xai/Xai areas.

Since early in the twentieth century [and perhaps before (Schrire, 1984)], cattle have been raised in the Dobe area, brought there for grazing by Tswanas and Hereros, generally located around the largest water sources where it is easiest to provide water for the cattle. A subgroup of the !Kung population turned their attention from hunting and gathering to earning their living by helping with cattle, and a few !Kung people had actually owned cattle, or (more frequently) goats and chickens, living as sedentary farmers, even in 1967–1969. We note that waterholes differ by the amount of the water available and also by the number of cattle and other livestock that live at them. Lee provided a tabulation of the number of cattle seen by the Botswana veterinary service in July 1968 (Lee, personal communication, 2003) and he has a tabulation of the number of Bantu living at each of the waterholes in 1964 (Lee, 1979: 53). Table 6.1 summarizes data about the waterholes that the Dobe area population was using at the end of 1968.

The waterholes listed in Table 6.1 are clustered along the ancient water course of the *!Kangwadum* in the area the !Kung call "*N/umsi*" (stones). Arriving from the East, one first comes to !Goshe, a large water hole where

3. Nowadays (1991 and later) people take donkeys and cloth bags when they go out into the waterless territories, and try to bring back enough food (especially mongongo nuts) to last for a substantial length of time.

4. It is interesting to note that one of the oldest men in the population, old Kase tsi !xoie (317) estimated at 82 years in 1968, was the central member of the group. For a photo of him and his descendants, see Howell (2000: 36–37). He was still alive in 1973. Photographers Peter Johnson and Anthony Bannister devote two pages (95–96) to Kase (who they call Old /Gashay) in Wannenburgh, A. (1979). The Bushmen. New York, Mayflower Books; and they noted that he died within a week of the photos, but they do not specify the year the photos were taken. Apparently he lived about 90 years.

TABLE 6.1. WATERHOLES AND THEIR CHARACTERISTICS

Waterholes	!Kung People	Villages	Cattle	% Clients
!Kangwa	59	6	976[a]	49
Bate	13	1		100
Karuwe	20	2		30
!Goshe	84	4	563	0
Mahopa	60	6	2387[c]	54
!Xabi[b]	0	0		0
Dobe	49	2	0	0
!Kubi	25	2	0	0
/Xai/Xai	130	10	542	49
Other (=Dabashe)	17	1	0	0
Total	416	34	4468	30

NOTE: See Figure 6.4 for map.
[a]The cattle at Bate and Karuwe are included in the !Kangwa count.
[b]The people who usually live at !Xabi went to Dabashe on this occasion.
[c]The cattle that would be counted at !Xabi were included in Mahopa.

TABLE 6.2. WATERHOLES AND THEIR NUTRITIONAL INDICATORS

	Mean CalBal	Mean BMI	Mean BMIDiff
!Kangwa	413	17.8	0.243
Bate	542	19.2	0.958
Karuwe	565	16.3	−0.817
!Goshe	132	17.7	0.287
Mahopa	225	17.9	0.182
!Xabi (=Dabashe)	340	17.1	
Dobe	449	17.3	−0.359
!Kubi	584	17.7	−0.178
/Xai/Xai	302	17.3	−0.170
Total Mean	314.36	17.4	−0.127
Standard Deviation	151.927	2.527	1.5914
Correlation Mean CalBal with		−.071	0.094
Significance Level		.171	.069
N individuals		376	376

SOURCE: http://hdl.handle.net/1807/17994.

there have been cattle for a long time, and where people are sedentary and comfortable combining cattle and bush sources of food. Few !Kung wore traditional clothing or made traditional-type houses at !Goshe in 1967–1969, although many of the families who lived there went out to bush camps for weeks at a time when bush foods were plentiful.

The next waterhole along the *malopo* (dry river bed) is !Kangwa (or Xangwa, as it is usually listed on maps in Botswana), which has been

the headman's village, and the location of the local court and delibera-
tive body (*kgotla*) (Holm and Molutsi, 1989).[5] While Lee is clear that
the !Kung have no headman of their villages, the Tswana administration
of Botswana appoints a headman to administer districts, and Isak Ituhile
was appointed by the tribal administration to administer the Xangwa
district in the 1950s. Isak (as all the local people in several ethnic groups
call him) imposed and administered Tswana law on the region until his
death in 1978. He demonstrated considerable understanding and respect for !Kung ways of life, no doubt derived in part from his !Kung
San grandmother. The !Kung often express positive attitudes toward the
benefits of Tswana law, feeling that the law prevents violence in their
community and permits people who are injured by others to obtain justice. Under traditional Tswana rules the !Kung would have been second-
class people at the *kgotla*, but under Botswana law (since 1964) the
!Kung are citizens of the country and thus entitled to equal rights under
the law, even though many Tswanas (including some government offi-
cials) continue to express discriminatory attitudes toward the San. The
!Kangwa waterhole was the location of the Botswana Trading Company
store in 1966–1968, and it was selected as the site of the new school that
was constructed in 1973 (the first in the area). In the 1970s (after this
study), !Kangwa became the location of the only permanent medical
clinic in the area, and the police post, and has clearly become an ad-
ministrative center as well as the place of residence of more than a hundred people, !Kung, Herero, and Tswana (Howell, 2000).

!Kangwa has two smaller waterholes nearby, Bate and !Kangwa
Matse (also known as Karuwe). Bate was the holding area for the cattle
purchased by the Botswana Trading Company from the local cattle
owners in 1968, and all of the !Kung living there (only thirteen in 1968)
were employees of the BTC.[6] It is striking that these well-employed people have the highest average body mass index, 19.1, of those at any waterhole, and have the highest average score on BMIDiff, at almost a full
BMI point greater than expected for their age and sex composition. It is
also striking to realize that Bate is the example used by Blurton Jones,

---

5. The *kgotla* is a traditional Tswana institution, in which the chief meets with the local citizens to discuss any policies that affect them, and to hear the evidence of any charges
that citizens bring against one another for the chief's resolution. The *kgotla* is an interesting and important democratic institution, but it has never had the power of making decisions by vote. See Holm, J., P. Molutsi, et al. (1996). "The Development of Civil Society
in a Democratic State: The Botswana Model." *African Studies Review* 39(2).

6. The residents of Bate are classified as a "client group" rather than as a living group
although they are not attached to a Bantu residential group.

Hawkes, and O'Connell (1994) as the only waterhole at which it is practical for children to gather food—marula nuts and baobab fruit—as there are trees near the water that are readily accessible to children. Lee's striking photo of boys bringing loads of food back to camp (Lee, 1979: 71) was taken at Bate in July 1973.

The other waterhole near !Kangwa, Karuwe, is also dependent on cattle, but the !Kung people there are not so prosperous: their mean BMI is 16.3, the lowest of all the waterholes, and they are also lowest in BMIDiff (−0.817). The cattle listed at !Kangwa in Table 6.1 are distributed between these three groups: !Kangwa, Bate, and Karuwe. If we combine these three waterholes into one group, they are close to the mean in BMI (18.6) and BMIDiff.

The next two waterholes, Mahopa and !Xabi, are so close to others that the groups that live at them are not able to reach open country without crossing the territory of another group. The hunting territories associated with waterholes are not necessarily bounded or exclusive, but the lack of uncontested territory would be a drawback for the !Kung living at these waterholes under traditional conditions. Mahopa was listed by the veterinary service as the location of the largest group of cattle, almost 2,400 head, most of which were owned by headman Isak Utuhile, in 1968. Without cattle, it seems likely that Mahopa and !Xabi waterholes might be left empty during the rainy season when people can camp close to their food sources, depending on seasonally available water sources. Mahopa people often use some of the territory around !Kangwa to have access to hunting and gathering territory near home.

Dobe is one of the smallest water sources, although Yellen's allocation of territories was focused around Dobe, so he describes it as having one of the largest hinterlands (Yellen, 1976:55). Dobe waterhole had no cattle in 1968, and largely for that reason it became a center of our anthropological studies of hunting and gathering. The Dobe people are close to the mean of the whole population in body mass index (17.2) and a bit under the average in BMIDiff (−.359). Having anthropologists living at your waterhole, as the Dobe people did from 1967–1969, may be entertaining for !Kung, but it doesn't seem to contribute to their physical well-being.

!Kubi is a medium-size waterhole, which in 1964 had many Bantu and their cattle living at it, but by 1968 the !Kung people living there were independent of Tswanas and were living entirely by hunting and gathering. Their BMIs were about average in 1968.

Table 6.1 shows us that one waterhole, /Xai/Xai, is much bigger in population (130 !Kung dwellers) than the others, and a look at the map in Figure 6.4 shows that /Xai/Xai is the only waterhole in our study region south of the Ahaha hills, so it has potentially the largest territory for exploitation around it. Sixteen percent of the !Kung population at /Xai/Xai is classified (Lee, 1979) as being "clients" of Bantu cattle owners rather than independent hunter-gatherers (who may visit cattleposts to drink the milk but do not organize their lives around the demands of cattle). Lee and I lived at /Xai/Xai most of the time during 1967–1969, and we may be better informed of events there than at other places.

The southernmost waterhole that we have studied is /Du/Da, the group of 140 or so !Kung, mostly unrelated to the people discussed above, who were found in 1968 to be living 60 kms south of /Xai/Xai, close to the border, with no cattle. Unfortunately, although Richard Lee and I went to visit the people and he did genealogical studies, and Pat Draper went to live with them for substantial periods of time and did child behavior and economic observations, none of us thought to bring the scale and height rod to measure body size in this population, so they have to be omitted from this study of BMI and its deviations. It is a real shame that we cannot relate their body size to the special characteristics of this group and to their totally hunting and gathering subsistence base.

On the level of waterholes, we see in Table 6.2 that there is little average difference in body mass index or BMIDiff (the measure that removes the effects of age and sex from body mass index). Differences might be due to the differing age and sex mixes of !Kung people at various waterholes, or it might be due to differing sources of food, cattle products versus reliance on bush foods, at the different waterholes, and we will look at these alternatives briefly.

Our measure for differences due to the age and sex composition of the !Kung population are incorporated in the variable "Mean Caloric Balance at Waterhole" (see Figure 6.1 above), which sums the individual Caloric Balance scores for everyone who lives at the waterhole, and divides that by the number of residents for a per capita score. The range in "MeanCalBalWh" (Average Caloric Balance of all residents at a waterhole) is narrow: 78 calories per day per person to about 300. And when we correlate this measure of waterhole well-being with individuals' BMIDiff, we get an r of only $-.084$, which accounts for only about 1% of the variation in individual well-being. Clearly the differences in the age-sex composition of the various waterhole populations are not a major factor in determining the well-being of the population.

Finally, in Table 6.2, we use the ANOVA statistical technique to evaluate whether the unit of waterholes is an important one for understanding the BMIDiff of individuals. ANOVA is a kind of analysis of variance that partitions the variance in BMIDiff (of individuals) into that which lies between the groups defined by waterhole residence and that which lies within the groups. For our nine waterholes,[7] there are eight degrees of freedom (df) between the groups (and 374 df within them). The F statistic compares the ratios of the Mean Squares of the variance: Table 6.2 shows that for BMIDiff by waterholes, we would expect to find a ratio as large as the one observed twenty times out of a hundred if there is no causal effect of waterholes on BMIDiff. We conclude that waterholes are not an important unit to understand in the determination of BMIDiff, our best estimate of well-being of individuals.

LIVING GROUPS, ALSO KNOWN AS BANDS, CAMPS, OR VILLAGES

The differences between the waterholes have not contributed much to our understanding of the nutritional variables, so now we shift our focus to the thirty-four groups of people who were living in face-to-face contact at the end of 1968, sharing the collection and consumption of food.[8] The traditional social unit that !Kung live in is the collection of households we are calling "living groups" here, which Lee calls "camps" when he is referring to people who are living by hunting and gathering (Lee, 1979), Marshall calls "bands" (Marshall, 1976) and we might equally well call "villages," except that "village" seems to imply a permanent place and the physical aspects of a residential unit, while living groups frequently move and consist more of the social relations than the houses the people live in. People can, however, change their living group when it seems to be advantageous. Often the two spouses in a marriage carry on a continual low-grade struggle about which living group their household will live with, each preferring to live with their own kin.

When several living groups are at a single waterhole, the people find it convenient for visiting one another, but they do not share food systematically, and they may not be well informed of the food resources of

---

7. Note that the waterhole of /Du/Da had to be eliminated from this analysis because we had no height and weight data for them.

8. For a cross-tabulation of Living Groups with the Households that make them up at the end of 1968, see Table 2.2 in Howell (2000: 44).

each family in the area. The living group is more important than the waterhole as an economic unit for the production and sharing of food, especially meat. Hunters from the living group go out, either in a group or individually, to track and kill animals, usually returning to the village to sleep at night.

When the hunters succeed in killing a large animal (which is not an everyday occurrence, but may happen in a village once a month or so), the residents of the living group (both men and women) may accompany the hunters back to the kill site to help carry the butchered meat back to the village, where it will be distributed by the owner of the meat (who is not necessarily the hunter, but may be the owner of the arrow that killed the animal) (Marshall, 1976; Lee, 1979). The distribution of meat is carried out under the observation of all of the members of the village who care to watch, and they usually watch closely to see if the distribution is fair. Each household (including that of the hunter and of the "owner of the meat") should be given a portion appropriate for their size. If the catch is very large (such as a giraffe or a kudu), the word will surely go out to members of other living groups to come and join the distribution, but most days food is shared only within the living group. Since the number of hunters differs from one group to another and the success rate of hunters varies widely, it is easy to see that there might be considerable differences between living groups in the adequacy of at least the meat portion of the diet of the members.

Gathered foods are not shared so publicly and equally as large animals are, but the women and men who go gathering frequently share some portion of what they bring back within the village, in an informal and less observed manner. So there is a real sense in which the living group, rather than the waterhole, is the unit of production and consumption of food, and there is more reason to expect that differences between living groups in age, sex, and diet choices will have an influence on the well-being of the members of living groups.

Living groups are smaller than waterhole groups. The size ranges from one to thirty-four, the mean size is twenty (standard deviation 8.2), but this picture is complicated by the existence of a number of fragmentary living groups, most of whom live with Bantu and work on cattle. Figure 6.5 shows the size distribution of the living groups in 1968 by the number of distinct households in each, providing most of the information for living groups that Table 6.1 provided for waterholes. Naturally the larger living groups have the most households in them. But we also see that the size distribution differs by the economic

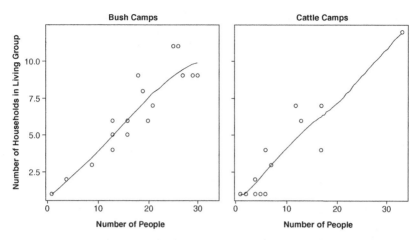

Figure 6.5. Number of !Kung households in living group, by number and size of living group, for bush and cattle camps. (Source: http://hdl.handle.net/1807/18000.)

base of the living groups, with "bush camps," traditional !Kung living groups, extending into larger sizes while "client groups" (consisting of San who live with and work for Herero cattle owners) are mostly smaller groups, one or a few workers and in some cases their families. The exception in Figure 6.5 is a living group that was hard to categorize, labeled as a cattle camp with twelve households and thirty-two people. This village [#26 in Lee's categorization (Lee 1979)] is headed by an old Tswana man, Halingisi, who raised children with each of two !Kung wives, and now has eight adult children with their spouses and children (and grandchildren) living in his village at /Xai/Xai. Most of the cattle camps are best described as some !Kung living in a Herero or Tswana village, but in this case, it is more like one Tswana man living in a traditional !Kung camp, supplementing their success as hunter-gatherers with food from the approximately two hundred cattle he had at the end of 1968.[9]

9. The same living group had forty-four members earlier in 1968 when Lee took the census reported in Lee, R. B. (1979). *The !Kung San: Men, women, and work in a foraging society.* Cambridge, England, and New York, Cambridge University Press, p. 58 and only ten members when he censused it in 1964. Clearly living groups can change a lot over a few years.

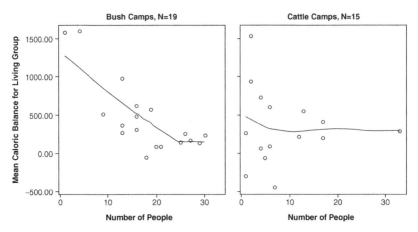

Figure 6.6. Mean Caloric Balance of 34 living groups by size, for bush and cattle camps. (Source: http://hdl.handle.net/1807/18000.)

Bush Camps and Cattle Camps

About two-thirds of the !Kung in 1968 were living in one of the sixteen living groups that are what Lee calls "camps," a group of adult siblings or cousins [descended either matrilineally or patrilineally from (usually) deceased ancestors,] and their spouses and children, organized into households that more or less provide their own vegetable foods and share the meat brought in by the hunters. The other third live in what we call "client groups" or "cattle camps," at least partially dependent upon cattle and cattle owners.

Figure 6.6 shows the size of the living group population by the mean Caloric Balance expected for the living group, based on its age-sex composition. We note that among the bush camps, mean Caloric Balance declines rather steeply in the larger groups. What this means is that the larger living groups contain most of the children, while the smallest living groups are dominated by adults. I would expect the small living groups with few children to be a temporary phenomenon. When there is a small group with many producers and few consumers, others may be attracted to join their group. Note, however, that the same relationship is not found in the client groups. Most of their living groups are small (ten or fewer members) but small groups are equally likely as large groups to contain dependents who drag down the mean Caloric Balance for the group. As I have pointed out before (Howell, 2000: 71), cattle posts attract !Kung who are either "pulled" (highly productive workers) or "pushed" (in great need due to sickness, injury, many dependent children, or frail elderly), leaving the bush camps drained of some of their expected components of the population.

Comparing Caloric Balance measures to BMI measures, we see that there are rather substantial differences in BMIDiff between living groups, much greater than those between waterholes. Partly this is because living groups are smaller than waterholes, and hence, there is less opportunity for extremes to be averaged into the group. Some of it is due to differences in the age-sex composition of these relatively small groups: some have more children and elderly dependents than others relative to the number of productive adults in the group. But there are probably also real differences between living groups that stem from the supply of good hunters (and to lesser extent gatherers) in the group who share their catch with the people in their living group.

We conclude our consideration of the role of living groups in determining the well-being of individuals by calculating two correlations. The first is the mean CalBal of the living group with the Mean BMI (body mass index) of the members of the living group. The correlation is $-.019$, an insignificant association. The second is the Caloric Balance of the living groups (the sum of the CalBal of each member) with the BMIDiff of each of the members of the living group (the BMI measure adjusted for age and sex composition of the living group). The result is $r = -.050$, again, an insignificant level of correlation, which accounts for almost none of the variance in individual BMIDiff measures. As we did when we examined the effects of waterholes on well-being, we calculate ANOVA for all the living groups together. The mean sum of squares of deviations between groups is higher than that within groups, which indicates that living groups are not strong predictors of the BMIDiff of individuals. The well-being of individuals cannot be readily explained simply by noting the characteristics of the village one lives in.

HOUSEHOLDS AND THEIR EFFECTS ON WELL-BEING

Finally, we come to the level of the household, which is the unit of food consumption, in which people are supposed to and usually do share all of their food, and in which adults have the obligation to meet the needs of each of the others in the group, adult or child, healthy or ill.

TABLE 6.3. LIVING GROUPS AND THEIR NUTRITIONAL INDICATORS

Number of Living Groups (in Dec. 1968)					
Count			34		
Number with one or fewer members			6		
Size of Living Groups (in Dec. 1968)					
Mean			20.06		
Range			1 – 34		
Mean Caloric Balance of Living Groups					
Mean			314.87		
Range			−445 – +1594		
BMI of Living Groups					
Mean			17.375		
Correlation (LG CalBal with)			−.019, ns		
BMIDiff of Living Groups					
Mean			−.029		
Correlation (LG CalBal with)			−0.50 ns		
ANOVA of BMIDiff by Living Groups	Sum of Squares	df	Mean Square	F	Probability
Between	91.193	31	2.951	1.141	.281 (ns)
Within	905.840	350	2.587		

SOURCE: http://hdl.handle.net/1807/18000.

The Household Cycle

Households often persist longer than the individuals who make them up, and households can range in size from one member to about ten in the environment of the !Kung. Household membership starts at birth for an individual. Everyone is born to a mother, who may share a household with her spouse and other children, and ego generally lives with that mother in her household, while additional children may be added to the family, until adulthood, leaving the parental household in the age range of 15 to 25 years. After what is usually a relatively brief period of living with grandparents and/or other adolescents, young adults form a marriage, which is likely to be fragile until the birth of the first child, which restarts the household cycle, now with ego as a parent rather than a child.

This alternation of "family of orientation" and "family of procreation" from the point of view of the individual is of course the same household unit from the point of view of the society. Couples tend to live in the same village as the parents of one or the other of them when they can and tend to live near one or more of their adult children after their dependent children are grown, to provide and to receive shared food and care between households. When a spouse dies, he or she may be replaced with another spouse, or the adult may continue to live alone (but usually close to other kin).

Households are fed primarily from the cooking pot of the mother, filled by food she collects, from the share of the meat of the hunters that is given to the household, and from the inputs from the father that he is not obligated to share with the whole living group, which might include vegetable foods he has gathered and small game (such as birds, porcupine, and springhare) that he has hunted or snared, plus whatever gifts of food, wild and domesticated, that the family receives. Incidentally, any adult who wants to can cook, although it seems that mothers take responsibility for most of it. Occasionally a nuclear family may obtain food from an older child still living in the household who is starting to hunt and gather and has not married yet, but the ability of young people to produce substantial amounts of food is usually quickly followed by marriage, so the parents do not profit by their children very long. When a daughter is married, and the young couple stays nearby her parents, the parental household may expect and receive regular gifts of food from the young couple as they observe the abilities of their son-in-law to provide for his coming family, but it may well be that equal or even greater volumes of food flow from the parents toward the young couple. Regularly (daily) almost every household will receive and make gifts of food from other households, in a pattern that makes it difficult for the analyst to keep track of the food economy.

It is in the household that we expect to see the adjustments of production and consumption so that families at all stages of the life cycle can flourish. The concept of Caloric Balance illustrates this process clearly. Couples who haven't had any children yet and those whose children are grown and independent while the couple is still strong and productive are expected to produce a regular surplus of several thousand calories a day of production over their need for consumption. This surplus will be invested, generally speaking, in their closest kin among those in their living group—parents or children, siblings or cousins—and only in more distant kin when closer kin have already received an adequate share of the surplus. But distance has several meanings when it comes to food sharing. A near neighboring household that is showing obvious signs of food shortage—thin children—may be considered for sharing purposes as though they were close kin. When a household has met all the immediate needs for a meal from the household members, the producers need to allocate their surpluses by some set of priorities. Hunters and gatherers can encourage consumption by their immediate household members (to maximize growth and fatness), can share with close kin who have shortages, can share with more distantly related people or their neighbors who complain of shortages, may take a day off from production to rest, or may attempt to save some part of their surplus for another day. !Kung ideas of proper behavior restrict individuals from excessively cutting their workload. An able-bodied person who does not hunt or gather for a long period of time will attract negative comment and criticism.

Household Composition

Figure 6.7 shows the relationship between the mean Caloric Balance of the household and the number of members of the household (from one

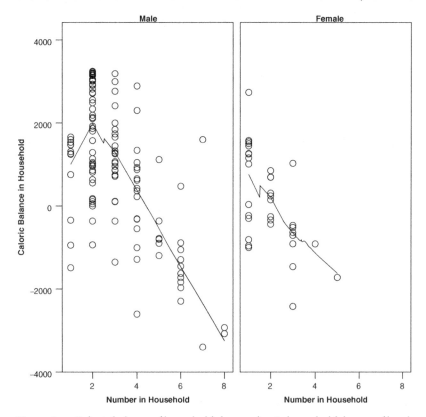

Figure 6.7. Caloric balance of households by number in household, by sex of head. (Source: http://hdl.handle.net/1807/18000.)

to eight), divided between two panels, one for those households headed by a male in the usual pattern, and another for those labeled as headed by a woman, divorced, widowed, or (in a few cases) married to a Bantu.

The households with only one member are mostly widowed older people, of both sexes, who generally live near adult children and may both give and take from the household of the adult child. In general, small nuclear families, hence, small households, are expected to be more prosperous (i.e., have a higher mean Caloric Balance) than large households. Adult couples can (usually) produce more food than they can consume. If they have no children to support, the mean Caloric Balance of their household is high, while families with many children necessarily have a lower Caloric Balance. Figure 6.8 shows that families who have two to four members are best off.

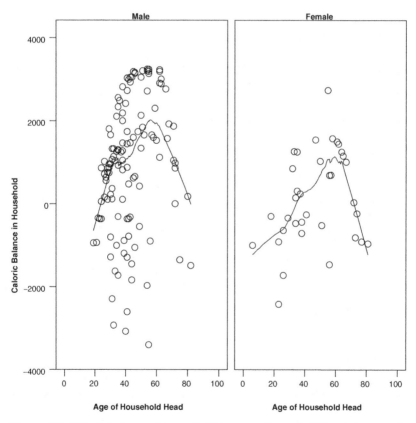

Figure 6.8. Caloric balance of household by age of household head, by sex of head. (Source: http://hdl.handle.net/1807/18000.)

Figure 6.8 also shows that there are many more households headed by a man than headed by a woman. In part, this is due to the method of classification: Women are only described as the head of the household if there is no !Kung man present, so it doesn't reflect actual decision-making power in the household. We see that the largest families are in male-headed households and that having a male head does not prevent a low mean Caloric Balance for large families. It looks like about half of the households with four members (usually a couple with two children) have a negative Caloric Balance and about half are positive, while households with five and more members are mostly in the negative range.

Figure 6.9 shows the Caloric Balance of households by the age of the head of the household, for male and female heads. We see that there is a "haystack" distribution, of increased mean Caloric Balance for the

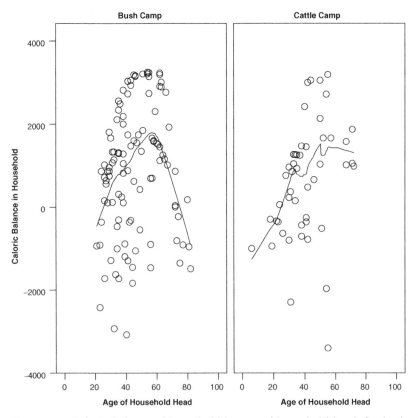

Figure 6.9. Caloric balance of household by age of household head, for bush and cattle camps. (Source: http://hdl.handle.net/1807/18000.)

household when the head is middle aged, say 40 to 70, with a lower level at the youngest and oldest ages for the head. This is more true for male heads than for female heads. Most of the households that can expect regular food surpluses are small households, headed by middle-aged males. We see from Figures 6.8 and 6.9 that females are sometimes the head of households across the age range, but that fewer of the women-headed households are at the extreme in Caloric Balance, either positive or negative, than the male-headed households. Incidentally, the extremely young female head of a household in Figure 6.9 is a little girl adopted into the household of her Bantu father.[10] This is an unusual situation: her mother remarried and is raising her half-sibs in another household. Ordinarily the child would accompany her mother into the new marriage, but in this case, the Bantu father's family requested that the little girl stay with them, and the mother agreed. We note that only a few of the heads of the households that we expect to have a regular deficit of calories for their members (i.e., are below −1,000 calories per day in Caloric Balance in household) are under 30 or over 60. Coping with scarcity on a long-term basis is likely to be the business of experienced adults.

Figure 6.9 introduces the complication of dependence on cattle or on bush foods to our understanding of the dynamics of !Kung households. The pattern of decline of Caloric Balance for larger households is slightly more pronounced for the bush camps.

Figure 6.10 shows the importance of the number of children who live in the household with one or more parents. Many households have zero children in them, and these households have the highest mean Caloric Balance score. Scores decline steadily with increasing numbers of children, crossing the zero line around two children and averaging a negative Caloric Balance after two. Having children and keeping them alive is probably the highest value seen in !Kung society. This data remind us that it is not easy and it is not automatic. Of course, it is not impossible, but we need to seek the ways that it can be done and how families adjust when food becomes scarce. Being in a household with parents does not guarantee that the resources needed to raise a child will be present. This conclusion holds up for both male and female heads of household.

Finally, we ask whether the Caloric Balance score for the household explains the BMIDiff scores, which is another way of asking whether

10. In retrospect, it was clearly a mistake on my part to totally exclude non-!Kung from my demographic study, which produces odd research results like this one. Bantu members of households are "invisible" in this analysis.

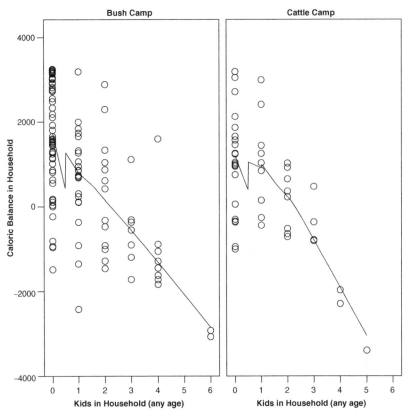

Figure 6.10. Caloric balance of household by number of children resident, for bush and cattle camps. (Source: http://hdl.handle.net/1807/18000.)

household composition determines the well-being of the individual. We saw before that CalBal for the individual did not have any correlation with BMIDiff for that individual. Table 6.4 presents the data.

We cannot simply correlate BMIDiff scores with the mean CalBal for a small unit like a household, however. Ego makes up a large proportion of the total, and we would be exaggerating the correlation between BMIDiff and CalBal for individuals. Instead, we remove the CalBal for the individual from that of the household before we calculate the correlation, in a variable we call "CalBalHHAdj" (Caloric Balance of Households Adjusted).

When we look at the individual BMIDiff scores with this CalBalHHAdj, however, we find no significant correlation. People who live in households that have relatively many net producers (adults) and

TABLE 6.4. HOUSEHOLDS AND THEIR NUTRITIONAL INDICATORS

Number of Households (in Dec. 1968)

Count	167
Households with one or fewer members	34

Size of Households (in Dec. 1968)

Mean	2.75 (S.D. = 1.6)
Range	1–8

Mean Caloric Balance of Households

Mean	347.04
Range	−3397 – +3246
Correlation (with Mean Number in Household)	.592

Adjusted Caloric Balance of Households (removes ego's CalBal from that of Households)

Mean	163.27
Range	−3635 – +2963

Correlation of CalBal and BMIDiff in Households	.036 (ns)
Correlation of CalBal and AdjBMIDiff in Households	.034 (ns)

ANOVA of BMIDiff by Households

Households	Sum of Squares	df	Mean Square	F	Probability
Between	501.539	153	3.278	1.507	.003
Within	493.757	227	2.175		

SOURCE: http://hdl.handle.net/1807/18000.

relatively few net consumers (children, especially adolescents, and old people) have only slightly higher BMIDiff scores than those who live in less favourably composed households, and those in the less favored households somehow manage to meet the needs of their members. The mechanism has got to be gifts that flow "from each according to his ability to each according to his need," as Marx and Engels famously phrased it. It seems that !Kung accept the obligation to share by giving gifts to others before they eat up their surpluses, increase their leisure, or save it for a rainy day as other people around the world may do.

Focusing on the Caloric Balance of the individuals within households and summarizing those balances into a score for each household draw attention to a basic fact of !Kung life that is easily overlooked: no parents can consistently provide the food needed by their children (as even the most productive parents are sick occasionally) and many families with dependent children cannot provide for all the needs of those children on a regular basis. The average couple cannot produce enough food on a daily basis to supply the needs of more than themselves and about three children. !Kung parents have no "savings" to draw upon to equalize fluctuations in the demands that their dependents place on them, and more than three children require more surplus than the average set of parents can produce. Of course, the balance achieved fluctuates from day to day, as parents are more or less hardworking, or lucky, or burdened with illness or handicaps. But the bottom line is that basically, among the !Kung, parents cannot count upon providing enough food to raise their children. Contributions from others are essential to the survival of the children, especially those of the most successful parents.

Figure 6.3 (above) reinforces this point by showing the relationship between the mean Caloric Balance of the household and the number of members of the household, and Table 6.4 brings together facts about households. In general, small nuclear families, hence small households, are more prosperous (i.e., have a higher mean Caloric Balance) than large households, but it doesn't follow that their members have higher BMIDiff. Apparently, any "surpluses" that exist on the household level are not consumed by its members to such an extent that they are fatter than others in the same environment.

What can a family do when their Caloric Balance as a household is in the negative range? Parents can work harder, by collecting more often and/or more efficiently, carrying more food home at the end of day, and perhaps by broadening the species they will collect and eat (Harris and Ross, 1987). In the short run, parents can consume less, so that there is more for their children, but that strategy doesn't work in the long run. In order to keep working, the parents must be well nourished. Mostly, families are forced to accept that there are periods of time in their lives when their households are not self-sufficient units, and that if they are net recipients of calories today, they and their household members may be net providers at other times in their life, so they need not feel guilty or humiliated by their needs. In the short term, parents of large families are both maximally successful (the winners of the competition for fitness) and are debtors to the community in which they live, harried and pleased at their situation at the same time.

I believe that it is from this conflict that the !Kung etiquette about modesty in hunting success and the fierce egalitarianism of the !Kung arises. When someone has more than they need immediately, whether it is a piece of clothing or a supply of food, they need to be aware of the people around them who have need for that surplus and share it without holding back. That person will be under scrutiny and subject to criticism as long as the surplus is held. Likewise, when one has a shortage of food or other possessions, the culture urges them to speak out, to ask for a share of what others have. The greater the need, the louder and longer the verbal demands for help should be, whether the giver is close, distant, or no kin at all, until the surplus is distributed.

But as we conclude our consideration of the geographically based social units, we have observed that the Caloric Balance of residential units is easily predicted by the age and sex of the residents, but we have not found that this predictable Caloric Balance necessarily predicts the BMIDiff of the same people. Let us look, therefore, at the mean BMIDiff of the members of households. Are members of the same household more like one another than they are like the general population?

Table 6.5 shows the analysis of BMIDiff at the household level. Members of the same household are more like one another on BMIDiff than they are similar to the total population. The ANOVA analysis confirms this. The household (but not the living group or the waterhole) exhibits more variability in BMIDiff between groups than there is within groups. The probability of finding F statistics this large for groups unrelated to the critical variable (BMIDiff) is estimated as three in a thousand. Presumably this means that the household unit is experiencing the same nutritional environment and that prosperity for one tends to produce prosperity for all in the household. At the level of the larger groups, the waterholes and villages, however, the differences in resources between households are largely averaged out at the living group level, and the waterhole level has little effect beyond that of the village. Table 6.5 shows us that households share the same environment but some kind of sharing of resources works to equalize the fatness of individuals among the living groups and the waterholes. This is evidence of sharing, but it doesn't show us how that sharing works.

To conclude, we come to the rather disappointing realization that Caloric Balance has not greatly increased our understanding of the role of food distribution in well-being of individuals and residential social groups. Clearly, Caloric Balance is so highly correlated with age that we are not learning anything new about BMIDiff from the composition of the groups. In large groups, it averages out so that all the groups are very similar, and in small groups it is a direct reflection of their age distribution.

TABLE 6.5. ANOVA OF BMIDIFF BY RESIDENTIAL
UNITS OF ANALYSIS

	Sum of Squares	df	Mean Square	F	Sig.
Waterhole					
Between groups	27.625	8	3.453	1.371	.206
Within groups	942.106	374	2.519		
Living Group					
Between groups	91.193	31	2.942	1.137	.286
Within groups	905.840	350	2.588		
Household					
Between groups	501.539	153	3.278	1.507	.003
Within groups	493.757	227	2.175		

SOURCE: http://hdl.handle.net/1807/18000.

MALTHUSIAN, DARWINIAN, AND COMMON-SENSE MODELS OF POPULATION CONTROL IN THE KALAHARI

Looking at individual well-being across residential groups reminds us of the Malthusian model of population control. Malthus (1766–1834) observed that population tends to grow until it encounters limitations of resources that increase mortality, to bring population growth under control.

The Malthusian model doesn't seem to explain the !Kung case very well, as fertility seems to be naturally low, population density is very low, and mortality does not seem to be driven by starvation. Cross-sectional data for a point in time are not ideal for observation of Malthusian process, and we look for more short-term solutions. The demographer tends to look at migration as a way of balancing resources and population in a given area over a short period of time, rather than to look to the long-run processes of fertility and mortality, and indeed, we note that migration between villages and waterholes is very frequent for some !Kung households.

Darwin (1809–1882) built upon Malthus's model of population outstripping resources to recognize that the generation emerging from a struggle for subsistence is not quite the same as the generation that gave birth to it, and that the accumulation of small differences can and does add up to large differences over time. Darwinian theory urges us to look for the differential reproduction of individuals in a generation, not only whether their cohort is larger or smaller than the previous one, but what heritable features have been passed on to the current generation from the past. Kinship is the key to understanding transmission of genetic material over generations, and we need to look at the contribution and investments that members of the population are making in their kin, as well as in other people. In the next chapter, we will continue this analysis by examining the kinship ties between households and living groups that provides the mechanisms of sharing for the !Kung people.

Consider the situation of a family who is struggling to get enough to eat, or an individual who is often hungry. Such people may assess their problem as having too few hunters in their living group, or too few highly successful hunters. They may consider moving to one of the other living groups with a better ratio of hunters to consumers, if there is one that would welcome them as residents, and they may think about moving permanently or temporarily. Or they may discuss with the owners of the *n!ori* whether it might be possible to recruit one or several good hunters to join their group and improve the diet of all of the residents. Older parents might ask a grown son who is a good hunter to come and live with them, or another resident might invite a brother or brother-in-law to come and live with them. Or someone in the group may try to recruit a good hunter to marry their daughter, so that he would come and provide the whole group with meat until the birth of a third child, which would be a long period of time. If none of these options is open to them, the family may decide to move to another group, or go to a cattle post, where there may be opportunities to earn or beg for access to domesticated foods. Clearly, an unencumbered adult will be welcomed much more easily than a single mother with a large family, or an elderly couple beyond the age of productivity. When people seek to move between living groups to improve their nutritional resources, the importance of kin ties comes to the fore. We will consider this factor in more detail in the next chapter.

These down-to-earth considerations remind us to depend upon our common sense, guided by theoretical models, to keep track of relevant behaviours in the population. We need to look for geographical and social boundaries of families and villages, for migration across groups, for gift giving and other pro-social behaviors in the group that do not otherwise seem to be economically rational, and for the rules that the group tends to follow. At the same time, we need to look for the ways that people get around the rules and the restrictions on their behavior when such rules interfere with their best interests. In the final chapter, after a consideration of the effects of kinship on well-being, we will return to some of these general questions of motivation and consequences of these behaviors.

CHAPTER 7

Kinship Relations as a Support System for Children

We saw in Chapter 6 that households and their characteristics are significant determinants of the well-being of this population. In this chapter we are going to look more closely at the exact composition of those households by the circle of kin around individuals to see if we can isolate the importance of each kind of kinship relationship.

We focus on the effects of kinship on children in this chapter rather than looking for effects on everyone, because we have seen how the correlation of age with some of the variables we are concerned with confounds the attempt to understand the whole population, and because the effects of kin on the well-being of children have long-term effects on their lives, their survival, and their eventual reproduction, whereas the effects of kin on adults and elderly, which may be crucially important at times of sickness and crisis, are more temporary, at best allowing adults to return to their full abilities. Theoretical questions and discussions of recent literature focus on consequences for children (Hewlett and Lamb, 2005; Hawkes and Paine, 2006). Also, the consequences of having some relatives may change over life history, so that having a grandparent alive and co-resident, for instance, may be a contribution to well-being for children, but can be a burden to mature adults, so we separate them here and look more closely at the effects on children.

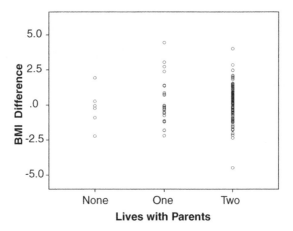

Figure 7.1. BMIDiff of children by number of co-resident parents. (Source: http://hdl.handle.net/1807/10411.)

RELATIVES IN THE HOUSEHOLD

We start, therefore, to explore the association between well-being of children, ages 0 to 19, and their kinship ties by looking at their household composition. Our first question is whether children who have two parents present in the household are better off than children who have only one.

Figure 7.1 shows the BMIDiff of the children who have one or two parents living with the child at the time of measurement. There were no children with zero living parents in 1968, although such a thing could occur. There are 162 children (age 0 to 19) alive at the end of 1968 for whom we have data on the living status of their relatives and measures of their BMIDiff. This is the population shown in the next group of graphs.[1] Eight of our 162 children have a deceased mother, and six have lost their father to death. Children who have lost a parent have lower BMIDiff than children with two parents, on the average. One orphaned child is plump (she has a high BMIDiff—her father and grandmother are raising her on a cattlepost); the rest are close to or below zero, including four who seem to be

1. In research with Pat Draper, we report on the living kin of 354 children alive in 1968, but many of those are lacking physical measurements (including the whole/Du/Da population). See Draper, P., and N. Howell (2006). Changes in co-survivorship of adult children and parents: Ju/'hoansi of Botswana in 1968 and 1988. *Updating the San: Image and reality of an African people in the 21st century.* R. K. Hitchcock, K. Ikeya, M. Biesele, and R. B. Lee. Osaka, Japan, National Museum of Ethnology. **Senri Ethnological Studies,** V. 70: 81–100.

very thin. The average for orphaned children is below that of those who have living parents but their numbers are sufficiently small that this cannot account for the overall extreme thinness of !Kung children.

Figures 7.2 and 7.3 show the BMIDiff of the children by the location of their two birth parents, relative to themselves. In Figure 7.2, the first column includes those whose mother is dead, the third column shows the single case where the mother is living at the same waterhole as the child, but the child lives with her otherwise childless aunt in a nearby living group. The fourth column is for children who live in the same living group as their mother, but in a different household (this is a teenager). Overall, distance from the mother clearly has a negative effect on the well-being of children, but the cases are few.

Figure 7.3 shows the more frequent case where the child is not living with the birth father. Fathers are more often absent from children's household environment because of the cultural rule that children stay with the mother when the marriage ends in divorce. Children always retain a tie to the father when he is alive, but often (about 10% of children) live separately from their father, and in this society where property and inheritance are not issues, there is little conflict between children of divorce and their parents.

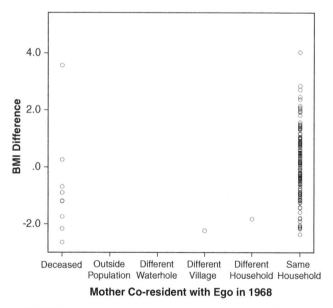

Figure 7.2. BMIDiff of children by residence status of mother. (Source: http://hdl.handle.net/1807/10411.)

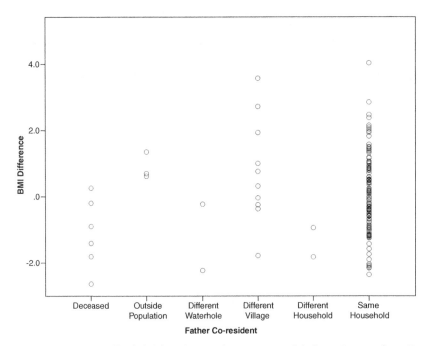

Figure 7.3. BMIDiff of children by residence status of father. (Source: http://hdl.handle.net/1807/10411.)

Those who are not living with two parents are usually missing their father, who might be deceased, divorced from the mother, or temporarily away from the household (for weeks or months, and in one case for many years, although the mother says they are not divorced) for work or travel. Children with only one parent in the household include some below the mean of BMIDiff, but only slightly more than those with two parents at home. And those categorized as having only one parent in the household who are above the mean in BMIDiff include several whose father is Bantu and is not counted as a member of this population. Women who marry Bantu are typically well off, with access to meat and milk from the husband's herd, and their children are likely to be well fed.[2]

Effects on Children of Parents in the Household

We want to know whether there is evidence for a correlation between the well-being of the parent and the child: When the parent is doing well,

2. See footnote 10 in Chapter 6.

is the child more likely to do well also? Figure 7.4 shows the scattergrams of the BMIDiff of the child and the mother, and Figure 7.5 shows the scattergrams of the child with the father (provided that the parent is in the household). The well-being of the parents does not predict the fatness of

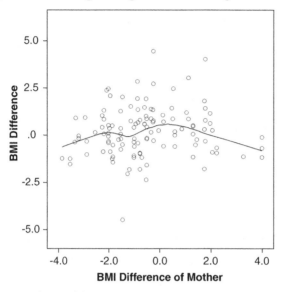

Figure 7.4. BMIDiff of children by BMIDiff of mother. (Source: http://hdl .handle .net/1807/10411.)

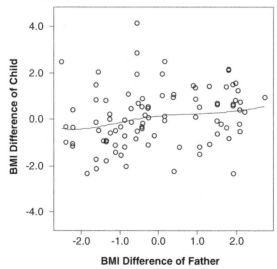

Figure 7.5. BMIDiff of children by BMIDiff of father. (Source: http://hdl .handle .net/1807/10411.)

the child with any consistency. The correlation coefficients of these relationships are insignificant. This suggests that children are often buffered from the causes of thinness (and fatness) in parents, such as the hard work of supporting a family.

In Figure 7.4, we see that there is a slight positive slope for children's nutritional status in the middle range for parents, but a negative slope for the very thin and also the relatively heavy mothers, with overall no significant relationship ($N = 128$; $r = .081$, ns). The relationship is the same for male and female children (not shown separately). A complicating factor in this relationship is that the BMIDiff of the mothers reflects not only her nutritional status but also her reproductive status. A pregnant woman appears to be better fed on this measure, when she is merely heavier due to the weight of the fetus, which suggests the generalization that children are best off when their mothers are neither very thin or pregnant or nursing.

Note that in Figure 7.5 there is less variability in BMIDiff for fathers (the range in BMIDiff goes from −2 to +2) than for their wives or for their children. None of the adult men are notably fat, but they differ in the degree of heavy muscles. No doubt, fathers contribute to the well-being of their children to some extent, but the custom that hunters share their catch across the village means that children are less directly dependent upon the productivity of their father than they are of their mother. Pat Draper, who quantified children's behavior in 1967 and 1968 (Draper and Howell, 2002), found that the thinnest children had low levels of physical activity, and they were also more often coded as being in physical contact with their father. She suggests that these children are often those being weaned during the mother's next pregnancy, or relatively neglected by the mother during nursing of a new baby, who attach themselves to their father for comfort.

Siblings in the Household

These data remind us that the household consists not only of parents but also of the other children of the parents, children who can be both helpers and competitors to the reference child. Figure 7.6 shows the total number of other children in the household, and Figure 7.7 shows the BMIDiff of ego by the number of older siblings in the household. It seems to be mildly beneficial to children to have one to three older siblings in the household, even though it is unlikely that these older siblings are actually supplementing the family larder in any significant way. We see that most children at a point in time have no older siblings. This group includes the first-borns

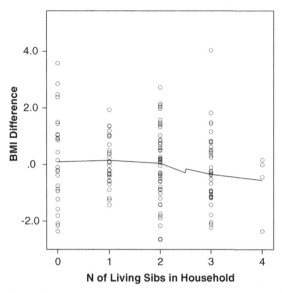

Figure 7.6. BMIDiff of children by number of siblings in the household. (Source: http://hdl.handle.net/1807/10411.)

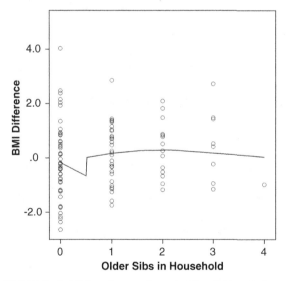

Figure 7.7. BMIDiff of children by number of older siblings in household. (Source: http://hdl.handle.net/1807/10411.)

plus those later born whose older siblings did not survive or are no longer in the household. At least Figure 7.7 does not suggest that the presence of older siblings is detrimental to the well-being of the younger siblings.

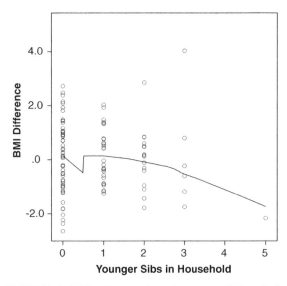

Figure 7.8. BMIDiff of children by number of younger siblings in household. (Source: http://hdl.handle.net/1807/10411.)

Figure 7.8 shows the effect of younger siblings on the BMIDiff of ego, and again we do not see much evidence of harmful effects of competition within the household, except at the extreme. The largest group has no younger siblings in the household and that group has the widest range of variation in BMIDiff (and in age). There is a small increase in this indicator of well-being for those who have one younger brother or sister, and a greater increase for those who have two younger siblings. This is rather surprising: If younger sibs are effective competitors for our reference child, we would expect a decrease rather than an increase in BMIDiff. If we were looking at the body mass index indicator rather than BMIDiff, which is adjusted for age and sex, the effect of younger siblings would appear to be even more important, as we have seen that body mass index declines through childhood to about age 10. The mean BMIDiff goes down when ego has three, four, and five younger siblings but there are relatively few such cases, and necessarily represent the oldest children still in the household of large families. Again, this would look different for BMI, as teenagers increase in BMI as they approach adulthood. Competition from siblings within the household seems to account for a very small amount of the variation in BMIDiff for children. Here we see additional evidence of the buffering of the effects of scarcity on larger families in !Kung society.

EFFECTS ON CHILDREN OF HAVING GRANDPARENTS
IN THE LIVING GROUP

When parents are unable to provide all the food that their children need, naturally they turn first to their closest kin for help. Hawkes and her colleagues (Hawkes, 1989; Hawkes, O'Connell, et al., 2000) have argued that the contributions to the survival of grandchildren and to the reproductive success of their adult children by grandparents, especially maternal grandmothers, have made a major contribution to human evolution, leading to the survival of our species into old age, past reproductive senescence. In !Kung culture, young couples are instructed to stay close by the bride's parents for a decade or so after marriage, so that the maternal grandmother can be of help to her daughter in pregnancy, childbirth, nursing, and learning to raise her children. The maternal grandmother does not only teach her daughter, but also contributes food and babysitting services that improve the diet of the younger family. At the same time, the custom is designed so that the parents can keep a close eye on their daughter's husband, to make sure that he treats her right, hunts enthusiastically, and shares properly.

In order to contribute to the well-being of children, grandparents have to be alive, robust enough to produce a surplus to share with the children, and have to live close enough to the child to provide meaningful goods and services. Under !Kung cultural rules, this means that they must be living (or at least visiting) in the same living group as the grandchild in question. Table 7.1 provides information on the parents and grandparents of the children of 1968, specifically their survival and residence

TABLE 7.1. PARENTS AND GRANDPARENTS OF CHILDREN

	Minimum Age[a]	% Alive	% of Those Alive Who Are Co-resident	% Co-resident[b]
Mother	18	94.6	98	92.7
Mother's mother	36	44.0	44	20.0
Mother's father	43	32.5	52	16.9
Father	25	95.8	87	83.0[b]
Father's mother	43	33.3	55	18.2
Father's father	50	23.6	80	18.8

SOURCE: http://hdl.handle.net/1807/10411.

[a]Minimum age refers to youngest age this person could be, assuming that women are 18 at first birth and men are 25. The average age for each group is about 20 years older than the minimum age.

[b]Co-residence means sharing the household with the child for the parents, and sharing the living group for grandparents.

status. This empirical data can be compared to theoretical distributions of the expected survival of grandparents and other relatives (Howell, 2000).

The help of grandparents seems to be a rather hit-or-miss affair. Children may have zero to four grandparents alive and resident with them, and grandparents may have zero to perhaps as many as twenty grandchildren to whom they could be contributing, who may all live in a single living group (unlikely) or be spread among many living groups in the vast area that is the Dobe area. Table 7.1 implies that grandparents can range in age from as young as 36 to as old as 85 at the birth of their grandchildren, and may be very helpful or, on the other extreme, very needy, a competitor with the child for the attention, nurturance, and food supplied by the parents. Column four of Table 7.1 shows the percentage of children who have the parent and grandparent in question co-resident with the child. And column three of the same table shows the relationship from the point of view of the older person: it shows what percentage of parents and grandparents who are alive are co-resident with the reference child.

Assuming that they are alive, what is the probability that the grandparents are co-resident with the child in question? Among the four kinds of grandparents, we note that the maternal grandmothers are both the youngest and the most often available to the child. But from the maternal grandmother's point of view, she is actually the least likely (44%) to be co-resident (in the same village) with the reference child, which is a bit unexpected. And the paternal grandfather, who is the oldest, is 80% likely to be living with the child, given that he is alive at all, which is almost as high as the rate of coresidency for the parents. From the child's point of view, however, there is only a 20% probability that the father's father will be living with him, because he is most likely not living at all. The mother's father and the father's mother, who are both intermediate in age, and in survivorship at the time the grandchild is needy, are also intermediate in the probability of living close to the child, and we will see below that they seem to have overall a distinctly negative effect on the child's well-being.

We want to know whether those children who have input from a grandparent do better than those who do not. Figures 7.9 to 7.12 show the BMIDiff of the reference child by the living status of each of his or her four grandparents. Figure 7.9 seems to indicate that children are best off when their maternal grandmother lives at another waterhole in the Dobe area, but that finding is based on just a few cases. Figure 7.10 shows that when the mother's father is living at the same waterhole but

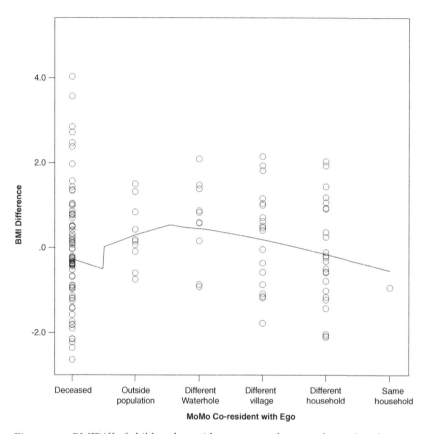

Figure 7.9. BMIDiff of children by residence status of maternal grandmother. (Source: http://hdl.handle.net/1807/10411.)

in another living group that children are distinctly worse off. Figure 7.11 seems to suggest that children are worst-off when their father's mother lives in the same living group, the so-called ideal arrangement. And Figure 7.12 shows a substantial drop in the child's well-being when the father's father (the paternal grandfather) lives in the same village with the child, compared to living more distantly. These findings lead us to think about the interpretation of coresidence: Does the grandparents' presence help the child, or is the grandparent attracted when the child needs help? In any case, the data do not support a strong positive effect of grandparents on the well-being of children. In fact, I believe that there is or can be a positive effect on the child, as we will discuss in the next chapter, but that the action is too subtle to be captured by looking only at the location of the grandparents relative to the child in cross section.

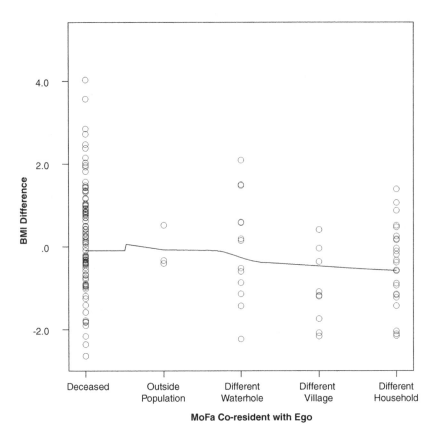

Figure 7.10. BMIDiff of children by residence status of maternal grandfather. (Source: http://hdl.handle.net/1807/10411.)

CORESIDENCE OF ANCESTORS
IN THE WELL-BEING OF CHILDREN

If we make a summary score of the presence of all of the caretakers (parents and grandparents) combined, and try to account for the effects on the well-being of the child, we find that the contributions from different directions add up to a substantial total: Table 7.2 shows the multiple regression of the contributions of these direct lineal ancestors of the child.

None of these ties has accounted for a great deal of the variance in children's well-being, but we haven't yet put them together to see if kin relations together may be a powerful predictor of which children thrive and which struggle for existence. It makes sense that relationships may be substitutes for one another. An only child of two competent parents may not benefit from additional help, but in a larger family, especially

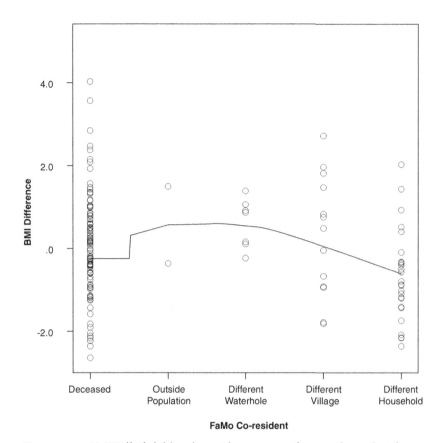

Figure 7.11. BMIDiff of children by residence status of paternal grandmother. (Source: http://hdl.handle.net/1807/10411.)

during a period of illness or absence of one of the parents, or just a period of bad weather or bad luck, children may be dependent on relatives outside of the household. It may not matter to the child's well-being which relative steps in to supplement the food and care that parents cannot supply, so parents' siblings (aunts and uncles of the child) may substitute for grandparents when needed.

In Table 7.2 we look at the multivariate analysis of variance of BMIDiff and data on the coresidence of ancestors, including parents and grandparents under that heading. The model combines the contributions to the explanation of the variance in BMIDiff (of children) from six sources of support to the child—the two parents and four grandparents—that we have examined one-by-one above. Combined, Table 7.2 shows that parents and grandparents together account for 12.3% of the variance in BMIDiff

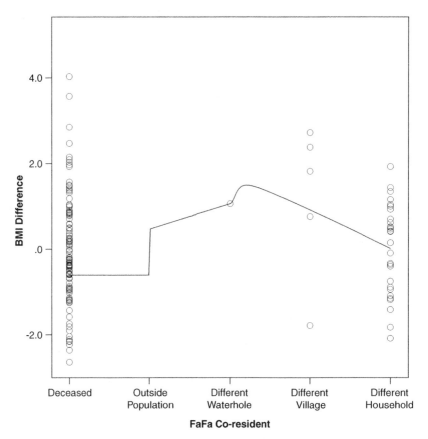

Figure 7.12. BMIDiff of children by residence status of paternal grandfather.
(Source: http://hdl.handle.net/1807/10411.)

(r = .399), which is a strong and significant contribution to our understanding. Of course, that still leaves 87.7% of the variance unexplained!

The effects of coresidence of children with their ancestors turns out
to be somewhat more complex than we expected. As predicted, mothers, fathers, mother's mothers, and father's fathers contribute to the
well-being of the child, but we found that mother's fathers and father's
mothers actually detract from the well-being of the child. Table 7.2
shows that the strongest contributors as measured by the beta score (regression coefficient) are the unexpectedly strong negative relationship
between mother's father coresident and the almost equally strong negative association between father's mother coresident, both with BMIDiff
of the child. When the maternal grandfather is living in the same village,

TABLE 7.2. MULTIPLE REGRESSION MODEL OF BMIDIFF
OF CHILDREN BY RESIDENCE STATUS OF ANCESTORS

Model 1: Multiple Linear Regression: Predictors — Co-residence
of Mother, Mother's mother, Mother's father, Father,
Father's mother, and Father's father

Dependent Variable—BMI Difference

R =	.399
R Square =	.159
Adjusted R Square =	.123
Standard Error of the Estimate =	1.1855

ANOVA	Sum of Squares	df	Mean Squares	F	Sig.
Regression	36.927	6	6.161	4.362	.000
Residual	194.917	138	1.412		
Total	231.883	144			

	Unstandardized		Standardized		
Coefficients	B	Std. Error	Beta	t	Sig.
Constant	−.834	.385		−2.165	.320
Father Co-resident	.206	.306	.059	.672	.502
FaFa Co-resident	.368	.288	.116	1.279	.203
FaMo Co-resident	−.987	.301	−.308	−.327	.001
Mother Co-resident	.955	.409	.200	2.338	.210
MoMo Co-resident	.183	.291	.056	.627	.531
MoFa Co-resident	−.772	.285	−.231	−2.704	.008

SOURCE: http://hdl.handle.net/1807/10411.

and when the paternal grandmother is living in the same village, the child tends to be poorly off by the measure of BMIDiff. The data do not tell us why this should be so, but we can speculate. We have noted that couples often seem to have a low-level conflict between living with the wife's family or with the husband's family, and perhaps each wants to maximize contact with the same-sex parent. This suggests that there may be an implicit competition between the needs of the spouse and the needs of the adult offspring's family for that same-sex parent, when the spouse is still alive. When the grandfather dies, the maternal grandmother may move closer to her adult daughter to both give and receive social support, and the widowed paternal grandfather may serve as a magnet to bring his adult sons to live nearby. When the child's maternal grandfather or the paternal grandmother are the surviving spouse, the elder may be drawn to live with their same-sex adult offspring.

THE GRANDMOTHER ROLE FROM THE POINT OF VIEW
OF OLDER WOMEN

We have explored the contributions that grandmothers provide to children
but now we leave that perspective and take a side trip to look at the relationship from the point of view of the grandmothers, not looking for
contributions to the BMIDiff scores of grandmothers, but simply considering the probabilities as generated by the demographic regime of the
!Kung that older women will have grandchildren to help care for when
they are at the stage of their life when they can contribute to their own
(and their adult children's) inclusive fitness.

There are sixty-one women over age 45 in the Dobe !Kung population
(at the end of 1968, when the data had been collected) for whom we have
complete data. Of these, the majority of the women (forty-seven) are less
than 65 years old, post-reproductive but relatively young; while fourteen
(23%) are in the age group 65 to 89 (the "old" post-reproductive women,
those who may require assistance from their adult children rather than
having energy and ability to give to the younger generation). Table 7.3
presents the basic data.

Forty-one of the sixty-one women are currently married. Of these, ten
have a husband who is classified as "weak," unable to work and needing
assistance (blind, crippled, frail, etc.) who may require care from the wife
that might otherwise go to the grandchildren. Twenty of the sixty-one
women are not married at this time, fourteen widowed, and another six

TABLE 7.3. POTENTIAL GRANDMOTHERS (61 WOMEN 45+)

Fre-quency	Women by Number of Adult Kids Surviving	Number of Adult Kids Surviving	Daughters' Surviving Kids Under 10	Dau's Kids Under 10 Coresident with Gr.Mo	Son's Surviving Kids Under 10	Son's Kids Under 10 Coresident with Gr.Mo
0	11	0	38	40	44	48
1	18	18	9	9	7	8
2	14	28	2	5	2	2
3	9	27	8	6	2	2
4	7	28	1	0	1	1
5	1	5	1	0	1	0
6	1	6	1	1	2	0
Total	61	112	68	33	49	22
Mean		1.99	2.52	2.43	2.43	0.38

SOURCE: http://hdl.handle.net/1807/17984.

divorced. These sixty-one women have 112 surviving children, in 1968. Most of these are adult children, fifty-six daughters and fifty-six sons. Forty-one have one or more grandchildren and of these forty-one, forty live with one or more of their grandchildren and can in principle contribute to the survival of the child. In other words, about two-thirds of the women past 45 are in a position to contribute to the well-being of at least one of their grandchildren. As we saw above, there may be multiple contenders among the grandchildren for the attention of the grandmother. It is clear that grandmothers are coresident with their grandchildren when they can be. It is too bad we don't have clear data on the amount of food collected per day by grandmothers, and the amount passed on to the adult child or directly to the grandchildren, but these data were not collected.

Among the twenty women who do not have a grandchild to live with in 1968, we note that some women over 45 are still too young to be grandmothers, but may achieve that status and play an important role in helping their grandchildren thrive in the future. Others may be too old to play a significant role in their grandchildren's lives now, but may have been important in the past. And some of those who don't have any grandchildren may be actively involved in supporting some other adult woman and her children [for example, see Shostak, 1981, on Nisa raising her niece (her brother's daughter, one of seven children), and later helping to raise her niece's children].

We find that 23% of the older women are widowed or divorced, while the majority are married and living with their husband only (44%), or husband and children (16%). Another 8% are living with a child or children as a sole parent, and 20% are living alone in their household. Only one out of sixty-one is living with and is the sole support of a grandchild.

Twenty-four women, 39%, have no living adult daughter, and another 25 (41%) have no living son. Overall, 18% have no adult children, and 38% have no living grandchildren (although some may be sufficiently young that they will have grandchildren later, especially from their sons). The older women may lose the opportunity to become a grandmother at each of several steps: they may fail to have children, or to have surviving children, or to have one or more children who marry, or fail to have any grandchild who survived to the point of observation. And those who have at least one grandchild are likely to have several (mean = 3.3), so that the effect on the child of grandmother's help and support may be diluted by division, or may shift from one child to another over time. Kinship is a reliable form of social organization on the average and over the long run, but it is unreliable in specifics and in the short run. Most "grandmothers," most of the time, will have too many or not enough grandchildren to make maximal use of their ability to help raise the grandchildren. Similarly, most children, most of the time, will find that they either have more caregivers than they need or not enough to provide food and guidance and comfort when they need it.

When there is "too much" capacity to care for children, the !Kung like all humans have no problem absorbing the surplus in the form of leisure and self-investment by the caregiver. When there is too little in the supply of caregivers, when parents and grandparents fail to be able to provide for children, other relatives are pressed into service or come forward at their own initiative. The siblings of the parents, the aunts and uncles of the child, are sometimes seen taking care of children or contributing food to the household, even if this is in competition with the child's cousins, the offspring of the parents' siblings. Evolutionary theory tells us to look at the effects on survival of the help provided, on the one hand, and to look at the closeness of kinship as measured by the proportion of genes identical by descent from the same ancestors on the other hand. Parents and siblings share .5 of their genes with the child; parents' siblings (aunts and uncles) and grandparents share .25 of genes identical by descent, and cousins and nieces and nephews share .125. Relatives who share fewer genes identical by descent can be referred to as "distant kin" and their genetic similarity to the child may be very similar to that of any "stranger" chosen at random from the !Kung population, because they may share genes identical by descent from distant ancestors even if they do not know one another. Close consanguine kin are the most valuable resource any !Kung person has in getting access to food and other resources during times of need, but others often fill in gaps when they are needed. Why and how that happens will be the topic of the final chapter of this book.

KINSHIP AS A RESOURCE FOR ALL !KUNG

We return now to a consideration of the ways that kinship influenced the !Kung in 1968 at all stages of the life history process. Like other hunter-gatherers, the !Kung live in a kinship-based society, in which all relationships are described as if they were a form of kinship, so we have to be careful what we mean when we describe kinship relations among the !Kung. Kin ties can be **consanguine** ("blood ties," formed by birth or "descent from common ancestors") or **affinal** (kin relationships formed by marriage rather than descent such as a spouse or in-laws, or by a combination of both birth and marriage, as when the husband of one's mother's sister is treated as a close "uncle"). Or kin ties can be fictive, a relationship described as though it were a consanguine or affinal tie, but is really just a metaphor for a kind of a relationship. The !Kung relate to people they cannot find a link to through the actual kinship system through the "name relationship," building on the kinship system as though the other is equal to a kinsmen with the same name. We will consider all three kinds of kinship to conclude this chapter, starting with the consanguineous.

Counting Consanguinial Kin

The !Kung live in a relatively small population (of five hundred to a thousand alive at one time) and virtually all mating has taken place within this group[3] for many generations. So the !Kung are necessarily closely related to one another, and their genes are descended from the same group of ancestors [as we saw in Chapter 16 of (Howell, 2000)]. Nevertheless, each person is more closely related to some of their consanguine relatives than to others. They share .5 of all their genes (identical by descent) with each of their parents, and with each of their siblings, and with each of their own children. Only identical twins exceed this level of close kinship. Parents' siblings, and siblings' and children's children make up the next circle around ego, sharing .25 of genes identical by descent. A third circle contains more distant relatives, with whom ego shares .125 of their genes identical by descent. This group includes what we call in English cousins, great-grandchildren, and great-grandparents.

Sometimes we extend these kin terms to the spouses of our relatives, but they are not consanguine ties in this sense of shared genes identical by descent. Cousin's children and others at further distances from ego do not have distinctive kin terms of address in !Kung, and other things (such as sex, age, and the name relation) being appropriate, ego can marry someone in this more distant group, which shares 6.25% of genes identical by descent. Let us start our investigation into kinship by looking first to see if it matters to ego's well-being in which consanguine kinship group he or she is located.

We generally think of kinship diagrams as being egocentric, so that you have to create one for each member of the population. !Kung culture would agree that kinship is egocentric, and they do not formally identify descent groups in the population. But the analyst is free to diagram kinship in more

3. For several decades before this study, some !Kung women mated with (and sometimes married) men from the Tswana or Herero groups who brought cattle to the Dobe area. At the end of 1968, seventeen of 134 marriages were to Bantu men. See Howell, N. (2000). *Demography of the Dobe !Kung*, 2nd ed. New York: Aldine de Gruyter, 234, 252.

objective ways, even if those groups are not recognized by the society. Consanguine kinship is traced through both the maternal and the paternal line, so each person is simultaneously a member of two descent groups.

Here is how we define the membership of descent groups in the living population. We count the living members of the maternal kin group (or maternal descent group) by looking at the oldest woman alive, and adding to her group all her children, male and female (living and dead, but the dead are only used to trace links: we do not count them as members of the group). We continue adding to this group by counting all the children only of her daughters (as the children of the males will be counted in the group of their mother). And if any of those daughters' daughters have had children, we count all of them (male and female) in the descent group of the old woman as well. The descent group is assigned an identification number, and we count the living members and their characteristics at a point in time to describe it. We continue with the next oldest woman, counting each of the living women and men descended from a mother alive at a point in time included in the analysis, and assign an identification number to each group along with the characteristics of the group. When we have exhausted the supply of mothers and their children and descendants of their female offspring, we assign an identification number to each of the living men who were not included in one or another of the women's descent groups and count each of them as a group of one member.

For paternal descent, we follow the same procedure, grouping the descendants of both sexes under their father, and the descendants of each of the male lines, ending by considering all of the women who are not included under their father as a group of one. In this way, each person (male and female) is counted as a member of two groups, a maternal and a paternal descent group.[4] Full siblings share the same memberships. Half-siblings share one but not both memberships. To arrive at the count of all the consanguine kin that each individual has, we add the two groups and subtract two (as ego is counted once in each group). A version of this procedure based on simulation can be found (Howell, 2000: 321).

We conduct an analysis of variance of the descent groups and BMIDiff for all individuals in the population (Table 7.4), and we see that the maternal and paternal kin group memberships are highly significant predictors of BMIDiff, our best indicator of individual well-being. This calculation is like

---

4. Diagrams of these maternal and paternal descent groups for the !Kung in 1968 are available in the data archive, drawing on genealogies collected by Richard Lee, along with the data files for each individual. See http://tspace.library.utoronto.ca, in the Dobe !Kung data sets.

TABLE 7.4. ANALYSIS OF VARIANCE (ANOVA) OF BMIDIFF
FOR MATERNAL AND PATERNAL DESCENT GROUPS

	Sum of Squares	df	Mean Square	F	Sig.
Maternal Descent					
Between groups	621.118	164	3.787	1.904	.000
Within groups	753.977	397	1.989		
Paternal Descent					
Between groups	679.171	199	3.413	1.687	.000
Within groups	695.924	344	2.023		

SOURCE: http://hdl.handle.net/1807/10406.

that in Chapter 6 where we explored whether waterholes and living groups were important predicts of BMIDiff (and CalBal), where we were disappointed to find that they are not. Here we discover statistically that it does matter to individuals which paternal and maternal descent groups they are in, and they resemble others in their group on the measure of BMIDiff more than the general population. The modal size of descent groups (the score at which there are the most individuals) is one, that is, just the ego. The mean size of the maternal descent groups is 9.84 and the mean for the paternal descent groups is 7.86. Most people have small descent groups (ten or fewer members) but the relatively few large groups include a substantial proportion of the population. The correlation coefficient of maternal descent groups with paternal descent groups ($r =.155$) is positive, indicating that those who have more maternal kin also have more paternal kin.

We might be tempted to jump to the conclusion that if membership in kin groups is significantly related to well-being that having many kin is better than having few kin, but the story is not quite that simple. Having prosperous kin is better than having poor kin, but the effects of numbers is not so clear. Figure 7.13 shows the distribution of group size for the maternal and the paternal descent groups, for 843 individuals, with a range of one to thirty-five for the maternal descent groups, one to thirty-one for the paternal groups, and highly statistically significant correlation (p. exceeds .01) between them.

In Figures 7.14 and 7.15, however, we see the association between the size of the maternal descent group and BMIDiff, our best measure of nutritional well-being, and paternal descent group size and BMIDiff. We see that the regression line for maternal descent group size is flat and near zero, with a correlation coefficient of $-.057$ (not significant). The regression line for paternal descent increases somewhat at the higher group sizes, and the correlation coefficient changes signs but is also not

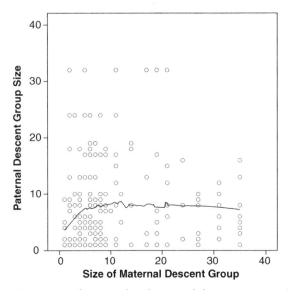

Figure 7.13. Group size of maternal and paternal descent groups, all !Kung in 1968. (Source: http://hdl.handle.net/1807/10406.)

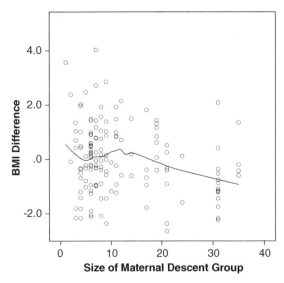

Figure 7.14. BMIDiff of children by size of maternal descent group. (Source: http://hdl.handle.net/1807/10406.)

significantly different from zero ($r = .016$). Note that we are counting individuals here, so effects on BMIDiff for the larger descent groups include reports from the many members of the group. When we proceed to disentangle the elements of kinship that produce the highly significant

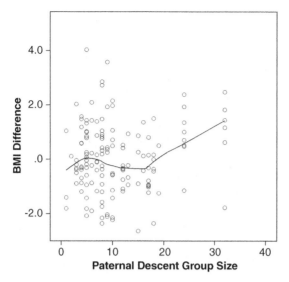

Figure 7.15. BMIDiff of children by size of paternal descent group. (Source: http://hdl.handle.net/1807/10406.)

relations with well-being, we find that the relationships are heavily influenced by age and sex, so that a relationship that is positive at one stage of life may well be detrimental at another stage.

Affinal Kinship

When we consider the difficulties of using consanguine kinship to solve problems of allocation of goods and services, we see the beauty of affinity in clear contrast. Pair-bonding was invented by birds long before humans found that they needed a solution to the problem of how to reliably allocate two caregivers to each set of dependent offspring.

Those who marry our consanguine relations are our first affine ties. Marriage choices allow a matching up of roles, one to one, which would seem to guarantee that husbands and wives will have their necessary reciprocal role partner when they need it. But what are affinal ties from the point of view of one parent of the child are just consanguine ties from the point of view of the child, and they are just as unpredictable as any other consanguine ties. As we saw in Howell (2000: Chapter 15), the inventory of kinship ties over the life span varies in predictable ways. Simulation showed that persons of all age and sex groups had an average of some sixteen close kin, and almost no one had more than forty such people in a model population like the !Kung. Children's kin inventory grows through childhood and jumps at the time of marriage when they gain not only the spouse but also all of the spouse's kin as new affinal ties. The kin inventory reaches a maximum for women in their 30s, and in their 40s for men, declining thereafter, as ties to the older generation are lost to death.

Aside from the marriage choice, people have very little control over their inventory of relatives, yet in a kinship-based society like the !Kung the quality and quantity of kin may be the most valuable asset people have. The functions of kinship seem to change over the life cycle. Providing food is most important to children, providing links to other communities and people become more important in early adulthood, and providing allies and supporters becomes more important as people reach their mature years. Yet there is very little any individual can do to change their inventory of kin.

Thinking about affinal kinship reminds us that individuals not only have a need for kin, but equally have a need **not** to be related to everyone in the population. !Kung kinship relationships are divided into respect-avoidance relationships and joking relationships, and a person needs to have some of each. A person with an enormous network of close kinship would have no one to marry, and his or her children would have no one with whom to joke or to marry. There need to be many dyads in the population that trace distant kin relation or cannot trace a relationship at all to keep the marriage system working.

Those with many kin and those with prosperous kin are more attractive on the marriage market than those who are isolated, who in turn may be more attractive than someone with many needy kin. And since parents make marriage choices rather than the young people (especially for first and early marriages), an abstract characteristic such as the quality and quantity of the kinship inventory is likely to be part of the marriage decision. The only way out of kinship isolation for an individual is to make a good marriage to someone with many kin, but the lack of kin is a negative factor in the person's attractiveness in the marriage market.

In the contemporary !Kung population, women (or at least premenopausal women) do not seem to have any difficulty getting a husband, and almost all of the women were found to be married throughout almost all of their reproductive period. Men, however, in the 1968 population sometimes failed to ever get a spouse, and many men were unmarried for long periods during their adult years. Partly this is due to the competition for !Kung men from Bantu men, who compete for the favors of !Kung women and who compete for their reproductive opportunities.[5]

---

5. Twenty-eight members of the numbered !Kung population ($N = 834$) have a !Kung mother and a Bantu father.

So we expect that availability of consanguine kin is a larger factor in the marital and reproductive success of men than of women.

Fictive Kinship: Creating Ties by the Name Relationship

On the other hand, people in face-to-face relationships in a kin-based society like the !Kung need to have some way to relate to strangers. Fictive kinship, based on the name relationship (Lee, 1979), is a means of forming predictable relationships with people for whom a consanguine or affinal relationship tie cannot be found. Ties of descent are traced through living people and through remembered people only, so that the genealogies are shallow. When there is no known relation of descent or marriage between two people, they construct a fictive relationship.

The elder of two otherwise unrelated persons has the initiative to use the kinship term for the other suggested by the other's given name. Each kin term has a reciprocal appropriate for relative age and gender. For example, if an older man meets a young man named "Bo," whom he doesn't otherwise know, the elder may reason that he had a father-in-law named "Bo," so he will call the young man "son-in-law" (the reciprocal term for father-in-law used for a younger person). And young Bo will be instructed to call him "father-in-law." This terminology will then govern relations between them, in terms of respect, avoidance, joking, and ability to marry one another's close relatives. Fictive kinship is a means to fill out the social structure when the rules would otherwise fail.

A person with few "real" kin in the immediate environment would necessarily want to emphasize fictive kin relations. Such a person can reinforce the ties by giving gifts, providing food, or arranging a marriage to link the families. The gift-giving relationship of *hxaro* (Wiessner, 1977) seems to function primarily as a device to emphasize certain relationships over others that might otherwise make competing claims. All !Kung do a certain amount of *hxaro* gift-giving, and these gifts seem to be important to individuals far in excess of their economic value. Most people start by establishing *hxaro* relationships to a few close relatives in childhood, under the guidance of parents and close relations. As a person gets older and takes control of their own *hxaro* decisions, he or she may use the relationship to publicly acknowledge friendship and close and warm feelings to particular relatives. At the same time, the selection of one person in a category to be a *hxaro* partner also signals to others in that category that ego is not reinforcing their relationship. A man with several aunts, for instance, might select one of them for *hxaro* to express and emphasize the thriving of his relationship with her and simultaneously encourage the withering away of surplus relationships (by not giving gifts) that are not seen by ego as essential to his well-being. As people become older, choices of *hxaro* partners may be more strategic. For example, one may reinforce the closest kin that he has at a waterhole that could conceivably be needed as a place of refuge at some time in the future if the water dries up at his own waterhole. *Hxaro* can be seen as a tool for simplifying and rationalizing the kinship inventory of a person, reinforcing relations that are needed and scarce and deliberately weakening surplus ties that do not seem to be needed. Of course, *hxaro* is a **reciprocal** relationship, which only strengthens ties when gifts are accepted and similar gifts returned at the appropriate time. So ego cannot use this tool to modify his kin inventory in his best interests without participation from others. It is interesting to see this rather mysterious social custom, which seems to have little or no strictly economic importance in the gifts that are given and received.

Instead of finding, in this chapter, that there are particular kinship relationships that determine the well-being of children in the !Kung society, we have found many small but probably cumulative effects from a range of kin in the society. Rather than a model of kin as wealth, for example, or kin as an insurance policy, we seem to be finding that there are a wide range of others who may play specific roles in supporting children in particular situations, where their help may be crucial but not regularly required. We will explore this idea further in the concluding chapter.

CHAPTER 8

Motives for Sharing Food and Other Prosocial Behavior

In this chapter, we conclude our consideration of a life history analysis of the !Kung adaptation. In the preceding chapters, we depended upon data collected in 1967–1969 for other purposes to explore issues of the production and distribution of food resources. Briefly, let us review what we have learned from the data before we go beyond the data to try to tie up some questions that naturally arose but cannot be answered empirically with the available data.

We saw that stages of life, as distinct from age and sex, are recognized by the !Kung and are quite strongly related to the production and distribution of food resources. We found that !Kung body sizes are quite remarkably small for such strong and active people, and that their growth is slow and maturity comes late. In the chapter on "calories required," we saw that the small body sizes and relatively low activity and reproductive costs keep the caloric requirements of individuals low across the life span. !Kung children and adolescents do very little productive work and are relatively very expensive for their population to support. The age at which young people begin to make significant contributions to the workforce is remarkably late in this group, and production is remarkably flat across the life span after that time, and this pattern continues on into old age. There is very little cost to the society of elderly people who cannot contribute to the food supply.

We found that the differences between individuals in relative fatness and well-being do not vary much between regions of their territory or the composition of the villages in which they live. Only the composition of households and kin groups has a substantial contribution to the well-being of individuals, especially of children, and even kin resources account for relatively little of the differences between individuals. Specifically we find little consequence of less-than-optimal household and kin composition on individuals, and we are left to explain the lack of consequences of bad luck by general notions of "sharing." People do not starve in this population because others, who are also thin, hard-working, and limited in calories, give of their little to those who have none. How and why this sharing persists to such a degree that deficits of income can hardly be seen in specific individuals in the population are questions that invite some speculation and some consideration of general theoretical ideas.

MODELS OF THE MOTIVES FOR SHARING

We wonder what else is going on that allows people with pressing requirements and scarce resources to meet the needs of their population over the long run. The simple answer is that the mechanism is sharing, not just with one's closest relatives but also with more distant kin, with affines, and with fictive kin—which amounts to everyone in the population. And this sharing is not random or automatic, but is targeted to the needs of the recipients as well as to the motivations of the givers that we will review shortly. In this chapter we will use a convenient review of the literature and theoretical perspectives on food sharing from a behavioral ecological perspective to guide our look at the dynamics of sharing among the !Kung and to try to understand the motivations of sharing from their point of view.

Gurven (2004b) asks, "Why do individuals engage in acts that incur personal costs and benefit others?" He points out that costly pro-social behavior is viewed by many researchers as violating the "axiom of rationality," which assumes that higher levels of consumption provide higher individual utility. Gurven asserts that research on sharing and cooperation among human hunter-gatherers may be important because common notions of fairness, equity, and punishment in many domains and in many societies may have been shaped in the food-sharing context of hunter and gatherer groups in early human history. He notes that psychologists, economists, and political scientists may find interesting hints from the studies of hunting and gathering people, and he points to the evolution of the "prosocial brain," which, he suggests, "may be at the root of the sexual division of labor and the origin of the human family with delayed childhood, long post-menopausal life spans, and large brains." From this study of the !Kung, we can put our findings on food sharing next to his summaries of what is known cross-culturally about food sharing in simple societies.

Gurven (2004b) organizes his review around four alternative theoretical models that have been proposed to account for the basic nature of food sharing. These hypotheses help us understand the !Kung situation, so we will discuss them in some detail below. The models, in the order in which we will consider them, are: (1) kin selection, (2) reciprocal altruism, (3) tolerated theft or scrounging, and (4) costly signaling.

All of these mechanisms can be at work in a single society to determine behavior: we do not have to choose only one between them. We will use the list of models to look at kinds of behavior observed among the !Kung that can be understood in this way. Perhaps on another occasion it would be useful to look at the variations between cultures as a consequence of the relative dominance of one or another of these models in determining the behavior of people in the different cultures, but here we are only looking at the !Kung. These alternative ways of looking at the motivation for a general class of behavior like sharing help us understand some of the puzzling behavior we have noticed along the way.

Kin Selection

"Kin selection" is obviously a powerful explanation for why people in small-scale societies engage in prosocial behavior (especially food sharing). The Dobe !Kung, like other hunting and gathering societies, use kinship as the metaphor for all social structure in their society. We saw in Chapter 7 the importance of kinship as a basis for sharing. Kin selection commonly explains sharing in the behavior of nonhuman animals, and it is surely an underlying process in human societies as well.

The basic principle of kin selection is expressed in Hamilton's rule (Hamilton, 1964) that an individual should give to kin when the benefits, B, to the recipient weighted by Wright's coefficient of relatedness, r, outweigh costs, C, to the donor (when $rB > C$). Wright's coefficient of relatedness reflects the proportion of genes identical by descent from recent generations, so that parents, children, and siblings are related by .5, grandparents and parent's siblings are related by .25, cousins by .125, and so on. When we ignore more distant relationships, we also ignore the effects of inbreeding over many generations in a small population.

Kin selection models predict that only consanguine kinship is important in sharing, but we know in the !Kung case (and probably in many others) that shared gifts of food may be provided to individual close kin but they are then redistributed through the household of the recipient to the spouse of the recipient as well as to their consanguine kin. The mean kin coefficient for the household is necessarily less than the closest tie in the household: Thus, if a hunter's daughter lives "next door" with her new husband and baby, their mean relatedness to the father-hunter might be .5 (daughter) +.o (her husband, unrelated) +.25 (grandchild), that is, .75/3 = .25 average for the household. The coefficient of relatedness could in principle be calculated for every households, every living group, even every waterhole, but of course, it is an egocentric measure and so it would generate a great deal of work to do so, and the payoff for doing so would not be clear. We have noted that the social structure of the !Kung (and perhaps all human groups) requires the presence and participation of non-kin as well as kin in the range of activities. Absence of either kind of ties presents problems to an individual, and there are frequently ways to get around these inconveniences (such as fictive kinship or "joking relationships" with kin).

As we think about the applicability of kin selection as a predictor of food sharing, we note the norm that spouses share with (eat out of one pot with) their spouse, who is never a close kinsman. All in-laws are distant kin, by definition, although cultural rules require a young hunter to provide for his in-laws as well as for his nuclear family until three children are born. These cultural rules and the theoretical model of kin selection remind us that people need distant kin as much as they need close kin in a society like the !Kung. A person can be handicapped by having few close kin, but can also be potentially handicapped by having so many close ties to large numbers of others that there are few people left with whom to joke and have sex. Imagine a person whose parents both happen to be drawn from the largest families in the population. This young person is forbidden to marry or to consider marriage with anyone in the position of first-cousin or closer kin, on any generation, which might be a substantial portion of the total population. In addition, he or she cannot marry anyone in the population who has the same name as his/her parents or any of his/her siblings. The first of these rules seems to be important and enforced, while the second is usually followed but can be finessed by changing the name of the offending spouse at the last minute if the couple really wants to marry. Clearly marital choice is wider for those who have fewer close kin.

It is certainly true that kinship provides the framework within which *hxaro* gifts are given and food is shared among the !Kung (Wiessner, 1977). Perhaps we should look at the *hxaro* relationship as one that specifies which among equally close kin are the particular individuals that ego depends upon for assistance. But whether the gifts go to nearby individuals whose coefficient of relatedness is actually higher than others in the village to whom gifts are not given is not altogether clear. There seem to be some forms of prosocial behavior among the !Kung that are performed primarily or even solely by close kin: intensive care of frail elderly or seriously handicapped individuals, for instance, has been observed from full sons or daughters of the elderly, or from mothers, fathers, or siblings of the handicapped, for instance, for sustained periods of time. But food sharing [and some other forms of costly prosocial behavior like curing (Katz 1982)] does not seem to be limited to close kin in this way.

Reciprocal Altruism

Reciprocal altruism is a classic explanation of why humans give to others who are not close relatives. The idea is that one may "invest" portions of food in gifts to others with whom one has shared in the past and expects to share in the future. Reciprocal altruism is seen as a means of reducing inequality in supplies from day to day and from season to season.

Gifts to others can be seen as payments on an insurance policy that protects against great need at some time in the future: "the potential receipt in the future is the motive for giving in the present" (Trivers, 1971). The selection of the recipient is up to the giver, and he or she may select a kinsman or an unrelated individual, depending upon that person's access to resources that may be needed in the future. Reciprocal altruism requires "scorekeeping" on the part of the participants, so that one knows what has been given and more or less what is expected in return (and when that is expected). In the !Kung case, we imagine the head of a household planning ahead by making a substantial gift to someone who is an owner at another waterhole, to protect against the possibility that one's own waterhole may go dry during the winter at some future time and the household may be forced to ask for permission to live at the other waterhole. The custom of *hxaro* gift-giving seems to be a classic example of reciprocal altruism, although Wiessner (1977) notes that many of the dyads that engage in *hxaro* transactions are close kin.

Analysts of reciprocal altruism commonly focus on the problem of "free-loading" or the danger of giving to another who does not reciprocate in the future. When reciprocity breaks down, the giver has the choice of continuing to give, retaliating against the other, or withdrawing from the interaction. It seems to me that !Kung express little concern about failures of reciprocity in the area of food sharing,[1] but show a great deal of concern about reciprocity in the area of *hxaro* gifts (which typically are of much less value to the recipient). *Hxaro* gifts seem to have as their purpose the labeling and reinforcement of specific relationships, and hence, the individuals who make the gifts are intensely concerned about whether their gift was received, appreciated, and will be properly reciprocated at the appropriate time. Individuals carry out these interactions publicly and talk about them openly with wide audiences. Meat sharing, on the other hand, is carried out publicly but is not necessarily appreciated or reciprocated, and other food sharing is carried out quietly and there doesn't seem to be any scorekeeping involved.

The central idea of reciprocal altruism has been extended and tested by Game Theory (von Neumann and Morgenstern, 1944), which applies the game known as Prisoner's Dilemma to understand the dynamics of human cooperation. Specifically game theoretical analysis has found that the strategy named "tit-for-tat"' is stable and maximizes success in this game, whereby the player starts by a cooperative response and afterward returns to the other whichever response was last given by the other, cooperation for cooperation, or defection for defection. Economists and economic anthropologists have explored the possibilities of better understanding cultural patterns in simple societies by carrying out additional experiments with people in a wide range of kinds of societies.

For instance, one game begins by giving a person a sum of money (or other valued goods) and asking that person to divide the goods between himself and another member of the society. If the second person accepts the division of goods proposed by the first person, they each get their share, but if the other rejects the division as inadequate or unfair, neither gets anything. It is possible to learn a great deal about attitudes toward goods and toward others in these games, and norms of fairness and punishment of violators can be inferred from the behavior (Henrich, Boyd, et al., 2004).

---

1. Lee has, however, noted that arguments about sharing meat sometimes lead to so much bad feeling that one or a few households leave the village and "resolve conflict by fission." [Lee, R. B. (1972). Population growth and the beginnings of sedentary life among the !Kung Bushmen. *Population Growth: Anthropological Implications*. B. Spooner. Cambridge, M.I.T. Press.] I have always seen this situation as a mechanism for Malthusian population reduction in the short run, whereby a perception that the village is overcrowded is expressed in the meat distribution, but it can also be seen as a failure of reciprocal altruism.

Researchers have carried out these games with a range of hunting-gathering and other small-scale societies, such as the Hadza (Marlowe, 2004) and the Ache (Hill and Gurven, 2004b). Personally, I wouldn't like the job of trying to explain one of these games to the !Kung. I anticipate their response would be a total rejection of the arbitrary rules and especially of the fiction that they are playing the game with another !Kung. I am sure that they would see it as an action by the anthropologist toward two !Kung, and would be willing to take any rewards promised, but puzzled and contemptuous of the "anthropologists' craziness" for proposing the game itself.

Gurven points out that **trade** can be seen as a form of reciprocal altruism in which the products given and received are in different currencies. We could equally well see reciprocal altruism as an early form of trade, before the values of different currencies are clearly established, in which gifts are given and received and in which both parties keep track of the value of those gifts and hope to receive benefits from the interaction in the future. Reciprocal altruism clearly has the potential to reduce risk or variance in the flow of goods or access to resources. It doesn't seem to have much power to explain why some people whose need is very great but who are not in a position to return favors are given gifts nevertheless. The name of the model seems to be ironic: interactions are not necessarily reciprocal, and the apparent altruism of gift-giving is reduced to a form of self-interest.

Tolerated Scrounging or Tolerated Theft

The third mechanism proposed for providing the basis for sharing initially sounds like the most unpleasant and selfish motive among the four, but the hypothesized motive turns out to be the most generous to the needy, the one most illuminating, and perhaps the most true of the !Kung. The tolerated theft model is especially applicable to situations where food comes in large packages on an unpredictable time pattern. The acquirer is therefore likely to have far more food than he and his immediate family can consume in the time available before it spoils, so giving away the excess is the only form of "saving" that the hunter or owner of the meat can engage in.

This mechanism was proposed by Blurton Jones (1984), who noted that when others in the group are hungry, a hunter may find that he would have to pay higher costs to defend a resource than it would cost him to give some of it away. The acquirer should cede portions of his resource

until all potential contenders have equal marginal consumption value
or utility. Gurven summarizes the argument:

> . . . "if individuals get smaller increments of value from consuming addi-
> tional portions of food, then remaining food portions will eventually be
> worth more to hungry individuals than to the sated acquirer. When one is
> unable to maintain control of a resource without paying a substantial cost
> to maintain control of the 'surplus', an acquirer should cede portions to
> other individuals." (Blurton Jones, 1987)

Since we rarely observed !Kung fighting to defend a catch against
others,[2] this mechanism would not seem to be in play. But on further
consideration, a lot of !Kung culture seems to be devoted to continual
reminders to hunters (and gatherers) that there are many hungry folks
in the village, and those who are lucky enough to find themselves strong
and healthy should be devoted to providing for those who cannot at this
stage of their life provide for themselves, kin, or otherwise. One of the
appealing aspects of this theoretical model is that it gives a great deal of
initiative to the recipient of giving or sharing, rather than concentrating
on the motives of the giver.

The key to understanding tolerated scrounging is a recognition that
need on the part of the recipient drives giving, and that recipients are free
to encourage gifts by asking for them, demanding them, or even stealing
them (although the latter is rare among the !Kung but see Howell, 2000:
52–53). "Asking for things" is a common activity among the !Kung and
can be seen as an art form that is performed with good humor, wit, charm,
and grace by many, and with desperation by a few. Rosenberg (1989) calls
it "complaint discourse" in her studies of the elderly, and Shostak (1981)
seemed to find it personally harassing. The theme of "asking for things" is
generally a comparison between the riches of the other and the poverty and
deprivation of the self, a refrain that is continued until something is given
and there is some balancing of the relative wealth of the pair, whether this
wealth is in the form of food, clothing, beaded decorations, or tobacco.

---

2. There is a particular delectable fruit called !no (oranges) that grows in trees, and is
harvested and claimed while green by the first !Kung to discover that the fruit is full-sized.
Bundles of fruit are wrapped in dry grass and left to ripen near the tree, and the owner
becomes irritated if others discover the ripened fruit and take it (or some of it) before the
owner returns. Whether this is precisely "stealing" is not entirely clear, but taking or consuming ripened fruit is certainly deviant behavior among the !Kung. Since it is possible to
"read" the footprints of others, the offender will likely become known. Most food resources
are plentiful in their season, and the cost of acquisition consists only of collecting them
and carrying them home, so the issue of control of wild foods doesn't often arise.

The ideal wealth distribution implied by "asking for things" is equality, and equality of resources is the only complete defense from "asking."

In the !Kung case, the frequency of visiting by young men or by a whole household to relatives in another living group is probably best described as tolerated scrounging, as the visitors will be fed for a day or so before being included in the hunting and gathering of the host village. The occasion for visiting is often noted to be a presentation of a *hxaro* gift by one of the members of the visiting household, which is an example of activation of strong ties that are probably kin-based but not applied to all kin of that degree of relatedness. The gift generally has no or little economic value[3] but is a token of the strength of the relationship.

Costly Signaling

Gurven completes his list of theoretical models of sharing with the alternative of "costly signaling." He explains this model by pointing out that the food quest often involves tasks that require great skill, risk, stamina, and vigor. Success in the food task thus not only provides the subsistence of the society, but also represents an honest signal to others of the phenotypic quality of the food provider. The signal is called honest because it cannot be easily faked, and it can therefore provide reliable information about the quality of the provider and can serve as a kind of "advertising" for partner choice as mates, allies, or other social partners. The sharing of the food acquired can be a (costly) signal of an honest intention to cooperate with others (Alexander, 1987; Gurven, M., and Allen-Arave, et al., 2000).

This model is the basis for the "show-off hypothesis" (Hawkes, O'Connell, et al., 1991), which says that men hunt risky game primarily because of social or mating advantages of success, rather than for its consumption benefits. We note that the general model of costly signaling is not reciprocal, which is to say that an individual gives to the needy and is rewarded by esteem from others (not necessarily the recipient). Hence, the model can be applied to situations like that of the !Kung where giving often goes to recipients who have little to offer in return.

From Gurven's point of view, the !Kung are an "assertive-egalitarian group," characterized by diets consisting of difficult-to-acquire bulky meat packages (and vegetable foods such as ivory hearts-of-palm bundles), supplemented by components of small, predictable, relatively

---

3. Examples of *hxaro* gifts might be beaded clothing, ostrich egg-shell beads, or a well-made knife or a tool. Typically weeks or months go by before a *hxaro* gift is reciprocated.

easy-to-harvest bundles, such as mongongo nuts, tsin beans, roots, and berries. Generally, the first category is harvested by men and the second by women. Both distribute their harvest, but men as hunters are more culturally protected from demands by others and from criticism by customs such as lack of control over the distribution. From the point of view of members of households that do not have adequate resources, the way to improve their access to food is to modify the composition of their household, village, or waterhole (on the one hand), and to aggressively make sure that others know of their need (on the other).

A prime example of costly signaling among the !Kung is the decision on the part of adolescents or young adults that they should shift their status from that of a very expensive dependent to that of potentially valuable producer by taking up the tasks of learning and then carrying out hunting and gathering. Young women often seem to decide to accompany women on the food quest and bring back a load of food during the adolescent growth-spurt, in advance of their first menstruation. Bringing back food is an activity that wins them approval from the adults in the group and may initiate consideration of the marriage of this young woman. And, more dramatically, young men, often after some years of loafing around and traveling widely to visit kin, apprentice themselves to their father or another good hunter and start the hard work of learning to hunt. Young men are publicly acknowledged by a ceremony and a ritual tattooing of their face when they succeed in bringing in the first male and female specimen of the prime meat species, kudu and eland. And significantly, people say that women accept men with those facial tattoos as lovers and potential husbands, while they are encouraged to laugh at the sexual advances of a boy who does not yet hunt. Given the power of the reward, it is surprising that so many young men put off starting hunting for many years. There is some evidence that this cultural rule, like others we see among the !Kung, is not strictly followed.

Costly signaling may also be the motive for already accomplished hunters to engage in the hard work and long hours of stalking and tracking game, even if the !Kung culture requires them to engage in modest demeanor when they come back to the village with the news of their kill. Men have an opportunity that women do not have, of increasing their reproductive success by having children with multiple mates, at the same time or sequentially. Young hunters may be motivated to impress parents and kin so that he can obtain a first wife, and an older hunter may be motivated to attract the attention and admiration of women who might be interested in having a surreptitious lover, or he might be anticipating the opportunity to have a second wife, especially if the first wife is subfecund or is approaching the end of her reproductive period. It is interesting that men's hunting prowess typically stays high through their 40s and 50s, at the time in their life when they might be seeking the opportunity to start a second family, either polygamously or after a divorce from the first wife.

We have noted the presence of customs that tend to denigrate the value of the meat of the hunter or to assign ownership of the meat to the one who provided the arrow that killed it (for example) rather than the hunter who killed it, but of course, everyone present knows who did the hunting and who brought the meat that the village is sharing and enjoying. The customs point to the awareness of the people that arrogance or bossiness could be a problem from a successful hunter and serve notice that there are limits on the power of a good hunter to control others. At the same time, no one begrudges the successful hunter some admiration, esteem, and sexual and reproductive opportunities.

How then, do we classify the !Kung on Gurven's scale? Following his logic, we characterize the !Kung (in contrast with other hunter-gatherers) as a group in which the amount of individual control that producers of food have over their surplus production is relatively small, and hedged around with cultural rules that restrict the freedom of donors (especially hunters) to distribute their gifts as they wish. The group size within which sharing occurs is small (with a range of fifteen to fifty and a mean of about twenty in living groups). The amount of privacy available to food producers that allows unobserved consumption of food is extremely small. Instead, everyone can see the distribution of meat, the amounts of food stored at the household fire, and the fatness (and thinness) of the members of the family. Gurven notes that the four evolutionary models considered ignore most characteristics of the production systems that generate the food items found in the diet. Among the !Kung, hunters are entitled to consume portions of their catch (especially the liver) at the site of the butchery of the meat, and sometimes have been known to cook and consume substantial meals of meat before they start the butchery if they are very hungry, but basically the meat is declared publicly, brought back to the village, and shared out publicly. Food that comes in smaller packages (birds, hares, and most vegetable foods), especially when collected and brought to the village by women, may be casually observed by others and may be given in small portions to others, but is not culturally controlled as large amounts of meat are.

The !Kung are well described by Gurven's characterization of most hunter-gathers as "assertive" or "fierce egalitarians," which includes leveling mechanisms such as ridicule of a hunter's ability or catch and explicit sharing rules. The !Kung are among those who consider refusal to share as the "ultimate sin" and who characterize those who do not share as "far-hearted." The ethos of sharing among the !Kung has made it difficult (but not impossible) for !Kung to succeed at horticulture and herding, as the demands for sharing by hungry others make it difficult (but not impossible) to retain seed from one year to another or to keep breeding stock from the domesticated animals from one season to the next.

WHAT DO WE MEAN BY A "SURPLUS"?

As we consider the motivations of the giver and the recipient in acts of sharing, we need to be clear about the nature of the concept of "surplus." We reviewed the essence of life history theory in Chapter 2 by saying that every calorie consumed can be put uniquely to the purposes of one of life's goals: maintenance, growth, reproduction, or mating effort, which is then not available to meet other goals. We did not discuss sharing at that point in the argument. If we had, we could have explained it as a method for increasing reproductive success (when we talk about sharing with children and close kin), or as a form of mating effort (as exemplified by the "showing-off hypothesis," for example).

It may be useful to think about designing a robot that would behave like !Kung people do, relative to all these competing demands on calories. To do so, we would have to be precisely explicit in our instructions to the robot, and hence, we need to be entirely clear in our observations of what people actually do. Let us start by considering an adult with a maximal ability to hunt and/or gather. Averaged over a week or so, the mean product per day is likely to be in the range of 2,500 to 4,000 calories a day output. A !Kung adult is likely to require about 1,800 calories for females, or 2,300 for males. Should we program our robot to set aside the daily needs for self out of the harvest produced before anything else? If that were true of !Kung, adult food producers would never lose weight in a time of scarcity, and the children and other dependents would absorb all the consequences of plenty and scarcity. Clearly this is not the case.

Let us consider what other demands there may be on the products of hunting/gathering. In the case of meat, we have noted that the product is not considered to be the private property of the hunter. It may belong to the maker of the arrow with which the animal was shot, and it belongs in part to those who helped on the hunt and in carrying the meat back to camp. It has to be formally divided and distributed throughout the village, and the culture dictates that the family of the hunter is not entitled to a larger share than others in the village. It is likely that both hunters and gatherers eat some portion (perhaps several hundred calories per day) of their food in the bush, in the course of the work, to sustain them through the work day, but the much larger balance of their diet must be shared and consumed socially.

In the household, food is cooked and processed and shared out. Do parents meet the needs of their children first and divide the rest between themselves? Do they meet their own needs first and provide the balance to be divided among the children? Do they meet the minimum requirements for basal metabolism for another day for every member of the family before distributing a second round to meet needs of growth, a third round to meet needs of reproductive and mating effort, and a fourth round to share with needy kin and neighbors outside the household? It is impossible to answer these questions with any precision, and indeed, even to specify how one would get the data to answer them factually under the best of possible circumstances. And yet we cannot program our robot to act as a !Kung adult acts without providing explicit instructions, and we can see that how this allocation process is carried out may have important consequences for the population.

A surplus of calories may be invested into fighting infection and strengthening the immune system; into healing wounds; into growth of brain, bones, or sinews; into pregnancy; into lactation; into courting or fighting to retain a marital relationship. A surplus may have the consequence of producing larger individuals who require more calories for maintenance every day for the rest of their lives or of producing more individuals who will be supported on the same amount of food. By decisions to invest resources in self and others, the population may be maximizing size, numbers, beauty, art, music, mythology, religious life, or healing or may be minimizing hunger, cold, suffering, infant deaths, stunting of growth, or handicaps.

These considerations do not show me how to program a robot to behave like a !Kung person, but they suggest that the programs should probably not be the same for all individuals and should be different at different stages of life. No doubt we would need some input from the needs of others in order to produce an outcome that resembles the !Kung solution in any way. Perhaps robots would have to be taught to "ask" others to give them what they need and taught to listen and respond to such requests (or demands) according to some nonobvious paradigm. All we can conclude about "surplus" at this stage is that it is not a simple concept. I suspect that most contemporary Americans would specify a level of minimum intake before a surplus would be recognized that represents a level of intake that few !Kung had ever experienced in their life.

SHARING DRIVEN BY SCARCITY

These considerations focus our attention on the low level of productivity and consumption experienced by !Kung. The decisions they are making about the allocation of resources occur in a context in which everything is scarce and in which everyone is (relatively speaking) in immediate need. Producers cannot afford to follow routine rules of allocation such as feeding oneself first or feeding the youngest children before the older ones, because the "needs" of almost any individual could be seen as requiring all or nearly all of the produce available, leaving none for others or for emergencies. Instead, there is a process of responding to a rather wide range of needs, before we come to what would be considered "surplus" in a situation of affluence. Long before we get to the level of consumption that would make people plump, or would lead to a feeling of satiety rather than gnawing hunger, or would result in maximal growth of children, the !Kung food supply is exhausted and people go to sleep hungry, hoping that the next day may produce more plenty.

Of course, there are times when the !Kung have more food than they can consume: when the hunters kill an eland or a kudu, for example, or when the group camps in the mongongo groves when the nuts have fallen from the trees, or when Nisa (Shostak, 1981) rejoices at eating her fill of juicy caterpillars at the time of the first rains in spring. On such a day, those who give food can afford to be irrational in their gifts. But most days, distributing food (also called sharing) is serious business, when excessive giving may cost someone else their chance at life.

We seek mechanisms that reduce the need for massive redistributions, that tailor giving to real need, and that depend upon the nearest provider (not necessarily the closest kin) to provide the needed calories to keep people alive and to provide for the minimum necessary level of growth for children. Effective giving responds to short-term needs, the occasional crisis that puts children in danger when their parents are acutely ill, for example, or when a waterhole dries up or a depended-upon species fails. The system of sharing is less able to cope with chronic scarcity caused by ineffective or incompetent parents or too many children. Neighbors may be continually giving small amounts of food to supplement children's diets, but it may not be enough if the parents cannot provide the core. We must remember that approximately half of the children born in this population fail to live to the start of their adulthood (Howell, 2000) and that it is only the survivors who provide information on the relationship between BMIDiff and kinship.

EVOLUTIONARY SPECULATION: THE PROSOCIAL BRAIN AS A PRODUCT OF DECISIONS ABOUT FOOD SHARING, PERCEPTIONS OF NEED, AND NURTURANCE

Evolutionary speculation is stimulated by comparisons across species, rather than within species. Following the lead of Hawkes and her colleagues (Hawkes, O'Connell, et al., 1998; Hawkes, O'Connell, et al., 2001a; 2001b), we note as a starting point that the life history stages of humans and chimpanzees are remarkably similar, with two striking differences. Birth size and gestational length is about the same; and infancy is similar between the species, with babies entirely dependent upon their mothers for lactation, transportation, protection, and care.

The first of the substantial differences between the species arises in childhood (postweaning, preadolescence). Chimpanzee children feed themselves from the day of their weaning, under the supervision and continued protection of the mother, with increasing independence and contact with other children and other members of the group. Human children, on the other hand, require being fed; that is, children need not only the collection of meat and vegetable foods by adults but also the processing of that food to make it palatable for humans, by cooking, pounding, cracking of nuts, and so on. And human children require this help in eating, along with the protection and guidance of adults, not for a short period of time while they make the transition from infancy to adulthood, but for almost two decades, which is about half the life span of chimpanzees and about 20% of the maximum life span of humans. Chimpanzee dependent children, who are necessarily infants, are sequential for their mother, who ends the intense investment in one child before she starts the next, while human children necessarily overlap in their dependency, because it goes on so long. The !Kung are extreme in the degree and duration of dependence of children on adults, but it seems to be true that all human children require substantial inputs of care from others to survive, although the contributions that children make to their own survival typically increase with age. This is true in that growth and development people note that humans alone have a biological adolescence, which in the !Kung seems to be that wonderful "loafing" period. With the exception of the case of the Ik

(Turnbull, 1972), who are said to turn their children out of the household at the age of 3 or 4 to fend for themselves, all human populations provide care and feeding for children. Reports of human children turned out of parental households to care for and feed themselves at an early age, as in the deviant case of urban street children, are always associated with poverty and extremely high childhood mortality, mortality so high that a hunter-gatherer population could not hope to have fertility high enough to compensate for it.

The second difference in life history stages between chimpanzees and humans is in the expansion of the post-reproductive, presenile period of maturity, as Hawkes has shown us (Hawkes, O'Connell, et al., 2000). Around age 40, chimpanzees end their reproductive ability, senesce into old age and die shortly. In the wild, few if any chimpanzee females survive to the end of their childbearing capacity, but it is seen in zoos and other protected environments. The demise of a chimpanzee parent has relatively little impact on the probability of survival of offspring, as parents are not provisioning them or doing much to educate them in any case, tasks that can be taken over by others in the group. Menopause for chimpanzees and human females is remarkably similar in timing. But the chimpanzees die at that time (if not before), while human females typically survive and are productive at least another twenty years (and occasionally as much as fifty years) before becoming senescent.[4] Hawkes has argued that the evolution of post-reproductive life among humans is a result of the contributions that people (especially women) can make to the increased survival of their offspring and grandchildren during that extra twenty years or more of life inserted between menopause and senility (Hawkes, O'Connell, et al., 1998). The argument is persuasive, although I think she underestimates the importance of the post-reproductive woman's contributions to the survival of her own younger children during the extremely long period of childhood dependency, in favor of contributions to the grandchildren. But increased survival of both generations—children and grandchildren—as a result of the added years of productivity of post-reproductive adults is plausibly the cause of the

---

4. The expectation of life at age 40 for females is 19.278 years in Coale and Demeny's *Model Life Tables and Stable Populations* at level 1, with an expectation of life at birth of 20 years, and is higher than that in all the other model life tables. On the average, men can only expect to live 16.9 years at age 40, under the same conditions, and !Kung men may be as old as 50 at the birth of their last child, when the expectation of life in MW1 is 12.6 years. About 30% of !Kung young people have lost their mother to death by time they reach age 20, and about half have lost their father at the same age.

increased longevity of all humans. This "grandmother hypothesis" seems to me to be a profound insight into the course of human evolution.

Fatness and Thinness as an Honest Signal of Need

While we are considering the contrast between the life history stages of humans and chimpanzees, let us also consider another model of sharing, which might be seen as targeted or strategic intervention in both kin and non-kin. Picture an adult female chimpanzee age 40 or so, standing next to an adult female human of the same age. Both have given birth to their children and are experienced mothers. The human will be taller and there are some changes in legs and pelvic structure that permit upright walking by humans, but many of the differences in their appearance are superficial.

One important difference in their appearance is that the chimpanzee is covered with fur, and the fat deposits of the chimpanzee are packed into the abdomen. The subcutaneous fat of the chimpanzee mother is evenly spread over her body. The human female has no fur (just hair on the head, underarms, and pubic area), and she has conspicuous fat deposits under the skin, especially in the area of the thighs, buttocks, and breasts, even if this hardworking middle-aged individual is thin overall. Let us entertain a "fatness hypothesis" to explain this difference between the species, which asserts that conspicuous fat deposits evolved in humans not only to provide storage of a surplus to get through periods of scarcity, as is often suggested, and to attract a mate because they are attractive (also frequently noted), but also to permit continuous monitoring of her nutritional state by others, so that food sharing can be tailored to need. Loss of fur and conspicuous subcutaneous fat deposits allow humans to assess the nutritional state of others in a glance.

Provisioning dependents is not and cannot be simply a state of continual efforts by some on behalf of others. Sharing instead requires a continuous decision-making process on the part of the provider. Adults must be able to decide: does this child need food? Does child A need more food than child B? If A and B are my own children, C and D are my adult daughter's children, E is my sister's child, and F is the skinny kid whose parents are visiting my mother-in-law, how shall I allocate my supply of food among them and me and my spouse?

Speech and increased capacity for subtle communications undoubtedly helps in this process, but whatever the level of deliberate communication, the provider needs to be able to assess not only the need for efforts to feed the dependents, but also the absence of need, the sufficiency of the dependent. Without the ability to evaluate when the dependent has had enough food, the ability to read the signal that no more provisioning is immediately needed, human mothers could not care for those overlapping dependent children, or make any contribution to the survival of adults and children other than their own offspring. The readily observable degree of fatness of self and others provides the basis for a silent communication of an honest signal of need.

There are at least three kinds of questions to be asked about provisioning children: (1) Is the provisioning needed, that is, will the child survive just as well without it? (2) Is there anyone else who might provision this child if I don't do it; that is, does the child have access to resources other than mine? And (3) What is my kinship to this child, or what is the calculation of inclusive fitness that influences decisions about investment? A child (like a sibling or a parent) shares half their genes identical by descent with the provider, while a grandchild shares one-quarter of the genes (the same as a niece or nephew), and an unrelated child shares no genes identical by descent (but a lot of genes are identical simply as a product of being in the same group and hence, descended from distant common ancestors, and simply from being human (Howell, 2000: 333–359). Although we do not suppose that early humans (or the !Kung) had a conscious awareness of the calculation of inclusive fitness, evolutionary theory shows that the consequences of investment decisions operate "as if" he (or she) does. In other words, providing food to one's own offspring is twice as efficacious as provisioning a grandchild for the purposes of inclusive fitness, provided that the two are identical in the other variables (degree of need and availability of alternative resources). And inclusive fitness is not simply a process of self-interest, but it is "the invisible hand" of evolutionary biology that ensures that a genetic trait, such as visible fatness, or the ability to perceive the need for food on the part of children, and/or sharing food with related and unrelated children when a need is recognized, will gradually become the typical genetic configuration of the human species. Prosocial emotions, including guilt, shame, remorse, and above all empathy (the ability to "read," identify with, and, to some extent, experience the emotions of others), has become a normal part of the human repertoire (Bowles and Gintis, 2003). Bowles and Gintis (in Gurven, 2004a) point out that without the prosocial emotions, we would all be sociopaths, and human society could not exist. They also point out that these prosocial emotions are most visible in the relationships between strangers, a kind of situation that is not frequently observed in hunter-gatherer societies, but may well be the birthing place of these mental traits.

Subcutaneous fat deposits in humans provide a valuable indicator to the provider about the condition of the dependent. Fat deposits play a role in hormone production and energy storage for adults, and simultaneously signal sexual condition to potential partners, so they play a role in pair-bonding and reproduction. But at the same time that fat deposits serve their primary purpose of energy storage and can be mobilized to smooth out short interruptions in the flow of food and nutrients, they also serve as signals turning on and off the impulse to provision children and, to a lesser extent, adults. When there is a longer range surplus of food, the fat deposits are added to, a little every day, to produce increased fatness, and when there is long-range shortage of food, the fat deposits are continually depleted. Because these fat deposits are located just under the skin, others can watch the process of weight loss and gain over a period of weeks and months, and learn to associate weight loss with negative condition. If the whole community is short of food and losing weight, the providers do the best they can to provision themselves and their dependents and survive the shortage. Seeing that a particular individual is losing weight while the community as a whole is well fed provides valuable information for the provider that some intervention needs to be made. Depletion of fat deposits may signal hunger but also illness, depression, overwork, or stress to the observer. Even if the observer has no medicinal treatment to offer for illness, for example, it is usually helpful to provide psychological support and comfort, extra food, and a reduction of high-energy activities.

Humans have deep-seated psychological responses to the observation of fatness and thinness. The sense of satisfaction and warmth that we feel when we see a fat baby may be universal, and the sense of anxiety and dismay that we feel when we see even a picture of an extremely thin baby is also widespread. Similarly, a plump child may be attractive, but it is also a signal to adults to leave that child alone and allow it to go off and play with its mates, whereas a thin child elicits intervention from adults to reduce the child's activity level, to treat any infections or wounds, and to provide a plentiful supply of food. In adolescence the short, thin, undeveloped young man is considered immature, whatever his age, and the similar girl is seen as not yet ready for sexual intercourse, whereas the blooming young woman with hips and breasts and thighs is signaling sexual readiness to the world and is considered very attractive. Thin and listless adults and elderly may be viewed with alarm by their closest kin, eliciting gifts of food and mobilization of the curers, even if the treatment is entirely magical. Visible fatness and thinness is thus a signal to others about nutritional well-being, and, in those who are dependent on others, thinness is a signal that the dependent needs to be fed and cared for.

Thinness is thus a prime example of what evolutionary theorists call "an honest signal," that is, a signal that cannot be faked. Complaints of hunger or requests for food are also signals to caregivers, but ones the recipient can manipulate at a low cost to get additional food, which might improve the fitness of the recipient but reduces the ability of the provider to allocate his or her efforts to the quarter where they will maximally increase the inclusive fitness of the provider. The ability to observe the honest signal of thinness is an indicator to potential providers that the dependent is not just talking about hunger, but is actually in need of additional food.

Mothers lactate in response to the amount of breast-milk the infant takes, not in response to the thinness of the infant, so lactation seems not to be primarily influenced by the infant's fat deposits. But the decision to wean the infant may be influenced by thinness, either that of the infant or that of the next older child. During the later stages of lactation, the mother may find that she can collect and carry back substantially more food if she doesn't take the increasingly heavy infant on her back during the collecting trip. So weaning the infant (so that he or she can be left behind in the village with others to supervise) may reduce the workload of the mother and improve the food resources of the older children and the family as a whole. On the other hand, a thin infant may continue to be offered breast-milk in supplementation to the family diet for many additional months, while the parents and the older children manage with a smaller supply of gathered foods and pay the price in their thinness. As Rose Frisch (2002) has taught us, the resumption of ovulation after a birth depends upon the critical level of fatness in the mother, so anything that contributes to the reduction of the food supply for the family is likely to have the consequence of longer birth intervals. We did not find much correlation between the BMI or the BMIDiff of a specific mother and that of her own children in the !Kung study. Still, it makes sense that all the members of a household, who share a supply of food, are likely to gain and lose fatness in synchrony, and indeed, we did find that the households were significant units for variations in BMIDiff. Observation by mothers that one or all of their children are thin can stimulate them to greater effort to collect food and to concentrate the available resources on their own family rather than volunteer help to support others.

Men, too, may be influenced in their behavior by observation of the fatness or thinness of their wives and children. We note that while women are depositing fat on their bodies during adolescence, men are depositing a similar amount of muscle mass on their bodies, so we expect that the signaling of need by thinness is going to be more effective when done by women than by men. Both sexes lose weight during scarcity, but it will show more on women than on men. Perhaps this is one of the roots of the protective attitude toward women and children that is seen in men in many cultures around the world.

Most !Kung hunters allocate only a few days a week to hunting, so there is a margin for increased effort when it seems clear that it is needed. Men can also reduce the labor of their wives by taking on more of the childcare, child carrying, hut construction, and so forth to spare the wife the added hours and effort of work. And Draper (1975) found that the thinnest "knee children" (the recently weaned child supplanted from the breast by a new baby) are often found in close association with their father in the village, whereas better nourished children of the same age are more frequently found playing with other children. So it seems that !Kung fathers are sensitive to the signals of thinness from their wife and children. In general, it seems that parents are maximally attuned to the monitoring of their young children's condition and do the best they can to provide a steady supply of the minimal requirements for normal health and growth.

The Grandmother Hypothesis

It is in the area of allocation of help and support to more distant kin where the honest signal of thinness comes into its most important consequences. Let us start by considering grandparents and the contributions that they make to their adult children and to their grandchildren. Women as young as 36 can be grandmothers, and men as young as 45 can be grandfathers, and we need to be reminded that it is very common that people are both parents of dependent children (their younger children) **and** grandparents relative to the offspring of their oldest children at the same time.

In order to contribute to the well-being of both generations of children, the older adults need to be in residential contact with the children, and able to perform work, especially food collection but also the tasks of the village such as water collection, hut construction, childcare, food processing and cooking, and so on to meet the needs of their own and their adult child's household. So calculations about the contributions that a person can make to the well-being of their own children and grandchildren (and ultimately to their own inclusive fitness) need to be made on a continuing basis concerning how much work needs to be done that day, what food needs to be procured and processed, and what travel and visiting can be done and needs to be done. Older adults with large households may use their influence to try to get their adult children, particularly their adult daughters, to live in the same village so that the grandparents can monitor the health and well-being of their child and grandchildren, and contribute to their well-being. Older adults with small households, especially if it is only the couple making up the household, may also try to influence their adult daughter to live in the same village, but may also exercise their option of moving to live nearby the daughter's family if they feel that their contributions are needed. Or they may at least visit the daughter's village for substantial periods of time when they feel they may be needed, perhaps at the time of the birth of a new child or in late winter when food is scarce. If the couple has several adult children, they may visit each in turn to assess where their contributions would be most needed or be most helpful. There is a natural bias toward helping their daughters rather than their sons, because sons marry later and because their son's wife is likely to have her own parents to help her, but societies vary on the prescription of whether parents should concentrate on helping their daughters or their sons.

It is rare that a grandmother has one and only one grandchild needing her care. As we saw in Chapter 7, most of the post-reproductive women have either none (which includes "none yet") or more than one. If the grandchildren are born to only one of the grandmother's adult children, she can contribute to the well-being of all of them by living nearby, but often the grandchildren are living in different villages and the grandmother must travel to be with them and must choose which among them to help. If the distances are great, the grandmother may not be aware that one or another of the grandchildren is thin and in need of her input. Short visits to adult children during the year have the function of continual assessment of where the grandmother or the post-reproductive couple's efforts are most needed. So the grandmothers, even more than the mothers, need to engage in a complex process of information processing and imagining the consequences of her various actions in order to invest in her grandchildren maximally. Note that we do not need to consider maternal grandmothers separately from paternal grandmothers: they are the same people and make choices between the targets of their investments in the context of the cultural rules of their people.

We do, however, have to distinguish between grandmothers and grandfathers. When women become widows, they are likely to concentrate all their efforts on assisting their adult children (and continuing to raise their own if any are still dependent), while men who are widowed are more likely to marry again and may be caught up in providing assistance to the new wife's adult children. No doubt these matters differ according to the cultural rules of the particular group, but they are likely to be important events in the lives of individuals from any hunter-gatherer group.

The Fatness Hypothesis

The fatness hypothesis consists of asserting that the woman will automatically assess the need of the child on the basis of fatness/thinness and its association with increased mortality. Continuing to look at events from the point of view of a youngish post-reproductive woman, we can consider her role vis-à-vis other relatives in the village. Assuming that her own children and her nearby grandchildren are thriving, what decisions will she need to make about her siblings' children, her cousins' children, and her husband's relative's children in the village? She can collect enough food for her own household and to supplement her daughter's household on several days a week and can rest from the rigors of food collecting, process the food she brought back, casually look after children in the village while others go out gathering, and carry out other household chores on the days between trips. She observes all the children in the village, those of relatives and those who are unrelated. In some way, she asks herself the three questions we raised earlier about these children. First, she asks herself whether the children are in need of her supplementation; that is, are they thin and at an age when thinness may make the difference between life and death for the child? Young children have higher probabilities of death from all causes than older children, and thin children are more at risk than plump ones. If, in addition, the child seems to be acutely ill, the need for food for a thin child may be immediate.

Second, the post-reproductive woman will consider who else the child at risk has in the village to provide for his or her needs. Is there only a single mother, or are there two parents to meet the child's needs? Do the parents have other close kin in the village who can help them when they are in need? Do they have many children and other dependents, or is this child the only one? Are the parents capable and experienced, or are they young and new to the area? Are they in good health, or are they handicapped or chronically or acutely ill? The answers to all of these questions contribute to the older woman's assessment of whether her efforts are needed to help this particular child through a food shortage that might otherwise prove fatal.

And third the potential helper will ask herself how this child contributes to her inclusive fitness, even if she doesn't ask the question in those terms. If the child is greatly in need, has no alternative providers, and is a close relative, the decision is likely to be to help with an immediate gift, by calling the child over to the providers' household and giving a bowl of prepared food for immediate consumption, or perhaps by making a gift of uncooked food to the head of the child's household for the whole family to share.

As we spell out the issues available to the provider, it is clear that she needs to add one more question to her list of queries. What are the opportunity costs for her of making a gift to a child in need? Will she need to go gathering a day sooner than she might otherwise have done? Will she need to continue her efforts another few hours the next time she is out gathering, and carry back a larger load of food? Will she be depleting her own fatness deposits by taking on the care of others, or those of the dependents that have come to count on her, her own spouse and young children, and perhaps the adult child and grandchildren? What price is she willing to pay to contribute to the survival of a thin child in her village?

We have been imagining this decision-making process for a post-reproductive woman and we need to think about how it might be different for others. The opportunity cost of helping is clearly greater for a woman in the reproductive years, as she may reduce her own fat deposits in the process and therefore lengthen the interval between the births of her own children, which might be a high price to pay (but also might not be, if she is fecund and well nourished and just as glad to leave a bit longer between the births of her children). And infertile women, even if they are in the prime reproductive years, are like post-reproductive women in their assessments and choices. A young woman with no children may find it easy to collect enough food to take care of herself and her spouse if she goes gathering several days a week with her mother, learning the skills of the trade and building her experience with the species of food available. She may indeed find herself contributing food to her mother's household rather than having her mother help her, especially if her mother still has several dependent children at home. And she may become an important contributor to families experiencing shortages during the years she awaits her own fertility.

Similarly, men have to decide how much effort to put into hunting and food gathering on the basis of their family's needs and those of others in the village. Men, of course, do not run out of reproductive opportunities with age the same way women do. They can marry a younger woman and carry on their family building phase when a first wife can no longer produce offspring. Hence, it seems plausible that older women respond to the direct observation of thinness in children, even if these children are not their own, but less plausible that older men do so. We note that men of any age who are seen to bring in a lot of meat from successful hunting will be attractive candidates on the marriage market and will be welcomed as a new resident of any village, other things being equal, no matter how the meat is divided in the village. Hunters generally have less control over the distribution of their meat than women have over the distribution of their vegetable foods. Perhaps this is one of the reasons why we do not tend to think of men as avid observers of the well-being of all of the children and contributors to those who are not doing as well as average.

The fatness hypothesis concludes, therefore, that human beings evolved to show their subcutaneous fat deposits prominently, in response to the development in the human population of a pool of surplus labor, consisting of post-reproductive men and women whose abilities to provide continue past the demands of their immediate families and who are capable of responding to the honest signal of fatness on the part of dependents, even those who are not close kin. These workers provide the cushion that human hunter-gatherers require to provide an adequate diet for children at every stage of their development, and for adults when they occasionally need to let up on their productive activities due to sickness or other problems.

The Nurturance Hypothesis

There is another hypothesis suggested by these same considerations, which we might call "the nurturance hypothesis." It seems clear to students of chimpanzees and other living primates that they are not very aware and concerned about hard times being experienced by conspecifics. Humans (or most humans) have the ability to imagine themselves in the state of others and sympathize with their situation. They may even imagine what can be done to ease the difficulties of others around them. And those who have this capacity are likely to contribute to a higher level of inclusive fitness in their kin group and, hence, encourage these capacities for nurturance of others to be increased in the population.

Human mortality seems to be significantly lower than that of our primate relatives at each stage of life history, even when we humans have no effective medical care or technological support to compensate for handicaps and illness. The cause of our improvement in survivorship probably comes from our social group and the general willingness of humans to share food, protection, and nurturance of individuals unable to care for themselves. Virtually all human adults have been severely ill at one time or another and required care from others. The probability of survival from a given level of infection or injury is probably always better for humans than for chimpanzees because humans can lie down and rest for days at a time in the home-base of the group, relying upon others not to move away and leave them behind except in extreme circumstances. Similarly humans can count upon others to provide them with food and drinking water while they rest from their illness, and others may provide whatever medical treatment they have available, such as supernatural intervention, herbal poultices, a sling for a broken limb, an extraction of a rotting tooth, or even primitive surgery when it is available. Studies of skeletal remains of early populations show an impressive rate of healed fractures and dislocations, suggesting that these populations were able to keep a seriously injured person alive long enough to heal from their injuries. This implies that others provided nurturance to the sick or injured party. Those with relatives who were willing to provide sustained care for the injured and sick lived longer and presumably had more surviving offspring than those whose neighbors and family members treated them as chimpanzees would, perhaps distressed by the sight of an injured conspecific, but leaving them to manage their own difficulties and, hence, more often succumbing to the predators of the neighborhood.

Finally, it seems clear that all three of these trends—the grandmother hypothesis, the fatness hypothesis, and the nurturance hypothesis—must have contributed to the evolutionary change in the human species toward the capacity for sustained abstract thought and communication. We can see that it is likely that the evolution of increased intelligence, which permits the development of language (or rather, many languages), grammar, kinship terminology, rules for marriage, and the religious constructions that make sense of human life in a stressful environment, can result from increases in inclusive fitness from all these traits—grandmothering, visible fatness signals, and nurturance, and no doubt by many others such as the increases in complexity in hunting and gathering, food preparation, and sexual selection. We humans became human by the small increments of fitness we accumulated by our observation and response to the nutritional well-being of one another, among many other processes. We could, of course, go on making lists of traits that must have evolved in the genome between chimpanzees and humans, but this would have little or no value, without detailed understanding of the processes involved and tests of the validity of any speculations such as we have made here. Such work is far from my area of competence.

It is encouraging to see the development of a science of the evolution of cooperation, of food sharing, of prosocial emotional development, and the capacity for nurturance and care of others. If this detailed presentation of the data on the !Kung can help those analysts to picture some of the concrete events and relationships in a simple society like those that must have been the stage for these evolutionary events, so much the better.

References

Alexander, R. D. (1987). *The biology of moral systems*. New York: Aldine de Gruyter.

Bailey, R. C., and N. A. Peacock. 1988. Efe pygmies of northeast Zaire: Subsistence strategies in the Ituri forest. In *Coping with uncertainty in the food supply*, G. A. Harrison and I. deGariere. Oxford: Clarendon Press.

Barclay, G. 1958. *Techniques of population analysis*. New York: Wiley.

Barnard, A. 1992. *Hunters and herders of Southern Africa: A comparative ethnography of the Khoisan peoples*. Cambridge, England and New York: Cambridge University Press.

Bentley, G. R., R. R. Paine, et al. 2001. Fertility changes with the prehistoric transition to agriculture. In *Reproductive ecology and human evolution*, P. T. Ellison, 203–231. New York: Aldine de Gruyter.

Biesele, M. 1990. *Shaken roots: The Bushmen of Namibia*. Marshalltown, South Africa: EDA Publications.

Biesele, M., and N. Howell. 1981. "The old people give you life": Old age among the Kalahari !Kung. In *Other ways of growing old*, P. Amoss and S. Harrell, 77–98. Stanford, CA: Stanford University Press.

Black, A. E., S. Jebb, et al. 1991. Validation of energy and protein intakes assessed by diet history and by weighed records against total energy expenditures. *Proceedings of the Nutrition Society* 50: 108.

Blurton Jones, N., L. C. Smith, et al. 1992. Demography of the Hadza, an increasing and high density population of savanna foragers. *American Journal of Physical Anthropology* 89: 159–181.

Blurton Jones, N. G. 1984. A selfish origin for food sharing: Tolerated theft. *Ethology and Sociobiology* 5: 1–3.

Blurton Jones, N. G. 1986. Bushman birth spacing: A test for optimal interbirth interval. *Ethology and Sociobiology* 7: 91–105.

Blurton Jones, N. G. 1987. Bushmen birth spacing: Direct tests of some simple predictions. *Ethology and Sociobiology* 8: 183–203.

Blurton Jones, N. G. 1994. Foraging returns of !Kung adults and children: Why didn't !Kung children forage? *Journal of Anthropological Research* 50: 217–248.

Blurton Jones, N. G., K. Hawkes, et al. 1994. Differences between Hadza and !Kung children's work: Original affluence and practical reason? In *Key issues in hunter-gatherer research*, E. S. Burch Jr. and L. J. Ellana, 189–215. Oxford: Berg.

Blurton Jones, N. G., K. Hawkes, et al. 1996. The global process and local ecology: How should we explain differences between the Hadza and the !Kung. In *Cultural diversity among twentieth-century foragers*, S. Kent, 159–187. Cambridge, England: Cambridge University Press.

Blurton Jones, N. G., and N. Howell. 1984. Birth spacing and !Kung reproductive success. *International Journal of Primatology* 5(4): 323–323.

Blurton Jones, N. H., K. Hawkes, and J. F. O'Connell. 1997. Why do Hadza children forage? In *Genetic, ethological and evolutionary perspectives on human development*, N. L. Segal, G. E. Weisfeld, and C. C. Weisfeld. Washington, DC: American Psychological Association.

Bogin, B. 1988. *Patterns of human growth*. Cambridge: Cambridge University Press.

Bogin, B. 1999. Evolutionary perspective on human growth. *Annual Reviews in Anthropology*, 28: 109–153.

Bogin, B. 2006. Modern human life history: The evolution of human childhood and fertility. In *The evolution of human life history*, K. Hawkes and R. R. Paine, 197–230. Sante Fe, AZ: School of American Research Press.

Bowles, S., and H. Gintis. 2002. The origins of human cooperation. In *The genetic and cultural origins of cooperation*, P. Hammerstein. Cambridge, MA: MIT Press.

Bowles, S., and H. Gintis. 2003. The origins of human cooperation. In *Genetic and cultural evolution of cooperation*, P. Hammerstein, 430–443. Cambridge, MA: MIT Press.

Bogin, B., and B. H. Smith. 1996. Evolution of the human life cycle. *American Journal of Human Biology* 8: 703–716.

Brown, P., T. Sutikaa, et al. 2004. A new small-bodied hominid from the Late Pleistocene of Flores, Indonesia. Nature 431: 1055–1061.

Caldwell, J. C. 1982. *The theory of fertility change*. New York: Academic Press.

Cartmill, M. 1993. *A view to a death in the morning: Hunting and nature through history*. Cambridge, MA: Harvard University Press.

Cashdan, E. 1985. Coping with risk: Reciprocity among the Basarwa of northern Botswana. *Man* 20: 454–474.

Chagnon, N. A., and W. Irons. 1979. *Evolutionary biology and human social behavior: An anthropological perspective*. North Scituate, MA: Duxburg Press.

Coale, A. J., and P. Demeny. 1966. *Regional model life tables and stable populations*. Princeton: Princeton University Press.

Divale, W., and M. Harris. 1976. Population, warfare and the male supremacist complex. *American Anthropologist* 78: 521–538.

Draper, P. 1975. !Kung women: Contrasts in sexual egalitarianism in the foraging and sedentary contexts. In *Toward an Anthropology of Women*, R. Reiter, 77–109. New York: Monthly Review Press.

Draper, P. 1976. Social and economic constraints on child life among the !Kung. In *Kalahari hunter-gatherers: Studies of the !Kung San and their neighbors*, R. B. Lee and I. DeVore, 200–220. Cambridge, MA: Harvard University Press.

Draper, P., and A. Buchanan. 1992. If you have a child, you have a life: Demographic and cultural perspectives on fathering in old age in !Kung society. In *Father-child relations: Cultural and biosocial contexts*, B. S. Hewlett, 131–152. New York: Aldine de Gruyter.

Draper, P., and H. Harpending. 1994. Cultural considerations in the experience of aging: Two African cultures. In *Functional performance in older adults*, B. R. Bonder and M. B. Wagner, 15–27. Philadelphia: F. A. Davis.

Draper, P., and N. Howell. 2002. *Kinship resources and growth of !Kung children*. B. S. Hewlett.

Draper, P., and N. Howell. 2005. The growth and kinship resources of Ju/'hoansi children. In *Hunter-gatherer childhoods: Evolutionary, developmental and cultural perspectives*, B. S. Hewlett and M. E. Lamb. New Brunswick: Aldine Transaction.

Draper, P., and N. Howell. 2006. Changes in co-survivorship of adult children and parents: Ju/'hoansi of Botswana in 1968 and 1988. In *Updating the San: Image and reality of an African people in the 21st century*, R. K. Hitchcock, K. Ikeya, M. Biesele, and R. B. Lee. Osaka, Japan: National Museum of Ethnology. *Senri Ethnological Studies*, 70: 81–100.

Draper, P., and M. Kranichfeld. 1990. Coming in from the bush: Settled life by the !Kung and their accommodation to Bantu neighbors. *Human Ecology*, 18: 363–384.

Durnin, J. V. G. A. 1991. Energy requirements of pregnancy. *Acta Paediatrica Scandinavica*, 10(Supplement): 33–42.

Durnin, J. V. G. A., and R. Passmore. 1967. *Energy, work and leisure*. London: Heinemann.

Dwyer, J. T. 1991. Concept of nutritional status and its measurement. In *Anthropometric assessment of nutritional status*, J. H. Himes, 5–28. New York: Wiley-Liss.

Dyson, T. 1977. *Demography of the Hadza in historical perspective*. African Historical Demography, Centre of African Studies, University of Edinburgh.

Early, J. D., and T. N. Headland. 1998. *Population dynamics of a Philippine rain forest people: The San Ildefonso Agta*. Gainesville, FL: University of Florida Press.

Early, J. D., and J. F. Peters. 1990. *The population dynamics of the Mucajai Yanomama*. San Diego: Academic Press.

Early, J. D., and J. F. Peters. 2000. *The Xilixana Yanomami of the Amazon: History, social structure and population dynamics*. Gainesville, FL: University Press of Florida.

Ellison, P. T. 2001. *Reproductive ecology and human evolution*. New York: Aldine de Gruyter.

Falkner, F., and J. M. Tanner. 1986. *Human growth: A comprehensive treatise.* New York: Plenum Press.

Food and Agriculture Organization. 1982. *Energy and protein requirements: Report of a joint FAO/WHO/UNU expert consultation.* Rome: World Health Organization.

Frisch, R. E. 2002. *Female fertility and the body fat connection.* Chicago: University of Chicago Press.

Frisch, R. E., R. Revelle, et al. 1971. Height, weight and age at menarche and the "critical weight" hypothesis. *Science,* 194: 1148.

Gordon, R. J. 1992. *The Bushman myth: The making of a Namibian underclass.* Boulder, CO: Westview Press.

Gurven, M. 2004a. The evolution of contingent cooperation. *Current Anthropology,* 47: 185–192.

Gurven, M. 2004b. To give and to give not: The behavioral ecology of human food transfers. *Behavioral and Brain Sciences,* 27: 543–583.

Gurven, M., and W. Allen-Arave, et al. 2000. "It's a wonderful life": Signaling generosity among the Ache of Paraguay. *Evolution and Human Behavior,* 21: 263–282.

Hamilton, W. D. 1964. The genetical evolution of social behavior. *Journal of Theoretical Biology,* 7: 1–16.

Hansen, J. D. L., et al. 1993. Hunter-gatherer to pastoral way of life: Effects of the transition on health, growth, and nutritional status. *South African Journal of Science,* 89: 559–564.

Harpending, H. 1976. Regional variation in !Kung populations. In *Kalahari hunter-gatherers: Studies of the !Kung San and their neighbors,* R. B. Lee and I. DeVore, 152–165. Cambridge, MA: Harvard University Press.

Harpending, H., and P. Draper. 1990. Comment on Solway and Lee, Foragers, genuine or spurious. *Current Anthropology,* 31(2): 127–128.

Harpending, H., and L. Wandsnider. 1982. Population structures of Ghanzi and Ngamiland !Kung. In *Current developments in anthropological genetics V. 2 ecology and population structure,* M. Crawford and J. H. Mielke, 29–50. New York: Plenum Press.

Harris, M., and E. B. Ross. 1987. *Food and evolution: Toward a theory of human food habits.* Philadelphia: Temple University Press.

Hawkes, K. 1989. Hardworking Hadza grandmothers. In *Comparative socioecology of mammals and man,* V. Standen and R. Foley, 341–366. London: Blackwell.

Hawkes, K., J. F. O'Connell, et al. 1991. Hunting income patterns among the Hadza: Big game, common goods, foraging goals and the evolution of the human diet. *Philosophical Transactions of the Royal Society of London,* 334: 243–251.

Hawkes, K., J. F. O'Connell, et al. 2001a. The evolution of human life histories: primate tradeoffs, grandmothers, socioecology, and the fossil record. In *Primate Life Histories and Socioecology,* P. Kappeler and M. Pereira. Chicago: University of Chicago Press.

Hawkes, K., J. F. O'Connell, et al. 2001b. Hunting and nuclear families. *Current Anthropology,* 42: 681–709.

Hawkes, K., J. F. O'Connell, et al. 1998. Grandmothering, menopause, and the evolution of human life histories. *Proceedings of the National Academy of Science*, 95: 1136–1339.

Hawkes, K., J. F. O'Connell, et al. 2000. The grandmother hypothesis and human evolution. In *Adaptation and human behavior: An anthropological perspective*, L. Cronk, N. A. Chagnon, and W. Irons, 231–252. New York: Aldine de Gruyter.

Hawkes, K., and R. R. Paine, eds. 2006. *The evolution of human life history*. School of American Research advanced seminar series. Sante Fe, NM: School of American Research.

Heinrich, J., R. Boyd, et al. (Eds.) 2004. *Foundations of human sociality: Economic experiments and ethnographic evidence from fifteen small-scale societies*. Oxford and New York: Oxford University Press.

Henry, C. J. K., and D. G. Rees. 1991. New predictive equations for the estimation of basal metabolic rate in tropical peoples. *European Journal of Clinical Nutrition*, 45: 177–185.

Hewlett, B. S. 1988. Sexual selection and paternal investment among Aka pygmies. In *Reproductive behaviour: A Darwinian perspective*, L. Betzig, M. Borgerhoff Mulder, and P. Turke, 263–276. Cambridge, England: Cambridge University Press.

Hewlett, B. S., and M. Lamb, eds. 2005. *Hunter-gatherer childhoods*. New Brunswick, NJ: AldineTransaction.

Hewlett, B. S., M. Lamb, et al. 2000. Internal working models, trust, and sharing among foragers. *Current Anthropology*, 41: 287–297.

Hill, K., and M. Gurven. 2004. Economic experiments to examine fairness and cooperation among the Ache Indians of Paraguay. In *Foundations of human sociality: Economic experiments and ethnographic evidence from fifteen small-scale societies*. Oxford and New York: Oxford University Press.

Hill, K., and A. M. Hurtado. 1996. *Ache life history*. New York: Aldine de Gruyter.

Hitchcock, R. K., K. Ikeya, et al., eds. 2006. *Updating the San: Image and reality of an African people in the 21st century*. Senri Ethnological Studies. Osaka, Japan: National Museum of Ethnology.

Holm, J., and P. Molutsi, eds. 1989. *Democracy in Botswana*. Gaberone: Macmillan.

Holm, J., P. Molutsi, et al. 1996. The development of civil society in a democratic state: The Botswana model. *African Studies Review*, 39(2).

Howell, N. 1978. Human reproduction reconsidered. *Nature*, 276(5686): 421–422.

Howell, N. 1979. *Demography of the Dobe !Kung*. New York: Academic Press.

Howell, N. 1986. Feedbacks and buffers in relation to scarcity and abundance: Studies of hunter-gatherer populations. In *The state of population theory: Forward from Malthus*, D. Coleman and R. Schofield, 156–187. Oxford: Basil Blackwell, Ltd.

Howell, N. 2000. *Demography of the Dobe !Kung*, 2nd ed. New York: Aldine de Gruyter.

Howell, N., and V. A. Lehotay. 1978. AMBUSH: A computer program for stochastic microsimulation of small human populations. *American Anthropologist*, 80(4): 905–922.

Isaac, B. L. 1990. Economy, ecology and analogy: The !Kung San and the generalized foraging model. *Early Paleoindian Economies of Eastern North America*, 5: 323–335.

Ivey, P. K. 2000. Cooperative reproduction in Ituri forest hunter-gatherers: Who cares for Efe infants? *Current Anthropology*, 41(5): 856–866.

Jasienska, G. 2001. Why energy expenditure causes reproductive suppression in women. In *Reproductive Ecology and Human Evolution*, P. T. Ellison, 59–84. New York: Aldine de Gruyter.

Jenike, M. R. 2001. Nutritional ecology: Diet, physical activity and body size. In *Hunter-gatherers: An interdisciplinary perspective*, C. Panter-Brick, R. H. Layton, and P. Rowley-Conwy, 205–238. Cambridge, England: Cambridge University Press.

Jenkins, T., B. I. Joffe, et al. 1987. Transition from a hunter-gatherer to a settled life-style among the Kung San (Bushmen)—Effect on glucose tolerance and insulin secretion. *South African Journal of Science*, 83(7): 410–412.

Kaplan, H. 1994. Evolutionary and wealth flows theories of fertility. *Population and Development Review*, 20: 753–792.

Kaplan, H. 1996. A theory of fertility and paternal investment in traditional and modern human societies. *Yearbook of Physical Anthropology*, 39: 91–135.

Kaplan, H., J. Lancaster, et al. 2000. A theory of human life history evolution: Diet, intelligence and longevity. *Evolutionary Anthropology*, 9: 156–185.

Katz, R. 1982. *Boiling energy: Community healing among the Kalahari Kung.* Cambridge, MA: Harvard University Press.

Keith, J., C. L. Fry, et al. 1994. *The aging experience: Diversity and commonality across cultures.* Thousand Oaks, CA: Sage Publications.

Kelly, R. L. 1995. *The foraging spectrum: Diversity in hunter-gatherer lifeways.* Washington: Smithsonian Institution Press.

Konner, M. 1976. Maternal care, infant behavior and development among the !Kung. In *Kalahari Hunter-gatherers: Studies of the !Kung San and their neighbors*, R. B. Lee and I. DeVore, 218–245. Cambridge, MA: Harvard University Press.

Konner, M. 1991. *Childhood: A multicultural view.* Cambridge, England: Cambridge University Press.

Konner, M., and C. Worthman. 1980. Nursing frequency, gonadal function, and birth spacing among the !Kung hunter-gatherers. *Science*, 207: 788–791.

Kurki, H. K. 2007. Protection of obstetric dimensions in a small-bodied human sample. *American Journal of Physical Anthropology*, 133: 1152–1165.

Lee, R. B. 1969. !Kung Bushman subsistence: An input-output analysis. In *Environmental and cultural behavior*, A. P. Vayda, 47–79. New York: Natural History Press.

Lee, R. B. 1972. Population growth and the beginnings of sedentary life among the !Kung Bushmen. In *Population growth: Anthropological implications*, B. Spooner. Cambridge, MA: M.I.T. Press.

Lee, R. B. 1979. *The !Kung San: Men, women, and work in a foraging society.* Cambridge, England: Cambridge University Press.

Lee, R. B. 1992. Work, sexuality, and aging among !Kung Women. In *In her prime: New views of middle-aged women*, V. K. and J. K. Brown, 35–48. Urbana and Chicago:.

Lee, R. B., and I. DeVore, eds. 1968. *Man the hunter.* Chicago: Aldine Publishing Company.

Lee, R. B., and I. DeVore. 1976. *Kalahari hunter-gatherers: Studies of the !Kung San and their neighbors.* Cambridge, MA: Harvard University Press.

Lee, R. D. 2000a. A cross-cultural perspective on intergenerational transfers and the economic life cycle. *Sharing the wealth: demographic change and economic transfers between generations*, A. Mason and G. Tapinos, 17–56. Oxford: Oxford University Press.

Lee, R. D. 2000b. Intergenerational transfers and the economic life cycle: A cross-cultural perspective. In *Sharing the Wealth: Demographic change and economic transfers between generations*, A. Mason and G. Tapinos, 17–56. Oxford: Oxford University Press.

Lee, R. D., and K. L. Kramer. 2001. Demographic influences on resource allocation in Maya households. Annual meeting of Population Association of America. Washington, DC.

Lee, R. D., and K. L. Kramer. 2002. Children's economic roles in the context of the Maya family life cycle: Cain, Caldwell and Chayanov revisited. *Population and Development Review*, 28 (3): 475–499.

Leslie, P. W., J. R. Bindon, et al. 1984. Caloric requirements of human populations: A model. *Human Ecology*: 137–162.

Lucas, A., M. S. Fewtress, et al. 1999. Fetal origins of adult disease—The hypothesis revisited. *British Medical Journal*, 319(7204): 245–249.

Lunn, P. G. 1985. Maternal nutrition and lactational infertility: The baby in the driving seat. In *Maternal nutrition and lactational infertility*, J. Dobbing, 41–64. Vevey, Switzerland, and New York: Raven Press.

Marlowe, F. 2004. Dictators and ultimatums in an egalitarian society of hunter-gatherers: The Hadza of Tanzania. In *Foundations of Human Sociality*, J. Henrich, R. Boyd, S. Bowles, C. Camerer, R. Fehr, and H. Gintis. New York: Oxford University Press.

Marshall, L. 1976. *The !Kung of NyaeNyae.* Cambridge, MA: Harvard University Press.

Martorell, R., and J. P. Habicht. 1986. Growth in early childhood in developing countries. *Human growth: A comprehensive treatise*, F. Falkner and J. M. Tanner, 241–262. New York: Plenum Press.

Migliano, A. B., L. Vinicius, et al. 2007. Life history trade-offs explain the evolution of human pygmies. *Proceedings of the National Academy of Science*, 104(51): 20216–20219.

National Research Council. 1989. *Recommended dietary allowances*, 10th ed. Washington, DC: National Academy Press.

Nurse, G. T., J. S. Weiner, et al. 1985. *The peoples of Southern Africa and their affinities.* Oxford, England: Clarendon Press.

Pawlowski, B. 2001. The evolution of gluteal/femoral fat deposits and balance during pregnancy in bipedal Homo. *Current Anthropology*, 42: 572–574.

Pfeiffer, S., and J. Sealy. 2006. Body size among Holocene foragers of the Cape eco-zone, South Africa. *American Journal of Physical Anthropology*, 129: 1–11.

Richerson, P. J., and R. Boyd. 2004. *Not by genes alone: How culture transformed human evolution*. Chicago: University of Chicago Press.

Robson, S. L., C. P. van Schail, et al. 2006. The derived features of human life history. In *The evolution of human life history*, K. Hawkes and R. R. Paine, 17–44. Santa Fe, NM: School of American Research Press.

Rosenberg, H. G. 1989. Complaint discourse, aging, and caregiving among the !Kung San of Botswana. In *The cultural context of aging: Worldwide perspectives*, J. Sokolovsky, 19–42. New York: Bergin and Garvey.

Roth, E. A. 2004. *Culture, biology and anthropological demography*. Cambridge, England, and New York: Cambridge University Press.

Sackett, R. F. 1996. Time, energy and the indolent savage: Quantitative cross-cultural test of the primitive affluence hypothesis. *Anthropology*. Los Angeles: University of California at Los Angeles. Ph.D.

Schrire, C. 1984. *Past and present in hunter-gatherer studies*. Orlando, FL: Academic Press.

Sealy, J., and S. Pfeiffer. 2000. Diet, body size and landscape use among Holocene people in the Southern Cape, South Africa. *Current Anthropology*, 41: 642–655.

Sealy, J., S. Pfeiffer, et al. 2000. Hunter-gatherer child burials from the Pakhuis Mountains, Western Cape: Growth, diet and burial practices in the late holocene. *South African Archaeological Bulletin*, 55: 32–43.

Shostak, M. 1981. *Nisa: The life and words of a !Kung woman*. Cambridge, MA: Harvard University Press.

Shostak, M. 2000. *Return to Nisa*. Cambridge, MA: Harvard University Press.

Tanaka, J. 1980. *The San: Hunter-gatherers of the Kalahari—A study in ecological anthropology*. Tokyo: University of Tokyo Press.

Tanner, J. M. 1960. Genetics of human growth. In *Human growth*, edited by J. M. Tanner, London: Pergamon Press.

Thomas, E. M. 1959. *The harmless people*. New York: Alfred A. Knopf.

Tobias, P. V. 1962. On the increasing stature of the Bushmen. *Anthropos*, 57: 801.

Trivers, R. L. 1971. The evolution of reciprocal altruism. *Quarterly Review of Biology*, 46: 35–57.

Trivers, R. L. 1974. Parent-offspring conflict. *American Zoologist*, 14: 249–264.

Trusswell, A. S. 1977. Diet and nutrition of hunter-gatherers. In *Health and disease in tribal societies*, C. Foundation, 213–226. Amsterdam: Elsevier.

Trusswell, A. S., and J. D. L. Hansen. 1968. Medical and nutritional studies of !Kung Bushmen in northwest Botswana: A preliminary report. *South African Medical Journal*, 42: 1338–1339.

Turnbull, C. 1972. *The mountain people*. New York: Simon and Schuster.

Ulijaszek, S. J. 1995. *Human energetics in biological anthropology*. Cambridge, England: Cambridge University Press.

von Neumann, J., and O. Morgenstern. 1944. *Theory of games and economic behavior*. Princeton, NJ: Princeton University Press.

Walker, R. S., and M. J. Hamilton. 2008. Life history consequences of density dependence and the evolution of human body size. *Current Anthropology*, 49(1): 115–122.

Watkins, S. C. 1995. Women's gossip networks and social change: Childbirth and fertility control among Italian and Jewish women in the U.S., 1920–1940. *Gender and Society*, 9(4): 469–490.

Wiessner, P. 1977. Hxaro: A regional system of reciprocity for reducing risk among the !Kung San. Department of Anthropology. Ann Arbor, MI: University of Michigan. Ph.D.

Wilmsen, E. N. 1978. Seasonal effects of dietary intake on Kalahari San. *Federation of American Societies for Experimental Biology Proceedings*, 37: 65–72.

Wilmsen, E. N. 1982. Studies in diet, nutrition, and fertility among a group of Kalahari Bushmen in Botswana. *Social Science Information*, 21(1): 95–125.

Wilmsen, E. N. 1989. *Land filled with flies: A political economy of the Kalahari*. Chicago: University of Chicago Press.

Wilmsen, E. N., and J. R. Denbow. 1990. Paradigmatic history of San-speaking peoples and current attempts at revision. *Current Anthropology*, 31: 489–524.

Wood, J. 1980. Mechanisms of demographic equilibrium in a small human population, the Gainj of Papua New Guinea. In *Anthropology*, 288. Ann Arbor, MI: University of Michigan.

Woodburn, J. 1968. An introduction to Hadza ecology. In *Man, the Hunter*, R. B. Lee and I. DeVore. Chicago: Aldine.

Wootton, S. A., and A. A. Jackson. 1996. Influence of under-nutrition in early life on growth, body composition and metabolic competence. In *Long-term Consequences of Early Environment: growth, development and the lifespan developmental perspective*, C. J. K. Henry, and S. J. Ulijaszek, 109–123. Cambridge, England: Cambridge University Press.

Yellen, J. 1976. Settlement patterns of the !Kung. In *Kalahari Hunter-gatherers: Studies of the !Kung San and their neighbors*, R. B. Lee and I. DeVore, 47–72. Cambridge, MA and London, England: Harvard University Press.

Yellen, J., and R. B. Lee. 1976. The Dobe—/du/da environment: Background to a hunting and gathering way of life. In *Kalahari Hunter-gatherers: Studies of the !Kung San and their neighbors*, R. B. Lee and I. DeVore. Cambridge, MA and London, England: Harvard University Press.

Index

Composition:	S4 Carlisle Publishing Services
Text:	10/13 Sabon
Display:	Sabon
Printer and Binder:	Thomson-Shore

Made in United States
North Haven, CT
27 May 2022